Absolute Tennis

The best and next way to play the game

• • • By Marty Smith • • •

NEW CHAPTER PRESS

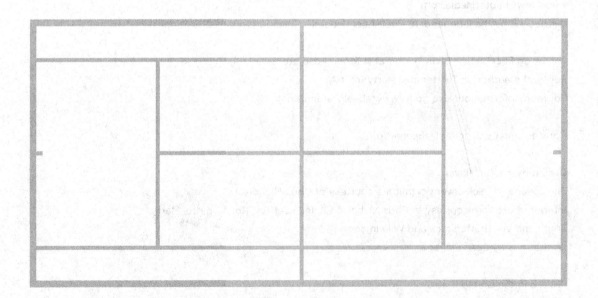

Absolute Tennis

Copyright © 2017 by Marty Smith

All Rights Reserved.

ISBN: 978-1937559748

Published by New Chapter Press, 1175 York Ave, Suite #3s New York, NY 10065

Randy Walker, Managing Partner RWalker@NewChapterMedia.com

www.NewChapterMedia.com

Distributed by the independent Publishers Group in Chicago (www.IPGBook.com)

Follow on Facebook and on Twitter at @TennisAbsolute

Follow the author on Twitter at @MartySmithAT

For more information, also go to www.absolutetennis.net

Copy editing by Jennifer DeLeonardo

Design by Kirsten Navin

The cover and back cover portrait are courtesy of Chris Nicholson

Interior photos are courtesy of Chris Nicholson, Lance Jeffrey, Ron Lopinto, Marty Smith and via Shutterstock and Wiki Images.

Illustrations by Sean Flanagan

Printed in the United States

CONTENTS

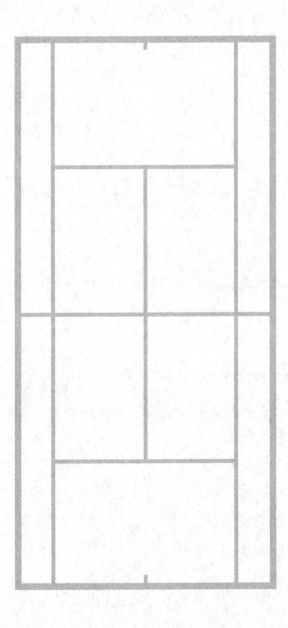

TENNIS PLAYERS MOVE UP, back, left, and right at varying speeds with different types of footwork. They hit the ball fast or slow, deep or short, high or low, flat or with heavy spin. They play against a variety of opponents whose style of play can range from relentlessly aggressive to incredibly patient. During a match, emotions can quickly swing up and down and concentration may fade in and out. The spectrum of physical and mental skills required in tennis is broad, so when Marty Smith told me about his plan to write a comprehensive tennis instructional book, I thought it was a terrific idea. His book *Absolute Tennis* appreciates the wide-ranging nature of the sport and is a great read for tennis enthusiasts both new and experienced to the game.

Acknowledging the fact that tennis is a very athletic game, Marty starts by discussing balance, the kinetic chain, and movement. Next, he takes you through grips and each phase of every stroke, giving you insights to improve your technique and play your best tennis. At each step, he pairs his instructional text with engaging individual and frame-by-frame photographs of the world's top players to illustrate his explanations. Federer's serve, Nadal's forehand, Djokovic's return, and Murray's backhand are a few of the strokes that are highlighted. Marty discusses not only the strokes of today, but also explores strokes that may be used in the future. Viewing tennis through the prism of the game's increasing speed, athleticism, and serving prowess, he explains how swings could evolve and makes a compelling case for three unconventional shots. Following the chapters on the key athletic principles and the strokes, Marty dedicates the last third of the book to strategy, the mind, and fitness. Successful tennis players "think" well on the court and his chapters on singles and doubles strategy provide tips on how to play smart. Additionally, his extensive chapters on psychology and fitness will teach you how to focus the mind to compete in a more consistent and confident manner as well as how to train your body to move faster and last longer. Back in my day, we did not have access to advice on psychology, stretching, nutrition, etc. that are now such an important part of training for the elite athlete.

Marty's goal is absolutely clear. He wants to teach you a tremendous amount, all while entertaining you with his holistic, practical, and forward approach to tennis. So read on to gain a deeper understanding of tennis and learn how to improve different parts of your game. If you put his advice into action, you will have more fun on the court and win more, just as his many students over his decades of coaching have done.

PREFACE

I WAS ONCE COACHING a determined 11-year-old named Katy, who was frustrated by one particular aspect of her game: her backhand, an awkward shot that often went into the net. "Marty," she told me, "I can't hit backhands." Wanting to lift her spirits and bring back her enjoyment of the game, I taught her a new approach to her baseline game, a shot that I call the Overlapping Dual Forehand. Almost immediately, Katy began to make more solid contact, sending the ball confidently over the net. Today, she considers this new shot her secret weapon, and she's energized by tennis and excited by her growing skill.

As I see it, Katy's experience is one to which tennis players of all ages around the world can relate. It's a story of hitting a roadblock and knowing that you are not yet the player you can be. Then, you get get a game-changing insight. It could be instruction on how to hit a different type of groundstroke, a new wrist movement or stance on the serve, or advice on how to better understand and refine a traditional stroke. Or your breakthrough could come from a less obvious angle, like guidance for improving your inner monologue or fitness. We all have the ability to take that step forward, sometimes we just need the right information. I hope this book provides you with it.

Absolute Tennis covers a wide range of topics. That's because I believe tennis players who possess a well-rounded knowledge of the game not only understand and appreciate it better, but also are more likely to take the right course of action to improve the fastest. You can read the book cover to cover or use it as a quick reference when needed. So, for example, if you're working on your serve, you can refer to Chapter Five. Or, for a more methodical (and recommended) approach to improving your game, you can work through the book from beginning to end. To help you understand the text, I have included more than 500 narrated photos of the world's best players and numerous side tips I call "Coach's Boxes." I also reference the top pros for learn-

Setting up for my favorite baseline shot — the forehand.

ing lessons and provide a list of exercises at the end of each chapter to invigorate your practice sessions or boost your fitness.

The book is divided into three main sections: the body, the strokes, and the mind. It concludes with a full chapter on fitness, a subject that is applicable to every aspect of tennis. The body section contains a chapter each on three important athletic fundamentals: balance, the kinetic chain, and movement. Here

you will learn how to use your body for improved poise, power, and court coverage.

Once you've worked through these foundations, the book delves into the next section (Chapters Four through 12) which explain grips and the stroke techniques for serves, return of serves, forehands, backhands, and volleys, as well as the different spins and derivatives of these shots. All of these strokes have critical stages, and I take you through each one and, when necessary, recommend the best approach for recreational players versus advanced players. I also describe the footwork needed to improve play. In fact, I consider the legs so critical to the success of a shot that when describing the strokes I start with the legs and then work my way up the body.

I conclude the strokes section with Chapter 12, which is devoted to potential "Future Strokes." In this chapter, I give a brief history of tennis' evolution in the modern era and raise an important question: namely, are there any shots not taught today that could evolve into commonly used shots in the future? As I and many others see it, tennis will become faster and more athletic, and the serve more essential. With this paradigm in mind, I present three shots for you to consider: the overlapping dual forehand, the reverse serve, and the volleyball serve. In short, the overlapping dual forehand offers players more power, time, and reach during baseline rallies. The reverse serve grants more variety and choices on the serve, while the volleyball serve produces a higher contact point and adds racquet speed to the service motion. These strokes, along with the hybrid backhand also described in the book, may be strokes taught to future generations, and I explain why.

In Chapters 13 and 14, I discuss how to tactically outmaneuver your opponents by using winning singles and doubles strategies. In Chapter 13, you will learn how to shift smoothly through the different phases of the rally, make the right court positioning moves and shot choices, reduce and entice errors, and form game plans to defeat different types of singles opponents. In Chapter 14, I explain the role of each of the four doubles players, court positioning, poaching, different serving and receiving formations, shot selection, game plans, communication, and how to chose the right partner. Next is Chapter 15, which is dedicated to tennis psychology. In this chapter I discuss the inner voice, concentration, focusing on the process, confidence, overcoming adversity, visualization, and other topics to give you a mental edge over your opponents.

I conclude the book with Chapter 16 on fitness. Few sports use the body as much, or in so many different ways, as tennis. It requires flexibility, agility, quickness, core stability, strength, and endurance, and in this final chapter I cover these components of fitness for tennis.

By reading what's ahead, I'm confident you will gather insight that helps you play at a higher level. Ultimately, my wish is that you not only elevate your game, but also play more frequently and experience the many rewards offered by tennis. A lifelong sport, tennis can help you maintain long-term health and fitness and make many friends along the way. Tennis can be a sanctuary: a game comprised of a racquet, balls, a net, and some lines that you can joyfully lose yourself in. It can improve your ability to focus, problem solve, and better appreciate the value of self-belief and introspection. In my career I've seen tennis give young players discipline, older players fresh inspiration, and players of all ages personal growth and satisfaction. With all this in mind, whether you are a seasoned player or swinging a racquet for the first time, I hope *Absolute Tennis* encourages and motivates you and you experience all the benefits and joy that can stem from playing this remarkable game.

Novak Djokovic works hard on his flexibility to help him maintain balance during the heated rallies of his ATP matches.

Balance

OVER THE COURSE OF A MATCH, you will sprint, jog, skip, shuffle, lunge, and jump in a variety of directions before, during, and after swinging the racquet. Certainly, tennis is a very athletic sport and knowing how to properly use your body to make your game as powerful and precise as possible is key. Thus, before discussing the strokes, the first three chapters are dedicated to the "anatomy" behind the strokes — balance, the kinetic chain, and movement.

A strong and reliable stroke starts with establishing good balance — keeping your back reasonably straight, shoulders level, and head upright — as you play the shot. Legendary coach Welby Van Horn said it well when he wrote, "Balance is the picture frame in which the picture (the stroke) is placed."[1] I believe it is important to conceptualize stroke production in this manner and understand that good balance leads to a rhythmic, consistent, and powerful stroke with less strain on the body. Of course, tennis is a game of near constant movement, so you must learn dynamic balance, that is, establishing balance on the move.

While balance my not be your first concern on the court, professional players know that to have superb racquet skills and movement, they must possess it — even under duress. Novak Djokovic, for example, is famous for the near leg splits he does during difficult situations to secure the balance needed to hit a forceful and controlled shot (*opposite*). He spends many hours each week working on his flexibility, partly to enhance his ability to establish good posture during a challenging rally. He knows, even as talented and skilled as he is, that he is likely to hit a weak shot if he fails to get balanced during the stroke.

In this chapter, I describe the various ways balance impacts your play and the important link between your center of gravity and balance. Next, I explain how your leg, arm, and head positioning influence your equilibrium and finish with exercises designed to improve your balance.

I. How Does Balance Impact Your Game?

YOUR DEGREE OF BALANCE will impact many facets of your game, including rally ascendency, stroke power, racquet control, vision, and recovery.

1. RALLY ASCENDENCY

The degree of balance you and your opponent have while hitting the ball will largely determine who is ahead in the rally. Your primary goal during baseline play is to move your opponent around the court and force them to hit off balance and defensively while you hit in a poised position and control the point.

2. STROKE POWER

As will be explained in greater detail in Chapter Two, it's very difficult to generate stroke power with your legs if you are off balance. Leaning too far forward, backward, right, or left during your swing limits your ability to set your feet and push forcefully from the ground.

3. RACQUET CONTROL

It is challenging to obtain a precise racquet head angle when you are off balance. When you lean, the angle of your hand in the grip

Even when Serena Williams is forced to hit with one leg either near or well off the ground, she still maintains good posture, helping her hit the ball with power and control.

stays consistent, but the angle of the racquet in relation to the ground changes. Therefore, if you lean backwards the racquet will open, often causing the the shot to sail long. Or, if you lean forward the racquet will close, often sending the ball into the net. Similarly, tilting to the right or left can make the ball veer too far in that direction.

Not only does being off-balance alter the angle of the racquet relative to the ground, but it also pushes body weight in unintended directions, a change that must be taken into account and adjusted for quickly during the swing in order to salvage the shot.

4. VISION

The more upright and steady your head is, the better your visual tracking will be. If your head tilts from being off balance, it can cause a mis-calculation of the height, speed, and distance of the incoming ball and hurt your ability to position yourself well and time your swing. Watch the top players and observe how they keep their head upright and still when pre-paring for their shots (*right*). This head posi-tion assists their vision and judgment, helping them to establish correct positioning to the ball and good timing on their stroke.

5. RECOVERY

Tennis is a game centered on movement and time management. The more balanced you are during the follow through, the better you will be at resisting the forces of momentum, allowing you to change direction and recover more quickly for the next shot. For example, leaning to the right while finishing a wide forehand, instead of being balanced and hav-ing your weight neutral, will slow down your movement to the left and ability to get back to the middle of the court.

Jo-Wilfried Tsonga's good balance sees his head up-right and steady as he sets up for this forehand. This helps his eyes feed good information to his brain regarding the incoming ball's speed and trajectory.

NOTE: For the sake of simplicity, when describ-ing footwork, swings, and grips throughout the book, I will be using the words "right" and "left" in the context of a right-handed player. Left-handers, please switch "right" with "left" and "left" with "right."

Rafael Nadal widens his stance and stretches his arms in opposite directions, helping him keep his center of gravity between his feet and maintain balance on this challenging shot.

II. Balance and Your Center of Gravity

TO PUT IT IN SCIENTIFIC TERMS, attaining good balance is dependent on placing your center of gravity (COG) over the middle of your base of support. What does that mean? Your COG is the point in your body where your body weight is evenly distributed. Because we have a little more weight in the top half of our bodies, our COG is located just above the waist. Your legs provide your base of support. Therefore, establishing good balance means keeping your torso aligned with the middle of your legs. And how do you do that? By adjusting the width of your stance, moving your arms in different directions, and keeping your head upright. Let's discuss in greater detail.

1. LEG POSITIONING

The best leg positioning depends in large part on the height of the incoming shot. The lower the ball, the wider your stance should be to keep your COG positioned above the middle of your legs and support equilibrium during the swing (*opposite*). As you widen your stance, you lower your COG and your base of support becomes larger and stronger. On balls hit above your head, the opposite should occur and your stance should narrow.

Bending your knees is also important for balance, especially on low balls. If you don't bend your knees and bend at the waist instead, your COG will move in front of your legs on low balls, causing you to tilt forward and stumble.

Keep in mind, your right and left leg will take on different roles during the swing to enhance balance. Many shots in tennis require one leg to anchor the stroke while the other leg pivots to balance out the body. For example, on most backhand groundstrokes, the right leg will anchor the body while the left leg swings around to the left for balance (*below*). The movement

COACH'S BOX:

In tennis, it is important to know how to use your body to maximize strength and balance. I sometimes illustrate the strength and balance that can be gained from using a wide stance by doing the "push" test with my students. To do the push test, stand with your feet side by side. Then, have someone push your shoulder firmly from the side; you will quickly lose your balance. Next, place your feet well outside your shoulders and have the person push your shoulder from the side again. This time, because you have a lower center of gravity and stronger base, you will remain stable.

Stan Wawrinka's backhand sees him anchor his right foot while his left foot pivots to secure balance.

The non-hitting arm plays an important role in establishing balance. Federer (*top*) raises and drops his left arm on his serve, and Caroline Wozniacki (*bottom*) moves her left arm right-to-left on her forehand.

of the left leg also allows the hips to rotate and weight transfer to happen fluently, as well as expediting the return to the center of the court.

2. TORSO POSITIONING

The torso is both the heaviest part of your body and the location of your COG, so its positioning is crucial to your balance. Because the torso itself is immobile, it is necessary to rely on the positioning of the legs and arms to get it in equilibrium.

Just as tightrope walkers use their arms for balance, so too should tennis players. For example, on the one-handed backhand, as you swing forward with the right arm, the left hand should move backward to equalize the body's weight distribution (*see Wawrinka previous page*). This not only enhances good posture in the torso, but also supplies anchoring counterpoint strength, or a base, for the right arm to push off, giving the shot more power and accuracy. On the serve, the left arm moves up to toss the ball and then moves down as the racquet swings up at the ball (*top*). Again, this motion balances the body as well as acting as a source of counterpoint strength. On the forehand, the left arm moves to the right during the backswing and then to the left on the forward swing (*bottom*). This equalizes weight distribution to help keep the torso upright as well as coil and uncoil the body to create power.

3. HEAD POSITIONING

While the head may only weigh eight to 12 pounds, a 30-degree tilt makes it feel like a 40-pound weight, significantly affecting your balance. Therefore, it is important that your head remains upright and aligned correctly with your COG during the swing.

III. Balance Practice

IT TAKES EXTENSIVE PRACTICE to be able to move quickly while maintaining the balance that allows you to strike the ball well. In Chapter 16, I provide some agility and flexibility exercises that will help your balance. For now, here are four on-court training exercises.

Modified
Mini-Tennis

1. MODIFIED MINI-TENNIS
Either place a pencil behind your ear or hold a small cup of water in your left hand. Then, hit slowly with a partner inside the service boxes (*above*). Gently hit the ball back and forth with good posture, trying not to allow the pencil to fall to the ground or the water to spill.

2. LOOSE HAT CATCH
Put your racquet aside. With a hat sitting loosely on top of your head, stand 15 feet from your partner. Have your partner throw a ball in various directions. Catch the ball after one bounce and then toss it back. The goal is to keep the hat from falling off of your head by moving smoothly and keeping your head upright. After successfully catching 15 throws, switch roles with your partner.

3. FREEZE TECHNIQUE
The freeze technique helps analyze balance and highlight what may need to be rectified to improve it. Ask your practice partner to feed a ball once every five seconds to random locations around the court. End each swing in a motionless position and hold, or "freeze," for three seconds. If you are wobbly or uncomfortable while "freezing," you either didn't pivot your back foot correctly during the swing or were positioned too far away from or too close to the ball.

4. ONE-HANDED VOLLEYS
With you and your practice partner standing 12 to 15 feet from the net, hit volleys back and forth with your left arm resting behind your back. Without the help of the left arm to assist balance, this drill will emphasize the importance of bending your knees and widening your stance to keep your equilibrium.

Please note there are many off-court fitness exercises that can improve your balance. Performing gym exercises on unstable surfaces (like doing squats on a BOSU ball or sit-ups on a stability ball) will improve your balance by activating the small stabilizer muscles in your ankles, knees, and core. Also, doing gym exercises that increase the range of motion in your muscles with flexibility exercises will help condition your body to maintain balance, especially when stretching for challenging shots.

Serena Williams coils her body on
her serve before uncoiling it
and unleashing the kinetic chain.

CHAPTER TWO

Kinetic Chain

PICTURE SERENA WILLIAMS at the U.S. Open, bouncing the ball, preparing to serve. She breathes in and begins moving the racquet backwards with her right arm while lifting her left arm to toss the ball. Now, focus on the important work that she does with the rest of her body once the ball leaves her left hand: the way she anticipates contact with the ball by turning her shoulders, bending her legs, pushing her hips forward, tilting her back, and essentially coiling her body to spring-load her energy (*opposite*). Then, she exhales and uncoils from the ground up, unloading that built-up energy onto a blurred racquet, squashing the ball on the strings, and sending it across the net at more than 100 miles an hour.

This incredible alignment and coordination is the foundation of Serena Williams' serving technique and the foundation of contemporary tennis: a full body windup designed to deliver a striking blow. It is known as the kinetic chain.

The kinetic chain reimagines the body as a system of chain links, whereby the energy generated by the legs is transferred and increased up the body, culminating in an end point power surge as you hit the ball. In this chapter, I will explain the benefits of the kinetic chain, including improved shot power and consistency, conservation of energy, and reduced likelihood of injury. I then teach you how to optimize the kinetic chain and finish with exercises designed to increase your kinetic chain strength.

Vorsprung dutch technik — Federer's superb use of the kinetic chain lifts him high above the ground on this serve. It allows him to hit with tremendous power without overexertion and is a contributing factor to his record of competing in 65 Grand Slam tournaments in a row.

I. The Benefits of the Kinetic Chain

1. ENHANCED SHOT POWER

While your arm and shoulder are the primary source of racquet speed on the serve, if you were to serve by just moving your arm, you would hit a mediocre serve. It is the big muscles of your legs and abdomen that comprise the driving force that supplies strength to your arm and speed to your racquet.

The power and contact height required for a good serve starts with the legs bending, straightening, and then pushing up from the ground, creating a *ground force reaction*. The energy in the legs then moves up the body and is increased by the rotation of the hips and shoulders. This energy, now located in the shoulders, is further amplified by a pronating forearm and wrist, which releases a burst of power that began in your legs out and onto the racquet (*opposite*). The same concept applies to your groundstrokes. The energy stored initially in the legs flows up the body and synchronizes with the forward swing to add racquet head speed and weight to the shot. In today's game, the serve and groundstrokes are the swings that determine the outcome of most points. Thus, it is vital that you are able to perform the kinetic chain well.

2. IMPROVED CONSISTENCY

If you use the kinetic chain incorrectly and depend primarily on the upper body and arm movement, you will lose racquet control and make more mistakes. If your arm moves vigorously without support from below, you will find it difficult to balance the racquet well at contact. On the other hand, if you use the kinetic chain correctly, you will not only gain more power but your strokes will also become more consistent. By deriving power from throughout your body, your arm and wrist can focus less on increasing power and more on stabilizing the racquet and establishing the precise angle of the strings needed to hit a consistent shot.

3. ENERGY CONSERVATION AND INJURY REDUCTION

Players who are stiff in the legs and core tense up their upper body muscles and make exhaustive arm movements attempting to gain racquet speed. Repetitively swinging the racquet in this manner will not only increase fatigue, but also intensify strain on the muscles and joints and, over time, possibly damage the arm and shoulder. If you use the kinetic chain well, you will place less stress on your arm and shoulder. Your arm will "come along for the ride" on the wave of energy surging from your legs and core, making efficient use of your whole body.

COACH'S BOX:

The serve is a throwing motion. To help my students understand the importance of the kinetic chain on the serve, I sometimes ask them to throw a ball four different ways: **first**, facing the net and throwing without moving the shoulders in a "shot put" motion; **second**, still facing the net but this time rotating the shoulders during the throw; **third**, the same way but now bending the knees and driving with the legs; and last, establishing a sideways stance and using a full throwing motion with some forward momentum. With each kinetic chain link that is added, the ball is thrown a longer and longer distance.

II. How to Optimize the Kinetic Chain

THE BENEFITS OF THE KINETIC CHAIN are clear, so how do we maximize its advantages? The kinetic chain works best when it is timed correctly and when you are balanced, prepared, and possess full body strength and flexibility.

1. CORRECT TIMING

The timing and sequence of the kinetic chain is important. The kinetic chain has a rhythm of the body lowering with the racquet close to the torso on the backswing, followed by the body rising as you exhale and swing the racquet out and away from the torso on the forward swing. Initiating the kinetic chain too early or too late will reduce its beneficial effects. During the serve, for example, if the racquet moves forward to the ball before the legs have begun to straighten, then the kinetic chain is incorrectly timed and will not function properly.

2. GOOD BALANCE

You must be in a balanced state for your legs to push up efficiently from the ground. Use poor posture or lean incorrectly during the swing, and your feet can't dig in the court (*left*) to establish the strong base needed to push forcefully up from the ground (*center*). If you position yourself too far away from the ball while hitting a forehand, your posture will be poor and your feet will shuffle during the swing, sapping your power. This is one of many reasons footwork is such an important feature

Simona Halep establishes a strong base before pushing up from the ground and landing balanced.

of tennis. Good footwork will get you in the correct position to be balanced, and only then with this good balance established can the power generated from the kinetic chain be uncorked.

3. EARLY PREPARATION

Do your best to establish good positioning early. This will allow you the necessary time to push well with your legs. By getting into position early and setting your feet, you can store more power in your legs during your backswing before unloading it upwards during the forward swing. If you are rushed and without time to set up properly, you will primarily use your smaller arm muscles, resulting in less weight behind the shot.

4. FULL BODY STRENGTH

Tennis players need to be physically strong throughout their whole body to perform the kinetic chain well. You can compare the energy of the kinetic chain to water flowing through the body. If one body part is weak in the link, it in effect creates a dam, and the energy produced before that link is diminished. For example, if a player has a weak abdomen, then the power that began in the legs will decrease through the torso as it filters up to the shoulders.

5. SUPERIOR FLEXIBILITY

You can enhance your kinetic chain by being flexible and by using the "stretch-shortening cycle" of muscles. The stretch-shortening cycle acts somewhat like a rubber band, where the stretching of a muscle is immediately followed by a more powerful shortening of the muscle. The greater your flexibility, the bigger the stretch, and therefore, the greater the amount of energy that can be forged by this

effect. For instance, at the end of your forehand backswing, your chest and shoulder muscles elongate as your hips rotate into the shot and the inertia of your arm causes the racquet to lag behind. This lagging of the racquet stretches the chest and shoulder muscles and stores energy, which is released as these muscles contract, powering the racquet forward faster to hit the ball.

III. How Much Should Your Body Move?

TENNIS IS A DYNAMIC GAME, so it is logical that the amount of body movement during the kinetic chain should and will vary depending on the shot. The kinetic chain is used on every serve and power groundstroke, but is used in different amounts on other shots depending on the speed of the incoming ball and the force of your swing. You must be responsive to the circumstances and use the right amount of body movement in your swing to achieve not only the most power, but also the best control.

The kinetic chain is more important on slower incoming balls, where you need to generate your own power. The best power forehands hit off a slow arriving ball are ones where you can set your feet, bend and then straighten your legs, uncoil the hips and shoulders, and unleash into the stroke (*next page, top*). On clay courts or any slow surface, where the occasions to generate your own power are more frequent, performing a full and vigorous kinetic chain is a vital component in hitting aggressively.

In contrast, on less aggressive shots — like drop shots and slice groundstrokes — you'll have less need for kinetic chain-induced power (*bottom*). The body will be more still on these shots, or "stay down" in coaching parlance. In addition, the kinetic chain is less important on volleys or when receiving fast balls because on these shots the ball has inherent power. For example, when returning a fast serve, there is power stored in the arriving ball and the need for strong sequential body movement is not required; on the contrary, it will only unnecessarily complicate the timing of the shot. For recreational players, staying down is a good groundstroke mantra because it simplifies timing, and it is a technique that agrees with the speed of their swings. Keep in mind, this reduction in body movement during the kinetic chain is done more often on hard courts, where the bounce of the ball is lower and faster than clay courts.

Djokovic uses strong kinetic chain power while hitting this aggressive topspin forehand off a slow ball.

However, on this slice backhand, he keeps his body more level and mutes kinetic chain power.

IV. Kinetic Chain Practice

HOW DO YOU BUILD a strong kinetic chain? Kinetic chain strength largely comes from building a solid core, the central third of the body that includes the spine, back, hips, and abdomen. The core is key to a strong kinetic chain; in order to maximize power, the kinetic chain's energy surge must flow through the core without being diminished. In addition, the hip and shoulder rotation stage of the kinetic chain relies on a strong core for support. Professional tennis players understand this and train hard to strengthen this part of the body, often turning to their favorite core workout tool: the medicine ball.

Medicine ball workouts train you to use your body as an integrated system due to the force required for the explosive throwing of the weighted ball. Also, you can copy specific swings, such as a forehand or backhand, and mimic the different movements that are used on the court.

Choose a medicine ball weight and number of repetitions appropriate to your fitness level for the following exercises.

1. GROUNDSTROKE MEDICINE BALL EXERCISES

Stand sideways to a wall (with the wall on your left) leading with your left foot in a crouched position. Hold the medicine ball behind your right hip with most of your weight on your

right leg. Mimic the loading position of the forehand and throw the ball to the wall following the forehand swing, maintaining good posture while rotating your torso. Follow through with both your hands finishing shoulder high and hips square to the wall. Then copy the backhand motion by doing the same movement but facing the opposite way and leading with the right leg. If you have a practice partner, it is a good idea to do these tosses while catching and moving around as you would during a baseline rally (*left*).

2. SERVING MEDICINE BALL EXERCISES

Stand facing a wall with your feet about shoulder width apart, place your hands on the sides of the medicine ball, and raise the ball high above your head. From this position, throw the ball against the wall in three different directions: upwards, straight ahead, and down to the ground in front of you. Next, change your leg positioning so that you lead with your left foot, finding yourself in the sideways serving stance. With the ball above your head, bend your knees, rotate your hips and shoulders in a similar fashion to a serve, and throw the ball upwards at around a 45 degree angle as far as you can against the wall or to a training partner.

3. VOLLEY MEDICINE BALL EXERCISES

Simply playing a game of catch with a training partner will strengthen the shoulder and arm muscles used on the volley. Throw the medicine ball using a chest-press motion, keeping the elbows near the body, while moving across the court with a partner. Next, throw the ball using the same chest-press motion while stepping with the left leg forward and then the right leg forward as you move across the court.

Tennis players need to be quick and agile in their movement. Here, Federer makes a ballet-like move to play this high backhand volley.

CHAPTER 3

Movement

T ENNIS FANS ARE SOMETIMES AWESTRUCK by a professional's spectacular stroke, but they often overlook what happened before the shot that made it possible: movement. In fact, movement has become increasingly more important on the professional tour as players hit the ball faster and the advent of poly strings has led to increased spin and more acute groundstroke angles. It is no surprise that the four players who have won the most ATP titles over the last decade — Roger Federer, Rafael Nadal, Novak Djokovic, and Andy Murray — are amongst the quickest players on the ATP Tour. The link between good movement and success at the professional level, however, is nothing new. The top players have always been quick and agile. When eight-time major champion Ivan Lendl was asked to name the greatest strength shared by the best players of any era, he didn't point to a big serve or a dominant forehand; he said superior movement. [1]

At any level, the impact of movement during a point can be seen in many different ways. On every stroke other than the serve, your movement hugely impacts the amount of time and balance you have to play the shot. It is only with ample time and balance that you can hit the ball consistently well. Movement allows you to reach a difficult ball and extend the point. It also sets up your position for the swing. If you take the wrong steps and swing while too close or too far away from the ball, your arms will under or overextend and your body weight will move in a different direction than the racquet. If you take the right steps, your arms will extend correctly and the movement of your body weight and racquet will be synchronized. Movement allows you to attack the ball and steal time away from your opponent or shift backwards and hit the ball at a more comfortable height. Simply put, tennis revolves around movement and every player should work hard to ensure it is an asset in their game.

Movement during a rally involves several different types of footwork including shuffles, skips, and slides as well as short, multi-directional sprints. You can think of court coverage as a dance where the ball is your partner and, because the ball comes at different speeds and lands in different locations, it is a partner adept at many different moves. On a high stretching backhand volley, your movement may resemble ballet, while the little steps recommended just before hitting a groundstroke may resemble the cha-cha. Making the right "dance" moves to the ball means reading the speed, spin, and trajectory of the incoming shot, predicting where the ball will land, and positioning your legs accordingly in the most comfortable stance. Players who have flexibility and adaptability in the way they move to the ball or, in dancing terms, the dancers that can change with the beat, are the ones who have the best footwork.

In Chapter 16, I explain the various components of fitness (flexibility, agility, quickness, core stability, endurance, and strength) that are important to overall movement. In this chapter, I focus specifically on the movement that occurs on the court and the different types of steps done sequentially that lead to a well-executed stroke: a split step, an explosive first step, small adjustment steps, and lastly, sliding.

I. Split Step

GOOD MOVEMENT STARTS with a strong split step (*opposite bottom*). Sometimes called the "ready hop," the goal of the split step is to heighten your state of awareness so that your body can react quickly at the critical moment when the ball comes off your opponent's strings.

The split step helps overcome the negative effects of inertia, making it easier to begin movement at a time when the body would otherwise be at rest. Pushing a stalled car is difficult, but once it starts moving, the car becomes easier to move. In tennis, the split step makes it easier to push the body.

The split step not only helps when there is little movement, but also when there is a lot of movement. It stops your body momentum from your recovery after playing a wide shot,

COACH'S BOX:

The panther is a great mover partly due to its malleable body and low center of gravity. The giraffe has opposite qualities. Playing in a panther-like athletic manner — staying loose and low to the ground — takes practice and good leg strength. This is why some players succumb to standing stiff and upright, giraffe-like during points, leading to a slow first step and less than ideal movement. During your practice sessions, allow your body to take on different shapes and remind yourself to crouch and lower your center of gravity. Making these athletic fundamentals a habit will speed up your movement, helping you to pounce faster on your prey, the tennis ball.

improving your ability to take off quickly for the next shot.

TECHNIQUE

You set up for the split step by getting into the athletic stance. The athletic stance places each foot several inches outside the shoulders with legs slightly bent so you stand around six to eight inches lower than your natural height (*right*). In this crouched position, you lean slightly forward with your upper body, but with your hips back and back fairly straight.

The athletic stance lowers your center of gravity and moves some of your body weight from the legs up towards the hips. This "lightens" the body and assists you in reacting quickly to your opponent's shot. Another helpful car analogy involves the design of Formula 1 racing cars. These cars have a wide wheel base and a very low center of gravity that hovers just above the ground. This design allows the car to move and change directions quickly.

After setting up in the athletic stance, the

Johanna Konta's athletic stance: feet outside the shoulders, knees bent, back reasonably straight, and weight slightly forward.

Andy Murray's explosive first step is partly attributed to his high and wide split step (*left and center*) and timing. He hits the ground (*right*) at the exact moment he knows which direction he needs to move.

At the end of this split step, Federer's left foot is touching the ground first, indicating he is anticipating moving to the right.

split step is done by hopping with both feet just above the ground an instant before your opponent makes contact with the ball (*previous page, left*). Your legs should open a little wider (i.e. split) as they lift off the ground (*previous page, center*). The higher off the ground you split step, the more force you apply with your feet to the court surface, and the more explosive your first step will be as a result.

The upward hop with both feet is followed by a lowering of the body with your weight forward and knees slightly bent when you hit the ground (*previous page, right*). Timing is a key aspect of the split step; your feet should hit the ground just as you first know which way you have to move.

This upward and downward movement of the body stores energy in the legs, allowing you to generate a more powerful first movement to the ball. Additionally, performing the split step shifts your weight forward to the front of your feet, naturally lifting your heels off the ground and eliminating the required step of lifting your heels to move.

Once you have mastered the basic split step, you can learn the advanced split step, whereby you land on the foot opposite the direction you anticipate you will need to move. For example, if you are anticipating the need to move right, then you will land with more weight on your left foot to allow you to push off aggressively towards the right (*left*).

II. First Step

AFTER THE SPLIT STEP, a good first step is critical because there is so little time to build up the speed necessary to reach your opponent's shot. If the first step is poor, all the subsequent steps also will be slower, hurting your ability to get into good positioning for the

After completing his split step, Nadal lowers his body, leans, and pivots his feet to help him take off quickly for his next shot.

To speed up her movement forward, Garbine Muguruza leans forward to match the push-off angle of her feet to the rest of her body.

stroke or reach your opponent's shot. This is why a well-disguised shot is so effective. When you get fooled by a deceptive drop shot, your weak first step means there is a good chance you will never gather the speed needed to run down the ball. If you can anticipate the drop shot you will take a stronger first step and run much faster.

In order to take a powerful first step, you need to simultaneously lower your body, lean towards the ball, and pivot your feet to open your hips in the direction you wish to move (*left*). It is important that your upper body leans forward slightly as you take the first step to match the push-off angle of the feet to the hips, spine, and shoulders (*right*).

Leaning with the upper body is also important in getting a strong first first step to re-

cover. To recover after hitting a wide ball, lean forward right or left against the momentum of the direction you were running (*next page, bottom*). If you are stiff in your trunk, you will find it difficult to put on the brakes and change course. Be flexible and have your body take on different shapes so that your trunk shifts in the direction that allows your legs to first move to the ball and then to recover.

While the great movers lean left, right, backward, or forward depending on the direction of their first step, they quickly straighten their backs to restore good posture once the first movement is completed. Watching Djokovic shortly after he completes his first move, you will notice how he stays low to the ground while maintaining good posture. The strength in his legs and core allows him to move quick-

Djokovic quickly regains his posture after a strong first step as he moves forward to reach a drop shot.

ly with his legs bent and his upper body fairly upright (*above*). This posture both enables him to slow down quickly once he nears the ball and helps him keep his head still to track the ball better and judge correctly where it will land.

TYPES OF FIRST STEPS

Because the ball arrives in different locations at varying speeds, there are many different first steps. For example, if there is only a short distance to cover, the the first step usually will be a small half-step out in the direction of the

With a long distance to recover, Nadal uses the crossover step followed by running steps.

With a short distance to recover, Jo-Wilfried Tsonga uses a crossover step followed by lateral side shuffles.

ball with the foot closest to the ball. But if there is a long distance to cover, the foot closest to the ball might slide underneath the torso and not in the direction of the ball. This slants the body in the direction you need to move, helping you accelerate to reach a difficult ball.

There are specific first steps to recovery as well. The crossover step, whereby the right leg moves in front and to the left of the left leg, or vice versa, is an important first step to learn in order to recover quickly. If there is a lot of ground to cover after returning a very wide ball, the first step will usually be a crossover step followed by running steps (*opposite bottom*). If recovering from a shot that is less wide, the the first step often will be a crossover step, but this time will be followed by lateral side shuffles (*above*).

III. Adjustment Steps

AFTER YOUR SPLIT STEP and first step, your movement to the ball continues with larger steps to cover ground and then, if time allows, small adjustment steps before your swing. These small adjustment steps allow you to compensate for any early misjudgments on where you thought the ball would land so that you end up the correct distance from the ball. Keep in mind, where you think the ball might land when it is 40 feet away may be quite different from where you know it will land when the ball is 15 feet away.

Adjustment steps will also improve your groundstrokes' rhythm and timing. As Nadal's coach Francis Roig once said, "The most important thing is how you read the ball and un-

Nadal takes little adjustment steps before unloading on this forehand.

derstand how it is going to bounce. In tennis, if you are too fast, it's bad. If you're too slow, it's bad. You have to be on time."[2] By using small adjustment steps as the ball approaches (*above*), you increase your chances of positioning yourself at the right spot at the correct time to hit with power and balance.

Next time you are watching a professional match, pay attention to the little steps the players take before their shots. On hard courts, you can hear their shoes squeaking on the courts as they use these steps to get into the best possible position. They play with "happy" feet. At the recreational level, the ball is traveling at a speed where there is time to take adjustment steps before most shots.

IV. Sliding

FOR THOSE OF YOU THAT PLAY on Har-Tru or clay courts, learning to slide on the court is important. It helps produce a quicker recovery, maintain balance, and save energy.

To slide well you must bend your knees, widen your stance, and keep the upper body straight. As you begin the slide, lean your up-

Jack Sock widens his stance and leans back to allow his right foot to slide after hitting this slice backhand.

per body back against the direction of the front foot to allow the foot to slide (*opposite bottom*). If your legs straighten or your upper body tilts forward, your sliding foot will grip on the court surface, causing you to come to a sudden stop and stumble.

The lead foot slides, pointing in the direction you are moving, while your back foot lines up perpendicularly to the front foot, anchoring your balance. On strokes described later in the book, your right foot will lead the slide on open stance forehands, slice backhands, and backhand volleys, and the left foot will lead on open stance backhands and most forehand volleys.

The timing of the slide on slice groundstrokes is different as compared to topspin groundstrokes. On slice groundstrokes, you will still be sliding as you play the shot and finish the slide after the ball has left your racquet. This type of slide is often used defending against a wide baseline shot or while moving forward to scoop up a well played drop shot. On topspin strokes, your slide should be complete before initiating the forward swing (*below*). As your slide comes to a stop on topspin strokes, you will push up with the legs and use the core of the body to swing with power. It takes practice to determine the optimal slide length that will allow you to stabilize your legs at the end of the slide and push up from the ground.

V. Movement Practice

PLEASE REFER TO CHAPTER 16 for exercises to improve your movement.

Gaël Monfils ends his slide before unleashing on this topspin forehand.

Two great forehand players who use different grips: Djokovic (*above*) uses a western grip while Federer (*below*) uses a strong eastern grip.

CHAPTER 4

Grips

N OW THAT WE HAVE DISCUSSED THE BODY, let's move on to discussing how to swing the racquet. First, before you hone your stroke technique, you must know to grip the racquet properly. You might think, "That's simple, right?" However, in my experience, many players hold the racquet in a way that hurts their technique and limits their progress.

Grips are the foundation of every tennis swing, or, as the great Rod Laver once put it, "The grip determines everything."[1] Your grip will influence the amount of speed and spin on each ball you hit. Some grips make it easier to angle the racquet face down, or be "closed," which is helpful for producing topspin on powerful groundstrokes. Other grips make it easier to angle the racquet face up, or be "open," which is helpful for creating backspin and controlling volleys and finesse shots. Your grip also affects where you make contact with the ball, and therefore, your body positioning and timing of your swing.

On some shots, like the serve, there is a very tight range of variability in how you should hold the racquet. On other shots, like the forehand topspin groundstroke, players have a wider range of choice in the grip used, with advantages and disadvantages to each. For example, Roger Federer and Novak Djokovic both have tremendous forehands, but each uses a different forehand grip (*opposite*).

I. Grip Tension

BEFORE DISCUSSING THE ALIGNMENT of your hand on the grip, it's important to stress that holding the racquet too tightly will hurt your game. Your grip should be firm but not tight. Control of the racquet comes mostly from the palm of the hand, *not* from the excessive squeezing pressure of the fingers. This is a subtle but important distinction.

If you feel your forearm and not the racquet head when you hit the ball, you are holding the grip too tightly and losing racquet speed, "feel" (sensitivity for the ball on the strings), and coordination. Using a slightly relaxed grip has the opposite effects. Let's discuss how grip tension affects power, feel, and coordination.

KINETIC ENERGY EQUALS ONE-HALF MASS
MULTIPLIED BY VELOCITY SQUARED MR. JONES!

1. POWER

It is a common misconception in tennis to equate muscle tension with power because that is generally the case in other physical activities. If you wanted to lift a heavy object you would tense your muscles and lift. However, tennis — in which a two-ounce ball is hit by a 27-inch-long swinging racquet — involves completely different physics.

The formula for kinetic energy is $KE = \frac{1}{2}mv^2$ (kinetic energy equals one-half mass multiplied by velocity squared). Therefore, doubling the velocity (racquet speed) will have a much larger effect on the energy delivered to the ball than doubling the mass. This is why a young junior can hit a tennis ball harder than some muscle-bound adults. The goal is to swing with speed, which can be done better with a relaxed arm. Additionally, on many shots, especially the serve and topspin groundstrokes, the racquet should lag slightly behind body movement, thus creating a strong "slingshot" effect for extra racquet head speed. This can only be done well if the muscles are relaxed.

2. FEEL

The way our body is designed results in our sense of touch being heightened when our muscles are looser. A surgeon, a concert pianist, a sharp shooter — occupations that require fine fine motor skills - will all tell you that to perform well they need their muscles to be slightly relaxed. Tennis is a fine motor skill sport and not being tense will improve your feel for the ball on your strings.

3. COORDINATION

When our muscles are tight, our coordination is adversely affected, and this leads to poor timing and more mishits.

Keep in mind, you will squeeze the grip to varying degrees at contact depending on the shot played. On a power volley, you squeeze more than on finesse shots. Regardless of the stroke, the grip should be relaxed during the preparation phase to allow your muscles to perform best.

COACH'S BOX:

Try rolling a ball around the edge of the racquet head while squeezing the grip tightly. Then do it while relaxing the thumb and index finger. You will notice how your feel for the ball and coordination improves when your hand is in a more relaxed state.

II. Types of Grips

A TENNIS GRIP IS OCTAGONAL with four main sides and four narrower bevels between the four main sides. I find the simplest way to explain how to find different grips is to assign a number to each of the eight sides of the racquet or racquet's grip (*below*).

I will use whole numbers to describe where to place the base knuckle of the index finger for most of the grips, but there is leeway to add or subtract half a bevel to find the grip most comfortable for you. Moving the knuckle half a bevel up or down from the original bevel makes the grip a stronger or weaker version, respectively, of that grip. With every grip hold the racquet low in the handle and sequence your fingers so your index finger is above your thumb.

1. CONTINENTAL GRIP

You can find the continental grip by putting the base knuckle of your index finger on bevel #2. The continental grip is versatile and is used on

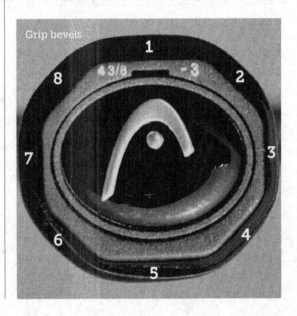

Grip bevels

Stan Wawrinka uses the continental grip on his slice backhand.

the serve, volleys, slice groundstrokes, finesse shots, and when defending low and wide balls.

The continental grip is used on the serve because it allows your wrist to pronate and accelerate the racquet best. It also gives you the ability to maximize contact height, take a full wind up, and hit heavy spins on the serve. By using the continental grip for volleys, where play at the net is fast, you are able to hit both the forehand and backhand volley without changing your grip. On slice groundstrokes (*above*) and finesse shots like the drop shot and lob, the continental grip increases the likelihood of accurate ball placement by al-

lowing you to comfortably open the racquet face and "cradle" the ball on the strings for better control. Lastly, the way the continental grip naturally opens the racquet face makes it a preferable grip for low balls, and its later contact point can help you when rushed for a wide shot.

Because the continental grip is used on many shots, it is vital to master. If you are not acquainted with the continental grip, commit to the exercises at the end of this chapter because a lack of familiarity with this grip can negatively impact your performance on many strokes.

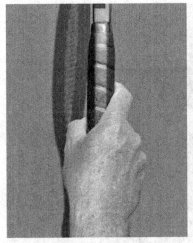

CONTINENTAL GRIP

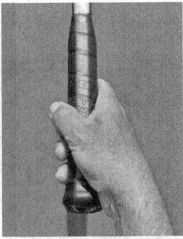

EASTERN FOREHAND GRIP

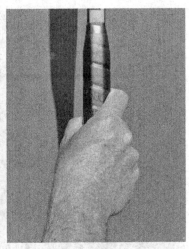

EASTERN BACKHAND GRIP

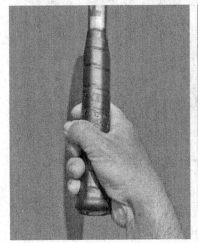

SEMI-WESTERN FOREHAND GRIP

WESTERN FOREHAND GRIP

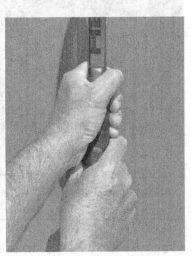

TWO-HANDED BACKHAND GRIP

2. TOPSPIN GROUNDSTROKE GRIPS

There are three topspin forehand grips (eastern, semi-western, and western) and three topspin backhand grips (eastern, semi-western, and two-handed) and they all have pros and cons. Spend time on the practice court to see which forehand and backhand grips work best for you.

A. EASTERN GRIPS

The eastern forehand grip (bevel #3) and eastern backhand grip (bevel #1) allow you to brush up the back of the ball to add topspin or easily flatten out your groundstroke for more aggressive intentions. The eastern forehand grip places the palm at the same angle as the strings, making it a suitable grip for recreational players to use as compared to the more closed western grips. The eastern grips are also good for net rushing players; since the change from the eastern to the continental grip is small, volleying is easier for these players than for other

Serena Williams' use of the semi-western grip allows her to change easily from hitting her forehand flat or with heavy topspin.

players who require a larger grip change. The negatives of the eastern grips are that high-bouncing balls are more difficult to return and groundstrokes may be less consistent because there is a smaller amount of topspin produced as compared to the western grips.

grips, they still provide a racquet face that allows the ball to be hit with less topspin when a flatter, faster shot makes strategic sense. It is also a comfortable grip for a wide range of contact heights, particularly on the high-bouncing balls common in the modern era.

B. SEMI-WESTERN GRIPS

Many consider the semi-western forehand grip (bevel #3.5 - 4) to be the ultimate topspin forehand grip, and it is the grip most used by today's professionals. The semi-western backhand grip (bevel #8) is for one-handed backhand players only. Although semi-western grips add more topspin to a shot than eastern

C. WESTERN FOREHAND GRIP

The western forehand grip (bevel #4 - 4.5) is the one that closes the racquet face the most and produces the greatest topspin. It is a comfortable grip to use on balls hit above the chest. The negatives are that it is a difficult grip on fast, low, or wide balls, and it is more challenging to hit flatter shots to produce winners.

D. THE TWO-HANDED BACKHAND GRIP

The two-handed backhand is the most popular way to hit the backhand at the higher levels of the game. The pros and cons of the two-handed backhand are discussed at length in Chapter Eight. There are different ways to grip the racquet for the two-handed backhand, but I recommend a continental grip (bevel #2) on the right hand and an eastern to strong eastern forehand grip (left index finger base knuckle at bevels #6 - 6.5) with the left hand. These grips allow the wrists to move freely and create good racquet head speed. Some players prefer an eastern backhand grip with the right hand, but I recommend the continental grip because it moves the contact point back slightly, allowing a precious split second longer to execute the shot. It is also easier to disguise a drop shot or hit a regular slice backhand because no grip change is necessary.

Murray uses the two-handed backhand grip favored by most professionals: a continental grip with the right hand and eastern grip with the left hand.

COACH'S BOX:

Young children sometimes begin using the western grip on the forehand because it feels more comfortable on balls hit above the chest, a shot they encounter frequently. However, this can lead young players to develop poor stroke mechanics, causing them to lean back, bend their hitting elbow too much, and cut their swing short. Although the eastern grip or semi-western grip may initially feel more awkward on the higher balls for young players, using these grips will help them in the long run as it encourages fuller swings. If they naturally gravitate to the western grip later on, that is fine.

III. Grip Practice

LEARNING ANYTHING NEW, including a new grip, should be done progressively. You don't learn algebra without first learning how to count. Similarly, in tennis it's best to start small and build up. If you are learning a topspin grip, start by hitting from the service line and move backwards towards the baseline three feet at a time as you become more comfortable with it. Learning the continental grip

Ball Taps

for slice groundstrokes can be done the same way. Due to the strong impact of the ball when hitting volleys, I recommend you first learn the continental grip off the bounce from the service line before you volley the ball out of the air. Learning this way also provides more time to turn the shoulders and develop good body positioning habits for the volley.

1. BALL TAPS

Using the continental grip, place the racquet in front of you at a 10 o'clock angle and dribble the ball down from a waist high position like a basketball player (*left*). This ball tap exercise will help you get familiar with the continental grip for the serve. Next, tap the ball up two to three feet in the air with the palm up and the racquet positioned at a two o'clock angle, and then do the same with the palm down and the racquet positioned at a nine o'clock angle. These two ball tap exercises will help your forehand and backhand volleys.

2. THE WALL

Hitting against the wall provides helpful repetition, which can quickly get you accustomed to any type of grip. If working on the continental grip, position yourself about 10 to 15 feet from the wall and hit gentle shots allowing the ball to bounce before you hit it. Serve practice with the continental grip can also be done against the wall. If you're learning a new topspin groundstroke grip, stand far enough away from the wall to allow the ball to bounce two or three times before hitting the ball. This will give you time to perform a full follow through.

BALANCE

"Your degree of balance will impact many facets of your game, including rally ascendancy, stroke power, racquet control, vision, and recovery."

KINETIC CHAIN

"The energy generated by the legs is transferred and increased up the body, culminating in an end point power surge."

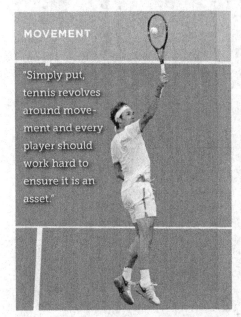

MOVEMENT

"Simply put, tennis revolves around movement and every player should work hard to ensure it is an asset."

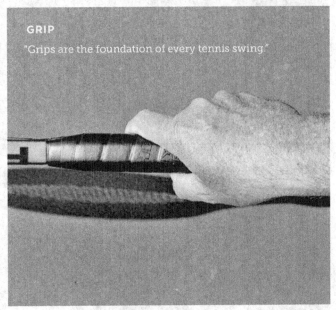

GRIP

"Grips are the foundation of every tennis swing."

BALANCE (Chapter One) underpins stroke control, THE KINETIC CHAIN (Chapter Two) boosts stroke power, MOVEMENT (Chapter Three) provides the time and positioning to get balanced and ignite the kinetic chain, and GRIP (Chapter Four) impacts not only stroke power and control, but also spin and technique. Now that the athletic principles and grips of tennis — the bedrocks of every great shot — have been covered, it's time to learn strokes, starting with arguably the most important one: the serve.

Pete Sampras' powerful serve was the cornerstone of his game.

CHAPTER 5

Serve

T HE SERVE SETS THE TONE OF THE POINT, and often the match. As Pete Sampras, who rode his serve to 14 major titles, once said of the importance of the serve, "You kind of live and die by the serve." [1]

Sampras' powerful serve allowed him to ace opponents or to put himself in a dominant position early in a point by either forcing a weak return or moving his opponent out of position. Thanks to his serve, he was able to save energy on his quick service games and, when receiving serve, he could relax and go for aggressive returns knowing that in most matches he only had to break serve once to secure the set. In contrast, players with a poor serve often have extended and tiring serving games and feel tremendous pressure to break serve; otherwise, they face the possibility of quickly finding themselves behind in the set. While of course we may never serve like Sampras, we all have the capacity to improve our serves — the only shot you completely control in a match and the only shot you can practice alone.

This chapter is split into three main sections: Serve Technique, Serve Tactics, and Serve Practice. The Serve Technique section makes up the bulk of the chapter, and I will break down the steps to teach you how to develop a powerful and reliable serve. I will cover establishing a routine, serving stance, backswing, ball toss, trophy position, racquet drop, wrist pronation, body positioning at contact, and follow through for the flat serve. After explaining these elements of technique, I describe how to perform the slice, the slice-topspin, and the kick serve. In Serve Tactics, I discuss how to be unpredictable with your serve and different strategies for deciding what serve to use based on your strengths and weaknesses and the score. In Serve Practice, I provide drills to help you improve this pivotal shot.

I. Serve Technique

I. ESTABLISH A ROUTINE

The first step is to establish a pre-serve routine. Sometimes the professionals' pre-serve routines are quirky, but even when they are, they are always regular. ATP player Ernests Gulbis asks the ball kid for three balls and proceeds to juggle them in one hand and tap them with the tips of his fingers before he throws his least favorite back. Rafael Nadal's infamously long pre-serve routine involves bouncing the ball several times with his racquet, picking at the back of his shorts, lifting his shirt on both shoulders, wiping his nose, moving hair behind both ears, and several more bounces of the ball with his hand. You certainly don't have to be as idiosyncratic as Gulbis or elaborate as

Nadal, but you need a pre-serve routine. It provides rhythm to the serve and can calm you down in a stressful situation.

As you are performing your pre-serve routine, you should be thinking about what serving spins and placements have been effective thus far in the match, what serve makes best use of your strengths, and what serve is best for the score (*see pages 64-65*). These factors should shape your decision when selecting the type of serve you will use.

Before you start the serve, make sure to place your hitting hand in the continental grip with a relaxed arm. The continental grip is a key component of a powerful serve. It is only by using this grip that you can obtain impor-

Federer contemplates his serving options before he serves.

tant qualities of the serve that I discuss in-depth later: deep racquet drop, high contact point, full wrist pronation, and the ability to hit strong spin serves. Last, imagine in your mind the ball landing in the service box where you intend to place it. Visualizing success like this on your serve will give you increased focus and confidence.

2. STANCE

There is no one perfect serving stance, otherwise all top players would use it and there would be uniformity in serving technique. The best stance is specific to the player and you need to figure out what works best for you through repetition and experimentation. The three main serving stances are the platform, the narrow platform, and the pinpoint stance.

Regardless of what stance you use, I recommend you begin your serve with your front foot pointing towards the right net post. The back foot is a more individualistic preference, but I recommend your back foot be lined up behind and slightly to the left of your front foot and angled parallel to the baseline to best anchor the weight transfer that occurs at the beginning of the serve (*below*).

Let's describe the three stances and look at the trade-offs with each stance in regards to power and consistency.

A. PLATFORM STANCE

In the platform stance, your front and back foot should be a little more than shoulder

Belinda Bencic begins her serve with her front foot pointing towards the right net post and her back foot angled parallel to the baseline.

width apart (*left*). Your weight starts forward and rocks back with your feet remaining stationary as you begin the backswing.

The platform stance has the advantage of a simple weight transfer and, therefore, leads to a more reliable toss and consistent serve. Also, the relatively wide base this stance provides during the top of the swing helps the legs push up forcefully from the ground. These advantages, coupled with the simplicity and naturalness of the platform stance, make it a good choice for recreational players. These qualities also help the elite pros and is partly the reason why players like Milos Raonic, a platform server, rarely has a bad serving day. The main drawbacks of this stance is that the wider base

reduces the power derived from the hip movement as compared to the other two stances, and it has less forward momentum than the pinpoint method.

B. NARROW PLATFORM STANCE

In the narrow platform stance, the feet start only a few inches apart (*right*). There is very little rocking back and forth from the front foot to the back foot. This narrow base and stability makes for strong hip movement and a steady ball toss, but it lacks the forward momentum of the other two stances. It's a serving style that was rarely seen before the year 2000. Soon after that, former U.S. Open champion Andy Roddick helped legitimize

Milos Roanic uses the platform stance.

Andy Roddick serves with a narrow platform stance.

this stance and proved that even without strong forward momentum, a blistering 155 mph serve is possible.

C. PINPOINT STANCE

The pinpoint serving style begins with the feet several inches wider apart than in the platform stance (*left*). As the hands go up on the backswing, you step forward with the back foot, aligning your feet together side by side before bending your knees and elevating to the ball (*right*).

Of the three serving styles, the pinpoint method has the strongest forward weight transference. Also, compared to the platform stance, the feet are closer together during the top of the swing, freeing up the hips for a larg-er hip push, pull, and rotation, and providing extra torque to the torso and power to your arm. However, because there is more body movement occurring as the left arm rises to toss the ball, the ball toss can be less dependable. Also, since it is a more athletic serve, it requires greater body control and timing. It is the most difficult of the three serving styles, but also the most explosive, which is why most ATP players and the vast majority of WTA players use this stance.

3. BACKSWING

Once you have completed your pre-serve routine and established your stance, you are ready to begin the serve and start your backswing. The serve needs to be rhythmic to be

John Isner utilizes the pinpoint stance.

powerful, so your movements during the back-swing are important.

There are three main types of backswings: pendulum, abbreviated, and waist-high. When determining the backswing that works best for you, remember that the purpose of the back-swing is two-fold: first, to produce a rhythm that allows energy to build up powerfully in your legs and second, to efficiently place the racquet in the correct position at the top of the swing.

A. PENDULUM BACKSWING

The pendulum backswing is the traditional wind up whereby the racquet drops down near to the ground (*opposite left*) before it moves back and then up into the top of the swing, tracing the circumference of a circle. Because the racquet follows the natural flow of a pen-dulum movement, it is an easy backswing and a good one for recreational players.

COACH'S BOX:

The top professionals appreciate the importance of the stance and backswing on the serve and often experiment and adjust their technique. Early in his career, Rafael Nadal changed from using the platform stance to the pinpoint stance on his serve. This adjustment increased his serving speed significantly. Similarly, Novak Djokovic's pre-2010 serve had a longer backswing that complicated his technique and led to a less consistent serve. In 2010, he shortened and moved his backswing to the right with his arm looser and more bent. This more efficient motion improved his balance and placed his racquet in a more comfortable position at the top of his swing. After making this change, Djokovic's upgraded serve helped him go on an impressive winning streak.

Certainly, if Nadal and Djokovic are prepared to refine their serve during their professional career, all players should be willing to make swing modifications and embrace the learning process of change that can sometimes mean taking one step back before going two steps forward.

Early in his professional career, Nadal changed from using a platform stance (*left*) to a pinpoint stance (*right*).

Djokovic's 2014 serve (*left*) has a more relaxed, shorter backswing than his 2008 version (*right*).

B. ABBREVIATED BACKSWING

On the abbreviated backswing, once the racquet goes back level with your back leg, it goes straight up past your chest into the top of your swing (*middle*). This shorter backswing works best for servers with a faster rhythm. It has the advantage of simplicity but requires significant shoulder strength and flexibility to use and hit a powerful serve.

C. WAIST-HIGH BACKSWING

On the waist-high backswing, the racquet passes by the hips horizontally before lifting up into the top of the swing (*right*). Some players find the pendulum backswing too long and not suitable for the serving rhythm, while others find the abbreviated backswing not long enough to build-up good energy in the lower body. These players are likely to use the waist-high backswing on their serve.

The teaching philosophy regarding how the arms should move up during the backswing has changed over time. Previously, the instruction was "arms go down together, and then up together," whereby the hitting arm and tossing arm lift together into the top of the swing (*middle*). This is a simple method and is still an effective one for recreational players and a minority of touring pros. However, in the modern serving technique used by most advanced players and touring pros, the hitting arm slightly lags the tossing arm. Here, your hitting hand is around waist level as your tossing hand releases the ball above your head creating a "see-saw" movement of the arms (*right*). While this technique is a little more complicated, the advantages are clear: it keeps the shoulders more relaxed, establishes a longer loading position for a stronger leg drive, and tilts the shoulders upward more to reach a higher contact point.

Andy Murray begins a pendulum backswing.

Richard Gasquet utilizes an abbreviated backswing.

Maria Kirilenko performs a waist-high backswing.

4. BALL TOSS

As your right arm performs the backswing, your left arm tosses the ball. It's a simple fact — in order to hit a good serve, you must have an accurate toss. An inconsistent toss will lead to awkward contact points and ruin the rhythm required for a powerful and reliable serve.

A. BALL TOSS TECHNIQUE

There are four components of ball toss technique to consider.

1. BALL GRIP

I recommend having the top half of three or four fingers on one side of the ball and the end of the thumb resting on the opposite side (*right*). Hold the ball lightly in this pincer-like grip. Don't hold the ball deep in your palm; your fingers may obstruct the release and cause your toss to go askew.

To toss the ball well, hold the ball towards the top half of your fingers.

2. ARM MOVEMENT

Your tossing arm should stay in front of you and drop only slightly before going upward (*opposite left*). If serving to the deuce side playing singles, the tossing arm begins its movement pointing towards the right net post to turn the shoulders (*opposite middle*) and then towards the center of the court as it continues its movement upward. Keep in mind that because the contact point is to the left of where the hand releases the ball, your ball toss will arc slightly from right to left. For recreational players, I recommend the tossing arm go up slightly left of the right net post. This way the toss doesn't arc, but goes up more in a straight line for a simpler toss.

Your arm should be straight, wrist still, and your palm facing the sky as you toss the ball. To help you keep your arm straight and wrist steady as you release the ball on your toss, try to imagine that instead of a ball, you are holding an ice cream cone that you raise while attempting not to spill the ice cream.

Remember to release the ball slightly above head level (*opposite right*). This will help keep your serve fluid and shorten the distance the ball has to travel, reducing the chances your toss will go astray.

> ## COACH'S BOX:
>
> **The importance of the toss was evident during Serena Williams' play at the 2015 U.S. Open. Typically, her very reliable toss places the contact point on her serve within a tight eight-inch range. However, during her first three matches at the 2015 U.S. Open, her toss was inconsistent, causing the range to increase to 19 inches. This variability upset her serving tempo and resulted in an almost equal number of double faults and aces. After her third match, she reduced the range on her contact height back to eight inches, and over the next three matches, her number of aces more than tripled her number of double faults.[2]**

3. BALANCE

Your weight will shift back during the toss, but this movement should be completed by the time the ball leaves your fingers (*right*). Keep your weight slightly on your back foot when you release the ball so as to establish a good position for the body's upward and forward push that follows.

4. FOLLOW THROUGH

After the ball's release, your tossing arm continues up to a position roughly perpendicular to the ground (*next page, left*). This produces a smooth, long motion and allows your arm to move at the proper speed at your release point. If you stop the follow through of your tossing arm abruptly, you will release the ball too low and too fast to have an accurate toss.

B. BALL TOSS PLACEMENT

The height of the toss will be affected by the speed and length of your wind up. Servers who use a slower or longer backswing will need a higher toss than those who have faster or shorter backswings. While everyone has a slightly different rhythm on the serve, a good guideline is to have the height of the ball toss peak one-to-two feet above the point of contact (*next page, right*). This allows enough time to execute your swing with good rhythm and a full build-up of energy throughout your body. A ball toss that is too high is difficult to time and less consistent, while a ball toss that is too low will cramp good arm extension and reduce the time allotted for the body to build energy.

The ball toss should be in front of you. The angle of your body leans into the court to ob-

Caroline Wozniacki's ball toss sees her left arm move down slightly, straighten, and then lift smoothly pointing towards the right net post.

To help her produce a smooth ball toss, Li Na continues to lift her left arm after releasing the ball.

Venus Williams tosses the ball approximately two feet above contact and into the court, allowing her time to build energy through the body and lean forward for added power.

tain the forward body momentum needed to hit an imposing serve (*right*). The distance in front of you will depend on your height and what type of serve you are hitting, but two feet in front of you on the first serve and one foot in front of you on the second serve are good general guidelines.

The direction of your toss also will vary right-to-left depending on what type of serve you are delivering (*see page 59*) and the side to which you are serving. If in front of an imaginary clock and serving to the deuce side, your

flat serve will have a toss around noon. On the ad side, because your target and momentum are more to the right, move the ball toss slightly more to the right.

5. TROPHY POSITION

After your backswing and release of the ball on the toss, you enter what is commonly referred to as the trophy position. In the model trophy position, your left arm is pointing straight up towards the ball, and your right arm is bent in an L-shape with your racquet pointing towards the sky and facing the side fence (*opposite*).

If looking at the trophy position from a back view, the right elbow should be left of the right shoulder. This elbow positioning places the

COACH'S BOX:

The ball toss would seem like an easy task to do well, but because other body parts are moving during the toss, it can prove to be an elusive skill for some. Fortunately, it's a skill that can be easily practiced almost anywhere. If your ceiling height permits, your ball toss can be improved from the comfort of your home, or if that is not possible, you can practice it outside at a nearby park. At the park, mark a spot on a fence with a piece of paper that represents your ball toss apex and practice tossing to that spot. Remember to move your hitting arm as you toss the ball and perform the toss as you would during a match.

David Ferrer sets up in the classic trophy position: left arm up and extended, right arm L-shaped, and racquet pointing to the sky. He also turns his shoulders and bends his knees to coil his body and load energy that will be unloaded when his body uncoils a moment later.

racquet in a good location to drop fully down the back and stretches your shoulder to spring the racquet faster to the ball later in the serve.

The trophy position is also sometimes called the power position because during this stage of the serve, the body coils to store power that will be unloaded when the body uncoils a moment later. Essentially, the body here becomes spring-loaded, preparing the arm to swing the racquet with explosive power and the body to lift up and forward towards the ball. This is how great servers deliver their serve with speed and consistency. They establish a strong power position and then release the stored energy and elevate the body to hit the ball at a height that creates a trajectory that clears the net by a good margin and lands well inside the service line (*next page, bottom*).

Four body movements occur together during the trophy position: the shoulder turn, knee bend, back tilt, and hip push.

A. SHOULDER TURN

As you move your arms up into the trophy position, your left shoulder turns to the right to point towards the right net post (*above*). Your shoulders should rotate more than your hips to produce an uncoiling of your shoulders that adds power to your swing.

B. KNEE BEND

The amount of knee bend will vary from player to player but an angle in the legs of somewhere between 30 and 40 degrees is considered ideal (*above*). The leg muscles are the strongest in the body; you need to use them well to hit your best serve.

C. BACK TILT

Your back should lean slightly backwards (*right*) to activate the abdominal muscles and allow your upper body to twist and drive your right shoulder both upward and forward (i.e. cartwheel). Without a tilted back, your right shoulder will move forward but be less able to move upwards. Tilting your back also deepens your racquet drop that follows and loads up more power in your legs, creating a stronger leg drive.

D. HIP PUSH

From a side view, the angle of your body at the completion of the trophy position should have a bow where your front hip pushes forward in front of your feet and shoulders (*right*). By leading with your front hip, you stretch your oblique muscles, tilt your shoulders upward, and place your chest underneath the ball toss. This places your body in a good position to lift yourself up and forward to the ball.

By tilting back and pushing his hips forward, Philipp Kohlschreiber creates a body angle that can spring him up and forward powerfully to the ball.

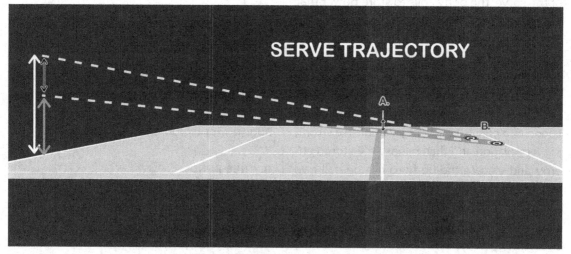

SERVE TRAJECTORY

Establishing a powerful trophy position and then lifting your body up and forward to the ball provides a higher contact point, and thus, a greater margin for error above the net (A) and inside the service line (B).

COACH'S BOX:

A common trophy position mistake on the serve is the racquet facing upward (*right*) rather than facing the side fence. This is caused by the incorrect use of the forehand grip and leads to an abbreviated wind up, low contact point, and poor racquet speed.

Making the change from the forehand grip to the continental grip on the serve will cause the ball to veer left. To fix this problem, try this drill. **First**, stand on the service line in your serving stance, place your hand in the continental grip, and lift the racquet head slightly above your head (*below left*). **Second**, toss the ball, drop the racquet down your back, and as you swing up at the ball, pronate your wrist. I recommend hitting to the ad side because the ball and the racquet are moving in the same direction to the right, making learning the continental grip on the serve easier than if hitting left into the deuce service box. At contact, focus on the arm being straight, with the racquet positioned roughly even with the front of your face, and your hips slightly closed to the net (*below middle*). Remember, you have to move the contact point up higher and less in front of the body than when you were using the forehand grip. **Third**, immediately following contact, freeze the racquet shoulder-high and make sure the wrist has turned the racquet face so it is facing towards the right side fence (*below right*). Once you get proficient at this racquet movement from the service line, move back gradually until you are successful from the baseline.

6. RACQUET DROP

Following the trophy position, the racquet drops down your back. The deeper your racquet drop, the longer the path your racquet can take to gather speed to the contact point and the greater the power created from the shoulder stretching and racquet lag (*below*). This is why it is vital to have a relaxed grip on the serve; your racquet won't drop fully if your shoulder is tight.

A full racquet drop requires a combination of torso rotation, leg drive, shoulder flexibility, and movement of the elbow. The rotation of your lower torso initiates the first part of your racquet drop, your leg drive propels the second part, and your upper torso rotation prompts the third part (*opposite*). As these movements occur, the rotation of your shoulder and your elbow's movement up and forward also adds depth to your racquet drop. This may sound complex, but it happens naturally if you use the continental grip, establish a good trophy position, and swing up at the ball.

At the end of the racquet drop, your back straightens and aligns with your straightening legs. At this point, your racquet remains stationary for a split second even though your chest started to go upward, producing a lag of the racquet that stretches your shoulder muscles and creates a powerful spring effect.

Murray's deep racquet drop stretches his shoulder muscles and lengthens his swing to add power to his serve.

GREAT SERVERS HAVE SIMILARITIES IN technique. Here we see the service motion of the right-handed Venus Williams mirror imaged with that of the left-handed Petra Kvitova. After establishing a strong trophy or power position (*images 1 and 4*), notice how their hitting elbows lift as their hips rotate up and around and their legs begin to straighten (*images 2 and 5*). These body movements produce a deep racquet drop (*images 3 and 6*), placing their racquet in a perfect position to lag and accelerate up to the ball.

Following the racquet drop, Nadal cartwheels his hitting shoulder over his non-hitting shoulder.

7. RACQUET DROP TO CONTACT

The body is sideways during the racquet drop, but begins to open as the hips swivel upward and around to the net as the racquet moves up out of the racquet drop. Once the hips fire, they quickly stop, which allows for the transfer of energy from the torso to the shoulder and arm.

As this hip movement is occurring, your hitting elbow elevates rapidly and straightens, taking an upward path above your ear as your torso rotates about your spine. Here, if you were to let go of the racquet while using the correct upward elbow motion, the racquet would fly over your opponent's baseline, rather than crashing before the net. To accommodate this elbow movement, your hitting shoulder must move over your non-hitting shoulder in a cartwheel motion (*above*). This cartwheeling of the shoulders helps lift your body to maximize your contact height.

A common issue among recreational players is that they do not cartwheel their shoulders. Instead, their shoulders rotate more horizontally, causing the elbow to pull to the side and the arc of the swing above the head to be more linear than circular. This results in a lower contact point and a poor ball trajectory into the service box.

8. WRIST PRONATION

As your elbow rises and straightens to reach up and hit the ball, your wrist pronates; that is, it turns the palm from facing the left side fence to face the right side fence. This is the last movement of your hitting arm before contact and a major factor in attaining fast racquet speed.

Each of the four types of serves uses a different wrist pronation. On the flat serve (I describe the wrist movement on the slice and kick serves later in the chapter), you pronate your wrist by first leading with the edge of your racquet near contact like you are going to karate chop the ball (*left*). Then, as the edge of your racquet head gets even closer to the ball, you rotate the racquet face around 90 degrees to square your strings to your target, effectively giving the ball a "high five" at contact (*center*). After contact, your racquet face continues to turn outward around another 90 degrees to complete the wrist pronation (*right*). This is one of the reasons why the continental grip is so important on the serve. It is only with the continental grip that you can "flip" the racquet face at a very high speed over such a short distance.

9. BODY POSITIONING AT CONTACT

As you reach up to hit the ball, your hips will rotate but should remain slightly sideways to the net at contact (*center*). If you do this correctly, your arm should be fully extended, with your racquet roughly even with the front of your face as you lean forward into the court

Federer accelerates out of the racquet drop with the edge of the racquet leading. Then, his wrist pronates to turn the racquet and square the strings up to the ball for contact. Following contact, his wrist continues its pronation, resulting in the racquet facing the right side fence.

(*right*). This body and racquet positioning will produce optimal serving power and maximize contact height.

In contrast, if your hips are too closed then the power from your leg drive and upper body rotation will be stifled and your contact point will occur behind the face, a physically weak spot. Or, if your hips are too open and parallel to the baseline, that same power created from your body will be decreasing instead of peaking at contact, and your contact point will be detrimentally lowered. Keep in mind, the amount your hips are closed will depend on what spin you are using and where you are directing your serve.

The positioning of your head and left arm is also important here. Remember to keep your head up and move your left arm towards your chest (*right*). If your head drops, the weight of your head will pull your shoulders down and lower your reach. Similarly, if your left arm moves down and away from your body, it will drag your right arm down and lower your contact point.

Djokovic reaches up with his arm fully extended and hips slightly sideways to hit the ball roughly even with the front of his face.

COACH'S BOX:

Just before contact on the serve, many recreational players fail to lead with the edge of the racquet and instead position the racquet to face the ball. It is understandable that players do this because it is hard to imagine approaching the ball with the racquet edge, especially since on many other shots you do place the strings behind the ball well before contact. However, the serve is a unique shot not only because of the swing itself, but also because you are hitting the ball as it moves at a very slow speed at an almost downward trajectory. These two characteristics allow you to rotate the racquet face more than 180 degrees quickly and still control the shot. On almost every other shot, the incoming ball has speed behind it and the ball is hit on a more horizontal trajectory. Consequently, on other shots, your racquet face must stay steadier through contact and command the collision of the ball. Don't let the technique needed on the serve adversely influence your technique on other shots or vice versa.

Nadal moves his racquet across his body and kicks his back leg up to finish his serve.

Moving your left arm inward also stops your hips from over-rotating and adds strength and stability to your right arm. Your left arm works as a decelerator to help your right arm accelerate and catapult your racquet out of the racquet drop phase with greater speed. Your two arms act in a way analogous to a jackknifed tractor-trailer. Your left arm mimics the tractor that puts on the brakes, while your right arm imitates the trailer that is slung powerfully forward.

10. FOLLOW THROUGH

After completing the wrist pronation, you finish the serve with the follow through. The follow through provides good information on how well you reached for the ball. A strong upward and forward push during the swing will elevate your front foot over the baseline and lift your back foot into the air to counter balance your upper body leaning forward (*right*). The deeper your knee bend and the stronger the cartwheel movement of your shoulders, the higher your back foot will lift to balance your body.

Your back foot should lift and finish pointing directly towards the back fence on the follow through. Your back foot acts like a "rudder" that guides the direction of the body. If it is pointing towards the right side fence, instead of the back fence, then your body rotated too much. Your front foot should point towards the target as you land on your follow through. If your front foot is pointing substantially to the left, this indicates an overly large body rotation, while pointing too much to the right indicates the opposite. You can "freeze" your follow through during practice to see the exact positioning of your feet and analyze what may need to be rectified.

Once your front foot lands forward into the court, the racquet swings down your left side behind you as your hips rotate through the swing. It is important to learn a smooth deceleration of your racquet on your follow through and avoid an abrupt stopping, which can lead to less power and potential injuries. Your left arm, which was tucked by your side, comes out at the end of your follow through and holds the throat of your racquet to prepare for the return from your opponent.

FORMER TOP FIVE ATP PLAYER AND ELITE COACH BRAD GILBERT once said if he had to pick one player to hold serve against a supernatural evil force with the end of the world at stake, he would choose Roger Federer. It's easy to understand why; Federer's serve is dependable, powerful, and extremely accurate.

Federer begins the serve in a relaxed manner with the racquet pointing down as he performs his pendulum backswing. In the second frame, he turns his shoulders and bends his knees in the trophy position to coil his body and store energy. Notice how high he raises his tossing arm. This not only helps him produce a smooth ball toss motion but also pushes his hips forward to help him lift his body up and forward to the ball. In frame three, he begins to uncoil his body and unload energy by straightening his legs and rotating his

hips. In frame four, the unloading of energy is complete, and the racquet begins its movement up to the ball with the edge leading. His racquet is the last to go up; that way, all the power created from his body is transferred into it. In frame five, he hits the ball with his hips slightly sideways to the net. We also see that his shoulders have cartwheeled, his hitting elbow has risen and straightened, and his wrist has pronated to rotate the racquet around 90 degrees from the previous frame. In the last frame, he follows through by continuing to elevate forward and high above the ground. His head remains up and his right leg moves backwards to balance out his body and help him land poised and ready for his opponent's return.

II. The Slice and Kick Serve

1. SLICE AND SLICE-TOPSPIN SERVE: USE AND TECHNIQUE

The flat serve described in the previous section is important for delivering power on the serve, but the slice and slice-topspin serves are also important for adding variety and consistency to your serve. These serves curve the ball to the left (or to the right for left-handers), create a lower bounce, and slow down the speed

Samantha Stosur's use of spin serves upsets the timing of her opponents' returns of serve.

of the ball. The slice serves are particularly effective when used in combination with other serves, as the changing curves, heights, and speeds can keep your opponent off rhythm and error prone.

The slice serve is typically used as a first serve and can be used to jam your opponents by serving into their body or to pull them wide off the court. The slice-topspin serve is a versatile one that can be used as a strong first or second serve. It is an effective first serve because of its good velocity and low, curving bounce and a good second serve because the forward rotation of the ball brings the ball down into the court, enhancing the control needed for a reliable second serve. The slice-topspin serve is a particularly good way for recreational players to hit the second serve, especially if the more difficult kick serve (described next) is proving troublesome.

The slice and slice-topspin serves have a similar technique to the flat serve except for the differences outlined below.

A. BALL TOSS

For the slice serves, you should place the ball toss slightly more to the right (*opposite top*). If in front of an imaginary clock and serving to the deuce side, your slice serve will have a toss around one o'clock and a little less to the right for the slice-topspin serve. On the ad-side, because your target and momentum is more to the right, move the ball toss slightly more to the right. Keep in mind, the more similar your ball toss is for all the serves, the less likely your opponent will anticipate and the more effective your serve.

B. BODY ALIGNMENT

Because of the more rightward path of your racquet at the top of the swing, your upper

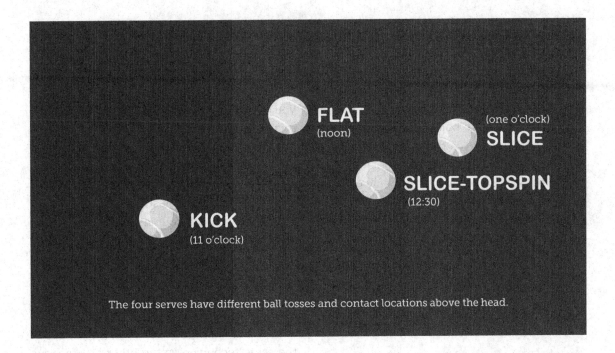

FLAT
(noon)

(one o'clock)
SLICE

SLICE-TOPSPIN
(12:30)

KICK
(11 o'clock)

The four serves have different ball tosses and contact locations above the head.

body will align more sideways to the net than on the flat serve during the backswing and at the point of contact.

C. RACQUET DROP TO CONTACT

The racquet is angled at contact on the slice serves, and because of this, your wrist pronation is less on your slice serves compared to the flat serve. Instead of pronating fully, your wrist movement on the slice serve is more of a tomahawk motion with the edge of your racquet heading towards the right net post after you hit the ball (*right*). Also, instead of hitting through the middle of the ball, as on the flat serve, on the slice serve, you brush around the two o'clock edge of the ball (*next page, left*). This causes a slightly forward and mostly sideways ball rotation. On the slice-topspin serve the strings meet the middle of the ball and brush up and over the one o'clock part of the ball (*next page, left*). This creates a mostly forward and slightly sideways ball rotation.

On the slice serve, the leading edge of the racquet moves towards the right net post as the strings brush around the two o'clock part of the ball.

2. THE KICK SERVE: USE AND TECHNIQUE

Developing a good kick serve will give you an assertive and dependable second serve - a crucial shot at any level. The topspin of the kick serve allows the ball to travel well above the net and curve back down into the service box, reducing the chance of a double fault. A successful kick serve involves not only getting your second serve in play but also hitting it with speed and spin that keeps your opponent on the defensive. Too many recreational players tap in their second serve, leaving them vulnerable to their opponents' weapons. A strong kick serve will bounce up high and twist away from your opponents, confusing them and taking the ball out of their preferred strike zone. It is particularly effective on the ad side, where the spin can force your opponent to hit the return outside the doubles alley. Furthermore, if you have a reliable kick serve, you can be more aggressive with your first delivery, making you a more dangerous server. Alternatively, without the kick serve in your repertoire, you may have less confidence in your second serve and serve more cautiously on your first serve. Lastly, it is a great doubles serve. Should you decide to deploy the popular serve and volley tactic, the slower speed of the kick serve allows you more time to move in closer to the net and establish better positioning for the first volley.

As noted earlier, the kick serve uses much of the same technique as the other serves; however, for a number of the elements, correct execution of the kick serve varies from the earlier discussion.

HOW THE STRINGS MOVE ACROSS THE BALL FOR THE THREE SPIN SERVES

SLICE SERVE

SLICE-TOPSPIN

KICK SERVE

On the kick serve, the racquet moves upward from horizontal to vertical as the strings brush up the back of the ball to create topspin.

A. BALL TOSS

The ball toss is more to the left than with other serves. When serving to the deuce side, the ball toss is around an 11 o'clock position. The ball toss is also less forward. If the ball toss for the flat serve is approximately two feet in front of you, then for the kick serve it should be around one foot in front of you.

B. BODY ALIGNMENT

Due to your racquet taking a more rightward path through contact, your shoulders turn more sideways to the net during the backswing (*below*) and remain more sideways as you hit the ball as compared to other serves. Also, because the ball toss is more to the left and less in front, the kick serve's trophy position has slightly more hip push and back tilt and less body weight centered over the front foot than in other serves.

Federer creates topspin on his kick serve by moving his racquet up from a horizontal (*left*) to 45 degree angle (*right*) at contact.

C. RACQUET DROP TO CONTACT

The kick serve's topspin is created by the racquet rising in a horizontal position behind your head, moving to the right to a 10 to 11 o'clock position at contact (*above*), and then a noon position just after contact. As the racquet moves up, the wrist will move forward and close the racquet face. Here, it should feel somewhat like you are rolling the strings over an imaginary beach ball suspended above you. The racquet movement on most kick serves will brush the strings up the seven o'clock part of the ball and move up and over the one o'clock part of the ball (*opposite left*). This is a "classic" kick serve typically hit to the right side of the service box; however, small changes in the path of your racquet and your ball toss can create different types of topspin. For example, if you want to hit a topspin serve to the left side to the service box, the racquet will brush up the ball from five o'clock to 11 o'clock and the toss will be less to the left.

Federer turns his shoulders more to begin his kick serve (*left*) than on other serves (*right*).

ONE OF NOVAK DJOKOVIC'S MANY STRENGTHS is his kick serve. He hits the ball deep in the service box and at a speed that differs less from his first serve than most players on the ATP.

He begins his kick serve in frame one with a good shoulder turn and a ball toss to the left about a foot in front of the baseline. He conducts his backswing in a relaxed fashion with the racquet dangling towards the ground. In frame two, due to the kick serve's less forward ball toss, we see his weight fairly evenly distributed between both legs rather than mostly on the front leg as with other serves. Next, he tilts back to get his body in good position to brush up the back of the ball. In frame four, the cartwheeling of his shoulders lifts his hitting elbow and ends the racquet drop phase. Notice the depth of the

racquet drop; his racquet head ends level with his waist. This full racquet drop permits a long swing path to build up acceleration to the contact point. It is important to acceler- ate the racquet on the kick serve at around the same speed as the flat serve; this creates good topspin for greater consistency. In frame five, we see that even though the ball has been struck, the racquet is still behind his head as it closes and continues its movement to the right after brushing up the back of the ball. He raises and tucks his left arm in to- wards the body. This balances the body, helps him swing up and reach high for the ball, and provides counterpoint strength for his right arm. He finishes the swing by landing on his left leg less inside the court and with his racquet more to the right compared to other serves.

III. Serving Tactics

YOU CAN HAVE A POWERFUL SERVE, but if you are predictable you may have a difficult time holding serve. On the other hand, if you keep your serve unpredictable, you will confuse your opponent and make it more difficult for them to return your serve well.

You can mix up the placement of your serve by serving wide, down the "T" (where the center line meets the service line), or directly at your opponent's body. Alternatively, you can vary your serve with different spins to change the speed and arc of the ball. You can also switch up where you stand on the baseline, the speed of your swing, or even how many times you bounce the ball before serving. If you feel your opponent is "dialed in" on your serve, make use of all the options available to you to disrupt their return rhythm.

Being unpredictable is one component of a well-considered serve; the second component is serving to induce a return that will play to your strengths. For example, top American professional Jack Sock sometimes stands several feet left of the center hash mark when serving to the ad side and kicks his serve wide to the right-hander's backhand. This serving strategy likely sets up a shot pattern that best utilizes his dominant forehand and begins the point in an offensive way. The importance of dominating play with the forehand after the serve is statistically clear in professional tennis. This was on display at the 2010 Wimbledon final between Rafael Nadal and Tomas Berdych. Although Nadal only hit five aces, he still never lost his serve, largely because he was able to use his strong forehand on 89 % of the first shots after his serve.[3]

The pros understand that if they want to control the point, they must consider their serve and strongest groundstroke as a single strategic unit. You should do the same. For example, if your forehand is a weapon, then serving down the "T" on the deuce side is an effective way to increase the likelihood that you can use that shot early in the point. This is because the angle of the return from the middle of the court is a difficult one to pull the server a long distance to the right (*opposite*). Knowing the limited angles that are

Nadal preparing to serve during the 2010 Wimbledon final.

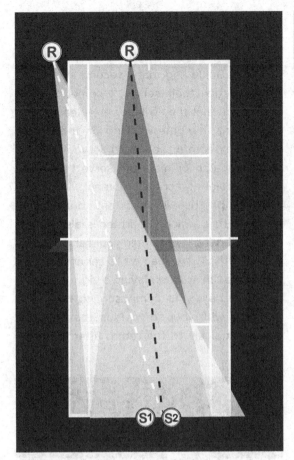

After serving down the "T," due to the angles available to the returner, you can move to the left (S1) and look to use your forehand more frequently. However, after serving wide, you must protect against the increased return angles available to the right and maintain your position (S2). This more rightward positioning reduces the chances that your first groundstroke will be a forehand.

available to your opponent to move you right, you can safely move a step left after serving down the "T" (*above S1*). This places you in better position to use your forehand. However, if you serve wide on the deuce side, you must be aware of the angle it creates for the cross-court return, and, therefore, position

yourself less to the left after the serve (*above S2*). Now, if you can serve wide on the deuce side at a speed that causes your opponent to be late on their return, then you can still safely move left and look to use your forehand. Your court positioning after the serve depends not just on angles, but serving velocity as well. You should understand your serving abilities and most successful shot patterns and execute your serve in a way that sets up the rally in your favor as much as possible.

You should also adjust your serving to the score. For example, if you are ahead 40-0 or 40-15 in the game, picking up an easy point with a powerful, but riskier, flat serve can make strategic sense. If you are down 30-40 or ad-out, using spin and placement that you have used infrequently during the match can surprise your opponent and induce a weak return. You have four main types of serves (flat, slice, slice-topspin, and kick) and three main areas of placement (wide, "T," and directly at your opponent's body) giving you 12 different possible combinations. It is often a good idea to keep one or two of these 12 serves "up your sleeve" to surprise your opponent at an important stage of the match.

Lastly, you want to get at least 60% of your first serves in. Enticed by the glory of an ace, some players like to blast their first serve, but if it goes in infrequently, any glory enjoyed through an ace will be short-lived as the chances of winning the match evaporate. If your first serve winning percentage is 65% and your second serve winning percentage is 40%, then missing four first serves in a six point game places the odds of you losing your serve at greater than 50/50. First serves are not to be wasted; use them wisely. If your first serve percentage dips during a match, increase the spin and aim for a bigger target.

IV. Serve Practice

SERENA WILLIAMS POSSESSES a great serve (*opposite*), but it didn't happen by luck. It happened by developing a good technique and repetition. Her coach Rick Macci recalls that from the time she was a kid, she would end her practice session almost every day with 450 serves. He said of Williams, "You put in the hard yards, the repetition, and you have the fast-twitch muscle and a very good technique, and this is what you see." [4] Many players neglect to practice their serve diligently because they feel it is less fun than hitting the other strokes. This is a mistake. The serve is a hugely important shot that must be given a high priority during your practice sessions.

To emphasize its importance, I sometimes deviate from the typical lesson protocol and start with the serve. After a dynamic warm up, I begin with the students serving shadow swings, that is, swings without using a ball, to warm up the shoulder and hone technique. Next, I have students practice ball tosses to reinforce the significance of this part of the

serve. Following the ball tosses, I set up targets in different parts of the service box and have students practice all the various types of serves, including many second serves. As they practice their serves, I sometimes remind them that they will be very pleased that they spent this time working on their serve when they comfortably hold serve in an important match or hit a big serve to quickly win the point at a critical moment.

Target practice is important, but playing points with a practice partner is also a vital part of learning how to hold your service game consistently. There is an art to serving well after you've run around playing a vigorous point and then gain your composure to begin the next one with your serve. Plus, the ability to respond quickly to the return after complet-

Placing cones on the court as targets can add focus to your serve practice.

COACH'S BOX:

Spend five minutes a day serving shadow swings for the first and second serve as fast as you can. Remember to keep your muscles relaxed during the swing and finish balanced. This training tip can build up serving strength and racquet speed. I recommend shadow swing training on all shots, not just the serve. It has the advantage of developing good technique through high repetition and without the stress of hitting to another person, which can compromise form.

ing the follow through on the serve is an important skill, especially on the second serve. This important third shot in tennis only can be practiced with someone on the other side of the net. Keep in mind when playing points during your practice sessions it is sometimes a good idea to change the rules (*see drill #2 and #3 below*) to place extra focus on your serve. This extra focus can improve the concentration needed to become a great server.

1. HORSE

Goal: Increase serving accuracy.

Using markers or cones, divide the service box into thirds. Then play a game of "Horse" by having your practice partner designate a third of the service box. If you are successful in hitting in that third and your practice partner isn't, they get the letter "H." First one to spell "H-O-R-S-E" loses. Add different spin serves or second bounce location targets that the serve must exceed as variations of the "Horse" game.

2. TWO FOR ONE

Goal: Enhance concentration when serving.

Play two points serving to the deuce side. You score a point if you win both rallies, but zero points if you win one of the two points. The receiver scores a point if they win one out of the two rallies and two points if they win both rallies. Repeat on the ad side. First player to 11 points wins and then switch roles.

3. SERVING HANDICAPS

Goal: Improve the second serve and learn to serve under pressure.

Work on your second serve by playing a set with your practice partner using second serves only. Or, play a set with second serves that allows first and second serves for only two points per game, chosen at the servers discretion, to better understand when the important points during a game occur. Another serving game to simulate pressure is to play a set with the server beginning each game at 30 - 40.

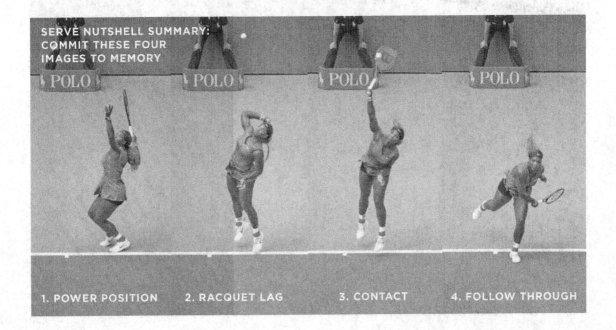

SERVE NUTSHELL SUMMARY: COMMIT THESE FOUR IMAGES TO MEMORY

1. POWER POSITION   2. RACQUET LAG   3. CONTACT   4. FOLLOW THROUGH

Murray said in 2015, "I just think the return is maybe more important than the serve now."[1]

CHAPTER 6

Return of Serve

IT WAS NOT LONG AGO that tennis fans worried the serve would become so dominant on the pro tour that the game would become less entertaining due to short points produced by big serving. However, the professionals adapted to the big serves by becoming much better returners, and rallies on the professional tour are as exciting as ever.

The return of serve has not only become a more skilled shot but also a more aggressive one. At Wimbledon in 2014, Eugenie Bouchard returned serve positioned inside the baseline an impressive 97% of the time.[2] By returning the serve so early, her opponents had very little time after their serve follow through to get balanced and move to cover her return. On the men's side, Roger Federer took return of serve aggressiveness to new heights in the summer of 2015 when he began to occasionally hit returns from just behind the service line then immediately attack the net. This tactic hurried his opponents and often took them by surprise, leading to poorly hit passing shots and easy volleys for him at net.

The return of serve has also evolved to become a bigger factor in a player's level of success. Statistics back up its growing importance. In 1990, none of ATP's top service returners were ranked in the top ten in the world. By 2014, four out of the top five service returners were in the top ten.[3] On the WTA tour, players' returns of serve have become so strong that it is sometimes more advantageous to return serve than to serve. Take for example, Bouchard's strong run at the 2014 Wimbledon mentioned above. During that tournament, she broke serve 25 times, sometimes two or three times in a set, on her way to finishing runner-up.

While the return of serve is hugely important at the professional level, its significance may be even greater at the recreational level. At the recreational level, an opponent's serve, especially a second serve, can represent an easy short ball where the returner has full knowledge of both when the shot will arrive and which service box it will land in. Therefore, the return of serve can be a great opportunity to hit a winner or set up a favorable situation to eventually win the point.

Good returners choose the right grip, anticipate, react quickly, employ good footwork, and use suitable backswing length. After discussing these components of the return of serve, I discuss how to make smart tactical and court positioning choices. I then explain why practicing the return is so important, how the return varies from regular groundstrokes, and finish the chapter with some practice drills.

I. Components of the Return of Serve

I. GRIP

Because returning serve is often a fast-paced situation and the topspin forehand and backhand require different grips, how you hold the racquet is a major consideration. There is no right or wrong way to do this; the grip here is an individual preference largely based on your groundstroke strengths and weaknesses and style of play.

Most players wait to return serve in their forehand grip because the left hand stays on the racquet longer during the backhand swing compared to the forehand, thus providing extra

Eugenie Bouchard steals time from her serving opponent by returning serve inside the baseline.

COACH'S BOX:

High speed analysis shows that to better their timing on the return, the pros typically cut the amount of spin they use by more than half compared to the spin they use during a baseline rally. The best professional returners of the past, like Andre Agassi and Jimmy Connors, used moderate forehand grips and hit flat returns. In contrast, players who use extreme forehand western grips can have trouble returning fast serves because their palm is more underneath the grip — not a good position to handle a strong serve's powerful ball impact. In addition, the western grip doesn't produce a comfortable arm positioning for the level swing required to reliably return fast serves. If you use a western grip on the forehand, you might consider using a semi-western grip on the return and hit with moderate spin.

Andre Agassi's moderate forehand grip
(and incredible eye-hand coordination)
helped him return fast serves with interest.

assistance to the right hand in establishing the backhand grip. Some players set up in the grip of their weaker groundstroke to help out that shot, while others prefer to wait with the continental grip, which reduces the grip change to either the forehand or backhand and is a good grip if they intend to block the return off a big server. Two-handed backhand players have an easier time deciding which grip to use. They typically wait with the right hand in their preferred forehand grip and their left hand in the grip they use when playing their two-handed backhand.

2. ANTICIPATION

Unless your opponent is very skilled at disguising their serve, the ball toss can help you determine what spin is coming your way. If the ball toss is to the server's right, you can expect a slice serve and should move right to cover its rightward curve. If the toss is to the left, then you can anticipate a kick serve and you should move to the left to cover its leftward bounce. If the ball toss is straight and in front, then a power serve is probably coming, and you can prepare a shorter swing for the return. Over the course of a match, you can pick up on your opponent's predilections for certain serves and remember that players often like to deliver their favorite serves on important points such as game and break points.

3. RITUAL AND REACTION

It is important to develop a return of serve ritual that helps you relax and focus before exerting the intense burst of energy needed to get a quick start on the return. Some players, like Federer, spin their racquet in their hands, while others, like Milos Roanic, bounce around on their feet, preparing their legs for action.

After establishing your location on the court for the return, set up in a wide stance with your feet outside your shoulders, knees bent, and upper body fairly upright. As the server tosses the ball, take a step or two forward, and then split step right before the server makes contact (*right*). The forward momentum going into the split step will give you a quicker jump on attacking a return.

4. FOOTWORK

After the split step, your first movement is to pivot with your outside foot, leaning right for a forehand (*opposite left*) or left for a backhand. The number of steps taken after the first step depends on the speed and direction of the serve. Wide serves will usually require a crossover step, with the left leg stepping across on a forehand (*opposite right*), and the right leg

crossing over on a backhand. Once the front foot hits the ground, the back foot will rotate around so you can square up into a wide base and lean in the direction you wish to move.

On serves that don't go wide, there typically isn't the time or need for the crossover step, and the return is hit with an open stance where your feet are parallel or close to parallel to the baseline. Due to the high bounce of kick serves, the open stance will also often be used on the forehand return as well as the backhand for two-handed backhand players. After hitting your return, move your feet quickly towards the middle of the court to set up for the rally.

Djokovic split steps to help him react quickly to his opponent's serve.

5. SWING TECHNIQUE

The role of the backswing is to produce a consistent contact point in front of the body. To achieve this the size of your backswing must adapt to the different serving speeds of your opponents rather than being stiff or robotic.

When returning a fast first serve you should take a lower, shorter backswing (*middle*) and use your opponent's power to hit the ball back. Stay low in a crouched position, keep your head still while swinging the racquet, and focus on making contact in front of you (*right*). Even though the backswing may be shorter, the follow through should remain full. Because the first serve return is usually hit flatter, the follow through will be high and extended. On the slower second serve, the backswing will be longer and more topspin likely used; therefore the follow through will usually be lower and

more horizontal, essentially replicating a regular topspin groundstroke (*see page 106*).

6. RETURN OF SERVE TACTICS

Depending on the caliber of your opponent's serve, there are a wide range of tactics you can employ on the return of serve. Your main goal is to make your opponent earn every single point by getting your return in play. Through the course of the match, a consistent returner will tire a server mentally and physically by making them work hard after their serve.

A. FIRST SERVE VERSUS SECOND SERVE RETURN TACTICS

Because the first serve typically is faster than the second, your tactical approach to returning these serves should be different as well. When receiving a strong first serve, your goal

Djokovic pivots and leans, and then uses a low and short backswing before making contact in front of his body on this wide forehand return.

1   2   3

IN 2015, NOVAK DJOKOVIC BROKE SERVE MORE OFTEN THAN ANY PLAYER on the ATP tour. He returns consistently and does so at a speed and depth that usually allows him to start the point in a favorable position.

In the first frame, Djokovic begins his return with a well-timed split step, helping him get a strong first movement to the ball. In the second frame, he pivots his feet, shifts his weight onto his left foot, and turns his shoulders. By frame three, his short back-swing is complete. Keep in mind his arms barely moved to arrive at this position; his backswing was largely achieved by his upper body turning as a unit. Djokovic drops

4　　　　　　　5　　　　　　　6

his racquet head to begin his low-to-high forward swing creating moderate topspin to control his shot. His left leg straightens to unload the power that was stored during the backswing. In frame four, he straightens his left arm and makes contact well in front of his body. Novak is not a passive returner. In frame five, we see him moving forward through the shot, attacking the ball. He drives through the ball extending the racquet out towards his target. In the last frame, he lands balanced on his right leg ready to recover quickly for his opponent's reply.

is to defend and neutralize the point. At the beginning of the match, especially against an opponent whose game you are unfamiliar with, you should aim your first serve return down the middle of the court. It's a good idea to strive for consistency and depth on the return until you're starting to read and time your opponent's serve. As the match progresses, you can start to aim closer to the lines.

In contrast to the first serve return, your goal on the second serve is to attack and return strong enough to put you ahead in the point. The second serve, especially a weak one, can offer a great opportunity for the returner because it effectively becomes a short ball that you can prepare for. Attacking the second serve is a tactic that often reaps larger rewards as the match progresses. It can cause your opponent to lose confidence and become disheartened at the prospect of defending the

point every time they miss their first serve.

Before your opponent begins their second serve, visualize a specific target on the court where you wish to hit your return. Remember the body performs best when the mind gives it decisive direction and clear purpose. Also, move your feet quickly on the second serve return so you can use your strongest groundstroke as much as possible. Keep in mind that it is advantageous for court position purposes if you can move left and use your forehand on the deuce side and move right and use your backhand on the ad side (*opposite*). This movement brings you towards the middle of the court after the return in good position for your next shot.

You can also move left and right to upset your opponent's rhythm by returning serves from different spots on the court. For example, if your opponent is hurting you with serves to

Federer defends against a powerful serve by shortening his backswing and aiming for a big target deep down the middle of the court.

your backhand, try standing more to the left and tempt them to serve to the "open" part of the service box. It will force them to hit a less grooved serve to what may be your strongest groundstroke.

B. FORWARD AND BACKWARD COURT POSITIONING TACTICS

Moving forward and backward can also upset your opponent's rhythm, but this type of positioning change plays a more important role in tactics. For example, if you wish to set an aggressive tone or shorten rallies, you can set up well inside the baseline (*below*) and return the ball early, robbing time from your opponent. Or, if you have better groundstrokes than your opponent, and extending the length of the rally works in your favor, you may want to position yourself further back and improve the chances you will make the return.

The final of the 2016 Sydney International between Viktor Troicki and Grigor Dimitrov demonstrated how a player's level of success can vary depending of the length of the rally. During that match, Troicki was almost twice as likely to win the point when rallies were three shots or fewer; the reverse was true when the rally went nine or more shots.[4] Perhaps if Dimitrov moved back to return serve and extended more points, he may have won that very close match.

What your opponent does after the serve can also affect return of serve positioning. During the 2015 Barclays ATP World Tour Fi-

Serena Williams uses her backhand on the ad side to gain better court positioning and stands well inside the baseline to set an aggressive tone for the rally.

At the 2015 Barclays World Tour Finals, Stan Wawrinka decided to stand closer to the baseline to return against Federer than he did against the slower serving Nadal.

nals, Wawrinka returned serve an average of 8.8 feet farther behind the baseline when playing Nadal, a deep baseline player, than Federer, an occasional serve and volleyer.[5] Wawrinka knew returning deep against Federer would create easy serve and volley opportunities for his compatriot, especially when defending against his wide serve. Although Federer serves significantly faster than Nadal, Wawrinka considered all the match variables and decided to return Federer's serve closer to the baseline than Nadal's.

The court surface also has a large impact on the level of aggression and court positioning on the return. In the last decade, particularly on clay courts, the pros have sometimes adopted a different type of second serve return whereby they drop back several feet towards the back fence to hit their shot (*opposite*). This deeper court positioning allows the speed and spin of the serve to slow down enough to hit a heavy topspin return. On the other hand, on hard courts they often move further forward and return the serve earlier. This strategy pays off because hard courts provide more reliable bounces and tend to reward aggressive shot-making.

Learn from the pros and adjust your forward and backward court positioning on the return taking into account not only the quality of your opponent's serve, but also the length of point that works in your favor, your opponent's tactics following their serve, and court surface.

On clay courts, Nadal (*background*) sometimes drops back to the fence to get the second serve return at a comfortable speed and height.

II. Return of Serve Practice

WHILE SOME POINTS LAST TEN STROKES and others last two, the average length of a point in most matches is around four to five strokes. Keeping this in mind, the serve and return of serve represent roughly forty to fifty percent of an average point. Now, what are typically the least practiced shots at the recreational level? You guessed it: the serve and, particularly, the return of serve. Don't make this mistake. Spend the appropriate amount of time on the practice court honing these two shots.

Many players don't give the return of serve the attention it deserves because they make the mistake of regarding it as just another groundstroke. However, the truth is that the return of serve is different from typical ground-

strokes in several ways: the serve is hit from a greater height creating a higher bounce, the ball speed is usually faster, the serve sometimes curves right-to-left or left-to-right, the distance your opponent serves from the net is always the same, and the area of the service box is much smaller to defend than the whole court. Therefore, in addition to the return of serve's huge impact in determining the outcome of the point, it is also in many ways a unique shot, and should represent a significant part of your practice sessions.

The pros fully understand this and hit thousands of returns in practice to improve the muscular and mental link that allows them to make the necessary tiny adjustments to return well. On the first serve they receive there is little time for deliberate action, so they operate along a range of reactions rather than premeditated thought. At the recreational level, serves are slower, and so there is a different thought process involved. Recreational players usually have the advantage of additional time, allowing them to plan ahead and hit a more premeditated return. Irrespective of the speed of serve you typically face, there is an art and rhythm to the return that can only be developed through practice.

1. UP AND BACK

Goal: Speed up return of serve reaction time.

Hit five serves to your practice partner from

Having your practice partner serve from several feet inside the baseline can speed up your return of serve reflexes.

six feet inside the baseline, five from three feet inside the baseline, and five at the baseline. They score a point for every successful return or return that lands past the service line, and you score a point for every unreturned serve or every return landing before the service line. The player with the most points after 15 serves wins, then switch roles. With this drill and all drills in the book, you can change the court positioning or scoring system depending on your skill level to make the drills fun and competitive.

2. TARGET PRACTICE

Goal: Improve accuracy of return.

Divide the singles court into four boxes by continuing the center line all the way to the baseline. You must return serve into a designated box. If the ball is returned successfully in the designated box or if your practice partner misses their serve, you score a point. However, if you fail to hit the correct box, your practice partner scores a point. First player to score 15 points wins, then switch roles. Variations include allowing two serves per point, dividing the court into two halves instead of four quarters, or allowing the returner to hit only topspin or only slice returns.

3. RETURN OF SERVE HANDICAPS

Goal: Emphasize the importance of defending against the first serve and attacking the second serve.

Play a set with your practice partner using regular scoring except that a failed return off the first serve results in two points for the server. Alternately — or additionally — if the returner hits a winner off a second serve, they score two points. You can add a variation in which the server is allowed three serves per point instead of two.

"The length of the point matters a lot more than fans may think. The first four shots, including the serve and the return, are by far the most important segment. You may think the point is just getting started, but it is often already over. During the 2015 U.S. Open, 71% of the points in men's singles matches and 66% of the points on the women's side came on rallies of four shots or fewer. And first-strike points have a much greater correlation to a match's result than extended rallies do. At the 2015 U.S. Open, the players who won more zero-to-four shot rallies won the match 90% of the time in men's singles and 83% of the time in women's. Players who had the advantage on rallies of nine-plus shots won the match only 56% of the time on the men's side and 59% on the women's."

- Craig O'Shannessy[6]

Jo-Wilfried Tsonga's forehand is, like most
ATP players, his baseline coup de grace.

CHAPTER 7

Forehand

THE FOREHAND IS MOST PLAYERS' WEAPON OF CHOICE. On the ATP professional tour, the majority of winners hit in any given singles match are likely to be forehands. The 2013 final of the BNP Paribas Open between Rafael Nadal and Juan Martin Del Potro exemplified the dominance of the forehand. The players combined to hit 40 forehand winners but only five backhand winners.[1] During the rallies, they repeatedly moved towards the doubles alley to hit their more dangerous stroke and, by turning backhands into forehands, changed neutral situations into offensive ones and often ended up winning the point.

The forehand is so dominant as compared to the backhand largely because of the superior physical force applied to the ball. The forehand uses the stronger chest and shoulder muscles as well as a more vigorous leg drive and hip rotation. Also, because the hitting shoulder lags on the forehand instead of leading as it does on the backhand, the forehand backswing is longer, allowing for a greater build-up of racquet speed. Furthermore, unlike the backhand, the body alignment on the forehand allows players to move

Federer and Nadal often move towards the doubles alley to use their forehand. Note the similarities in the way they establish balance, position their racquet and non-hitting arm, and flex their legs to store power.

quickly away from the middle of the baseline while still hitting a well-balanced shot. Players like Federer and Nadal like to move away from the middle of the baseline and control play with their forehand, often dividing baseline play into two-thirds forehands and one-third backhands. If they take control of the point, the division of the court can grow to be three-quarters forehands or even more.

Federer and Nadal not only share the desire to dictate play with their forehand, but also share commonalities that all great forehand players possess (*left*) and that are discussed in this chapter. Briefly, they draw on each body part to establish balance and strong kinetic chain power. They use a circular backswing and lag the racquet before the forward swing to maximize racquet head speed. For consistent shot depth, they use good extension through contact and "windshield wiper" racquet movement to control their powerful strokes with topspin. And they follow through in a manner that decelerates the racquet smoothly and facilitates quick recovery. These are the fundamentals of a great forehand. While Federer and Nadal make a range of creative choices on their forehand — their individuality is evident when you dissect their strokes and observe differences in style and technique — all is within the parameters of the fundamentals.

This chapter has four main sections. I begin with the advantages and techniques of the three main stances. I then explain the upper body phases of the forehand swing: the unit turn, backswing, forward swing to contact, contact, and follow through. Next, I go through the different types of forehand and then finish the chapter with some suggestions for groundstroke practice and forehand drills.

I. Forehand Stances

A GREAT FOREHAND BEGINS with good positioning. To obtain proper positioning, you must utilize the best stance for the given circumstance and align your legs to provide balance and power for the swing in the least amount of time. While certain stances are recommended for specific shots, the choice of stance is dynamic. It will depend mostly on the height but also the width, depth, spin, and speed of the incoming ball. As Nadal once wrote: "From the moment the ball is motion, it comes at you in an infinitesimal number of angles and spins; with more topspin or backspin or flatter or higher. The difference might be minute, microscopic, but so are the variations your body makes — shoulders, elbows, wrists, hips, ankles, knees — in every shot."[2]

The shorter and more defensive David Ferrer is predominately an open stance forehand player.

This unpredictable nature of tennis means you must have adaptable footwork and make use of all the stances.

Because the height of the ball is a key factor, your height will play a role in what stance you use. Your style of play will also have an influence. For example, players who like to rally from deep in the court will use the open stance more often than players who enjoy moving forward and attacking the ball. These intricacies influence forehand stances on the ATP Tour. For the same ball, David Ferrer, Novak Djokovic, and Tomas Berdych may each use a different forehand stance. The shorter, more defensive Ferrer likes the open stance (*left*), Djokovic, a counter-puncher, prefers the semi-open stance (*next page, left*), and the taller, more aggressive Berdych uses the neutral stance more than most players (*next page, right*), Their stances are a function of their height and style of play, as well as their natural proclivity.

Which forehand stance should you favor? As you will learn below, the open stances are quick and explosive while the neutral stance has the advantages of simple weight transfer, compact swing structure, and straighter extension through contact (*see page 102*). And while you may favor some stances more than others, because tennis is such a dynamic game, you will need them all. By using the guidelines, and through practice, you will learn how to make use of the best stance for all the shots.

1. THE OPEN STANCES

The two predominant stances used on the forehand at the higher levels are the open and semi-open stances. The open stance sees your

Djokovic's semi-open forehand stance is well-suited to his aggressive counter-punching style of play.

The taller and more aggressive Berdych uses the neutral stance frequently.

feet parallel to the baseline (*opposite top*) whereas in the semi-open stance your feet are staggered at roughly a 45-degree angle with your left foot in front of your right foot (*opposite bottom*). In both stances, your feet should be wider than your shoulders with your knees bent and back fairly straight. This wide stance and good balance distributes body weight up towards the hips and makes for a sturdy balanced position. You need this strong foundation to effectively handle the large amount of force and momentum generated by pushing up from the ground during an aggressive forehand swing.

The open stances have three main advantages. **First**, tremendous power is produced from the kinetic energy generated by the legs pushing up from the ground and the torque created by the "corkscrew" swivel of the hips and shoulders. **Second**, the execution

is quicker because fewer steps are required compared to other stances. **Third**, they produce a comfortable body position for playing balls above the waist.

The open stance is typically used on balls that are wide, high, or fast, while the semi-open stance is normally used on balls that are above the waist and hit towards the middle of the court and on inside-out and inside-in forehands (*see page 110*). If you have time, use the semi-open stance rather than the open stance because it will produce greater power. Although your chest will face the net at contact in either stance, in the semi-open stance your hips begin more sideways to the net and therefore uncoil more for increased power. Moreover, because the left foot is in front of the right foot, there is more forward weight distribution into the swing than on an open stance stroke.

On this wide ball, Serena Williams' open stance forehand sees her loading up weight on her right leg before pushing off it, adding power to her swing.

On this middle ball, Simona Halep moves left before establishing a strong base in a semi-open stance, loads up weight in both legs, and pushes off, mostly from the left leg, up and forward into the shot.

TECHNIQUE

During the backswing, the open stance loads up energy in the right leg before releasing it up the body on the forward swing (*previous page, top*), while the semi-open stance loads up energy more evenly between the legs before pushing forward and up mostly off the left leg and into the shot (*previous page, bottom*). On the majority of semi-open and open stance forehands, your left foot finishes pointing towards your target, while your right foot ends resting lightly on the toe with the heel off the ground. On defensive swings, your feet will stay more grounded, but when hitting a powerful forehand, your feet will pivot and elevate to allow the body to rotate fully through the shot.

It is best not to lock your feet down during semi-open or open stance forehands, especially your right foot, but instead let them rise and flow to a natural position. The pivoting of the feet not only lets the power flow naturally and helps you maintain balance for a speedy recovery, but also places less stress on the leg joints as the shoulders rotate against the hips during the swing. It is the release of energy from the legs, combined with the aggressive upward arc of the swing, that result in the pros sometimes hitting these shots in an airborne fashion.

2. THE NEUTRAL STANCE

Not all balls should be hit with an open or semi-open stance; sometimes it is best to use the neutral stance. In a neutral stance, your left foot will be positioned in front of your right foot with your feet set slightly wider than shoulder width apart and your body aligned in a sideways position perpendicular to the net (*below*).

There are several reasons why the neutral stance is a good choice, especially for recreational players. **First**, the forward transfer of weight from the back foot to the front foot adds power. This forward linear power is less complicated to perform than the open stance's upward angular build-up of power. **Second**, it guarantees that the key fundamental of the shoulder turn happens. **Third**, because the arc of the swing is more compact and stays closer

Maria Sharapova uses the neutral stance on this low ball towards the middle of the court.

to the body, it keeps the swing structure more consistent. **Fourth**, having the body sideways to the net naturally produces a straighter and longer extension to hit "through" the ball during the critical contact phase. There is a reason why other sports like baseball and golf use the neutral stance — the stance provides a straight, long extension through contact to the target as well as reliable weight transference. **Fifth**, by stepping down the court, you hit your shot earlier, robbing time from your opponent, and have better court positioning to launch an attack to the net.

The neutral stance is typically used on slow, low balls hit towards the middle of the court. For example, if the incoming ball is hit with backspin, then the neutral stance is probably the best option due to the slower and lower bounce of the ball. Recreational players can use the neutral stance more often because of the slower speed of the game and less frequent use of high-bouncing, heavy topspin balls. This is particularly true in doubles, where the reduced court area a player must cover makes for fewer wide balls, and therefore, less need for the open stances.

TECHNIQUE

When using the neutral stance, it is important to line up your back foot almost behind the flight of the incoming ball (*opposite, far left*) because you want your front foot's forward momentum to push towards your target (*opposite, center left*). If you are stepping across the court with your front foot, then it probably means you should have used a semi-open or open stance.

The front foot should be angled towards the right net post (*opposite, center right*) to keep the upper body in correct alignment during the swing. If the front foot is perpen-

dicular to the net, your hips will open too much (your hips should be at a roughly 45 degree angle to the net at contact). If your front foot is parallel to the to the net, you will hinder the forward momentum of the weight transfer through the shot.

As you swing, your front foot should hit the ground a moment before contact to secure forward momentum (*opposite, far right*). At contact, the front foot stays still to anchor the stroke and your back foot slides to the right. This movement of the back foot allows the hips to rotate and produces a contact point in front of the body. While finishing the stroke,

COACH'S BOX:

The neutral stance has returned to favor after being in the tennis teaching doghouse for a period. In the 1990s, while working at a renowned tennis facility, I was told by the tennis director to teach students to use the open stance only, even when receiving lower and slower balls. This was during the time when the Williams sisters were dominating with their open stance style, and many top coaches were taking heed. This tunnel vision focus of using only open stance groundstrokes is an example of instruction being influenced by the "flavor of the month" mentality, instead of instruction being logically responsive to the game's dynamic nature and forged in sound fundamentals and optimal biomechanics. Today, there is agreement in the coaching community that the neutral stance is the best choice in certain circumstances. Interestingly, I've seen the Williams sisters hit more neutral stance groundstrokes later in their careers.

Caroline Wozniacki performs her recovery step as she swings on this aggressive neutral stance forehand.

swing your back foot around level with your front foot (*right*). This is the recovery step.

Tennis is a changeable game, so the timing of the recovery step will vary. Sometimes a deliberate recovery step is not needed because it happens naturally. For example, if you need to move quickly sideways to play a neutral stance forehand, your back foot will pivot around to the right from the body's momentum. Or, on a powerful swing, the fast movement of your racquet to the left on the follow through will naturally pull your back foot to the right (*above*). However, if your forehand requires less movement to the ball or is less aggressive, which is often the case at the recreational level, your recovery step can be later and more deliberate. The later recovery step has the advantage of both stabilizing the hips and helping balance the racquet correctly at contact.

3. THE HOP STEPS

Most groundstrokes will be hit with your feet in one of the regular open or neutral stances;

however, there are other times when your feet should move and pivot in less conventional ways to establish balance, power, and recovery in the most efficient way. If you focus on learning the three main stances in a static form only, you are leaving out a substantial part of the vital footwork component of the game. It is important to learn the dynamic derivatives of the regular stances: the hop steps.

Hop steps, where one foot hops through contact while the other foot lifts in different directions to balance out the body, are used in various situations when time is limited and the shot is best hit with only one foot on the ground.

A. FORWARD HOP

A forward hop is used when moving forward to respond to a short ball. Here, the front foot is grounded during the backswing as it steps towards the net in a neutral stance. It then lifts and hops forward during the swing and follow through while the back foot remains in the air (*opposite, above*). This hop happens natu-

Federer uses the forward hop before attacking the net.

rally due to the momentum from the forward movement combined with the low-to-high arc of the topspin swing. After the follow through, continue the forward momentum so that the back foot ends up in front of the front foot. This will help you gain speed to move quickly to the net to volley.

B. FOREHAND SEMI-OPEN HOP
After moving quickly left to play a semi-open stance forehand, the weight transfer into the shot usually will begin from the left foot and, due to the sideways movement, propel the body sideways in an airborne fashion during the swing (*right*). As the racquet moves forward to meet the ball, the left foot hops sideways to the left as the right leg kicks back behind to balance out the body.

Jo-Wilfried Tsonga moves left, sets up in the semi-open stance, and hops through the swing.

Marin Cilic uses the open stance hop, ending well to the right of where he began the swing.

Jo-Wilfried Tsonga defends against a high-bouncing ball by employing the backward hop.

C. OPEN STANCE HOP

The open stance lateral hop is used on wide shots where the energy created by the sideways movement lifts the outside foot during the swing, landing it some distance away from the inside foot. While airborne and finishing the swing, you lean your legs to the left on the forehand and to the right on the backhand as the upper body stays upright (*left*). This helps reverse the directional momentum and facilitates quick recovery.

D. FOREHAND BACKWARD HOP

The forehand backward hop can be useful on a deep, high bouncing topspin shot. From the semi-open stance, the right foot will push off and move backwards through the shot while the left leg lifts and moves backwards behind the right foot (*top right*). After the left leg lands, the body pushes forward towards the baseline to recover.

E. FOREHAND LUNGE HOP

There are times when a ball is too wide and you are unable to set your feet for an open stance shot. When this happens, an elevated,

Caroline Wozniacki uses a forward lunge hop to power through a wide forehand.

lunging crossover hop is best. When using the lunge hop on the forehand, the last step before contact loads up the weight on the right leg, which thrusts the left leg forward with a large powerful step as you swing the racquet (*bottom*). During the swing, the right foot lifts and the left arm pulls backwards to balance the body. As you follow through, the right foot hits the ground, slowing down the body and beginning your recovery.

II. The Five Phases of the Forehand

NOW THAT WE HAVE COVERED the stances, let's discuss the forehand swing in regards to the upper body. There are five main phases of the swing: the unit turn, backswing, forward swing to contact, contact, and follow through.

1. UNIT TURN

To maximize power and consistency on the forehand, it is important to use the larger muscle groups of the hips, chest, and shoulders effectively. The best way to efficiently use these muscles is to start the swing well with a unit turn. You do this by turning your body as a unit, keeping your arms relatively still while pivoting your right foot, lifting your left heel, and turning your shoulders with your left hand holding the throat of the racquet (*right*).

There are four reasons for your left hand to stay on the throat of the racquet during the unit turn. **First**, it forces your shoulders to turn so your body can uncoil powerfully later in the swing. **Second**, it guides your racquet into the correct path for the rest of your backswing. Letting go with your left hand too early allows the racquet to enter swing paths that may be higher, lower, shorter, or longer than ideal. **Third**, your left hand can turn the racquet as you place your right hand in your preferred forehand grip. **Fourth**, your left arm feeds information about the racquet's height and angle to your brain during the backswing, freeing your mind to focus on the ball.

As you set up in the unit turn, point the racquet upward with the strings around eye level and your hitting elbow comfortably bent a few inches lower than ninety degrees. Pointing the

Maria Sharapova starts her forehand with the unit turn.

racquet upward like this creates more racquet speed into the end of the backswing as compared to lower backswings. This is analogous to a ball dropped off a table having greater energy than a ball rolling down a ramp.

Unless the ball is wide, thus requiring you to pump your arms to run fast, you should do the unit turn quickly and prepare as early as possible for your forehand. The backswing will begin at different times, but the timing of the unit turn to initiate the swing should occur quickly and with a more consistent timing.

Once you have prepared your arms in the unit turn, move your feet and set your stance for the swing. After setting their stance, some players pause the racquet and lock their hips

COACH'S BOX:

It is important to begin the swing well — this coaching mantra holds true for every stroke. Without a strong unit turn to begin your forehand, the steps that follow will be less effective and powerful. Fortunately, it is a movement every player can do; we can all start our forehand like the pros.

Below in frames one and five, we see Federer and Djokovic start their swings with a strong unit turn. Now their racquets are in good alignment to end the backswing in the power position (*see page 97*) and lag the racquet (*frames two and six*). Next, their hitting shoulders combine to drive the racquet forward to contact as their wrists lift the racquet head to create topspin (*frames three and seven*). Their swings end with a full follow through and good balance (*frames four and eight*) and it all started with and flowed from a technically sound beginning.

to end the unit turn. Nadal (*below*) and Federer do this, while others like Djokovic and Murray are more fluid. For advanced players, I recommend the pause method because I feel it loads up energy in the legs more powerfully and disguises the drop shot better. For less advanced players, it is simpler to keep the racquet moving during the unit turn. As long as the shoulders are turning and the racquet head is pointing upwards, the unit turn can be executed well either way.

After his forehand deserted him for much of 2015, Nadal said he spent many hours on the practice court working on a stronger unit turn to produce a more technically sound stroke.[3] In the spring of 2016, his improved forehand helped him clinch tournament victories in Barcelona and Monte Carlo.

2. BACKSWING

After setting up with the unit turn, the backswing begins. Most backswings will be similar, but it is important to remember that the backswing on the forehand will vary depending on the situation and purpose of the shot. The backswing on a powerful forehand off a short ball will be longer, while if the shot received is fast or your balance is compromised, a shorter backswing will be more appropriate.

A. TIMING

When you begin the backswing is a key factor in establishing good timing for the shot. If you start too early, it will reduce your potential to accelerate the racquet on the forward swing. If you begin the backswing too late, your ability to gather power will be limited and negatively impact your racquet control.

When do the top players start their backswing? During a baseline rally on clay courts, most players delay the start of their backswing until just before the bounce of the ball. This is the timing that permits the greatest racquet acceleration and allows them to make last second adjustments that would be difficult if the backswing began earlier and their left hand was off the racquet. On the faster hard courts, they prepare sooner. Recreational players have a much slower swing and should begin the backswing well before the bounce of the ball while still preparing the racquet in a way that keeps the swing fluid.

B. THE LEFT ARM AND RACQUET POSITIONING

After determining the timing of your backswing, the backswing itself begins with your left hand separating from the racquet and moving to the right, ending parallel to the net. This left arm positioning ensures that the shoulders turn more than the hips, allowing

Federer starts his "outside" backswing with his left arm parallel to the net and his strings facing towards the right side fence.

the upper body to uncoil more powerfully during the forward swing.

As your left arm moves across, the right arm moves the racquet back in a circular fashion with the strings of the racquet facing towards the right side fence (*above*). Having the strings face this way during the first half of the backswing places your wrist at a comfortable angle to drop the racquet efficiently into the power position at the end of the backswing.

C. THE OUTSIDE BACKSWING

As the racquet goes back in a circular fashion, it should stay to the right or to the "outside" (*above*). This gains time by having the racquet take a shorter path to the end of the backswing versus the longer path taken by larger, more "inside" (or to the left) backswings. Even though the outside backswing is shorter, it is more powerful because the wrist can flex back more at the end of the backswing. It also re-

Nadal and Federer end their backswing in the power position, a commonality of all great forehands.

sults in a straighter path to contact, creating a longer extension for increased accuracy.

D. THE POWER POSITION

At the end of the backswing, your hitting arm straightens and your racquet should point towards the right side of the back fence with the racquet head above the wrist and strings facing towards the ground (*above*). This is referred to as the "power position." It is a commonality seen in all great forehands. With this position established, you have the body fully coiled and the racquet in a powerful slot to transition from the backswing into the forward swing.

As the racquet sets in the power position, the left arm straightens, providing anchoring

---

COACH'S BOX:

On the professional tour, the emphasis on the forehand shot has evolved from creating power with a longer backswing to handling and returning shots with power using a shorter, outside backswing. It is partly for this reason that players like Federer have plenty of time to play their forehand. It also allows them to play closer to the baseline and move quickly forward to attack short balls.

Some players have adjusted their backswing over time and adopted this technique. Early in his career, Nadal struggled to win big tournaments on the faster court surfaces. Then he began taking the racquet back slightly lower and preparing the racquet more to the outside of the body. This change reduced the time he needed to execute a powerful forehand and allowed him to play more aggressively and closer to the baseline. Since then, he has won several Grand Slams on the faster surfaces.

Following the power position, Djokovic rotates his hips and lags the racquet.

counterpoint strength for the hitting arm to move the racquet forward with greater force. It also stretches the oblique muscles, preparing them for the hip rotation that follows. The hip rotation adds power through leverage; the force it creates multiplies as it is transferred to the arms, much like the lever system that allows a toy propeller to fly.

3. FORWARD SWING TO CONTACT

With the backswing and the setting of the power position complete, the left arm that was stretched at the end of the backswing begins to bend and pull left, and the hips rotate causing the racquet to lag (*above right*). The word "lag"

usually has negative connotations, however in tennis, it means extra "sling shot" power. Racquet lag stretches your shoulder and arm muscles, generating extra momentum to thrust the racquet powerfully towards contact.

During the racquet lag, the forearm and wrist will circle around in a clockwise direction. The more topspin desired, the larger the circle. This circling of the racquet turbocharges the swing and occurs without conscious muscle manipulation. It happens naturally from establishing the power position with an outside backswing and your hitting elbow holding its position as your hips rotate.

Following the racquet lag, your forward

The path the racquet takes on the forward swing will vary depending whether you are hitting a topspin or flat forehand. On Jo-Wilfried Tsonga's topspin forehand (*top*), his racquet lifts at roughly a 45 degree angle, while on his flat forehand (*bottom*), his racquet takes an almost level path to the ball.

The decision to hit a flat forehand versus a topspin forehand is largely dependent on your desired level of aggressiveness and court positioning. For example, if you are looking to take control of the point and are positioned near or in front of the baseline, the flat forehand is likely the right shot choice. On the other hand, if you wish to stay in the neutral phase of the rally and are positioned beyond the baseline, then using the topspin forehand often makes strategic sense.

Djokovic's racquet butt points towards the ball before it turns towards the body to square up the racquet for contact. The forehand swing sequence is outside for quick preparation, inside to lag the racquet (*left*), and outside again to meet the ball (*right*).

COACH'S BOX:

Always remember that because your wrist is your body's closest joint to the racquet, how it aligns and moves through contact has a huge influence on the success of every shot. When you break it down, tennis technique is quite simple. You have three main shots — serves, topspin groundstrokes, and volleys — with three different wrist movements. Of course, there's a lot more to it than that, but basically if you can learn to pronate your wrist on the serve, lift your wrist on topspin groundstrokes, and hold your wrist steady on volleys, you can play a very good level of tennis.

swing continues with hips rotating and the racquet head dropping below the ball. After the racquet head drops, the racquet butt cap moves forward to point towards the ball, lagging the racquet for a second time.

After the racquet butt cap moves forward, it turns towards the body, causing the racquet head to move closer to the body and then away, or inside-to-outside (*above*), as it gets closer to contact. It's natural to think, because the ball moves in a linear fashion, that the forehand should be linear type swing. However, to maximize kinesthetic power, the forehand swing should arc and curve; arc up on the backswing, and then curve forward to meet the ball.

As the racquet moves towards the ball, your

Djokovic moves his wrist forward slightly for power and then steadies it at contact to direct and control his shot.

wrist moves forward from a 60 to 70 degree angle to the forearm (*left*) to around a 45 degree angle at contact (*right*) This forward movement (or "catching up") of your wrist to your forearm adds racquet speed and squares up the racquet face to your target. Keep in mind, the wrist is the final moving part of the body to influence the speed and direction of the racquet. Its motion is the crucial final link of the forehand's kinetic chain, whereby the build-up of energy throughout the body reaches a final crescendo.

As the arm and wrist move the racquet forward, the wrist also moves slightly upward to lift the racquet head and add topspin to the shot. From a front view on a waist-high ball,

the racquet head that was below the ball at around an eight o'clock angle before contact (*next page*) moves upward to meet the ball at a nine o'clock (or horizontal) angle to start the windshield wiper motion discussed next in the contact section. While the wrist moves upward and forward, that forward motion slows down an instant before contact, allowing you to master ball impact and direct the shot.

4. CONTACT
At this point, you are roughly halfway through your forward swing and it's time for for the moment of truth — the contact point and its three main considerations: the "windshield wiper motion," the point of contact, and extension.

A. THE WINDSHIELD WIPER MOTION

As mentioned, the racquet head moves forward and tilts upward to meet the ball at a nine o'clock angle. It continues to move forward and tilt upward following contact before finishing across the body at a three o'clock angle (*opposite top*). This upward rotation of the racquet is commonly referred to as the "windshield wiper" motion because the racquet takes a path that somewhat mimics car windshield wipers as the top edge of the racquet on the forward swing becomes the bottom edge on the follow through.

The windshield wiper motion allows the strings to brush up the back of the ball and makes the ball rotate forward, giving it topspin after it leaves the racquet. The amount of topspin you produce is determined by the steepness of the racquet's low-to-high gradient and the speed of the racquet head — a sharp upward brushing of the ball with a fast racquet will produce a lot of topspin. Or, put in windshield wiper terms, strokes with heavy topspin will rotate the racquet head more quickly than flatter shots.

Stan Wawrinka begins the windshield wiper motion with the racquet head below the ball just before contact.

COACH'S BOX:

The correct combination of windshield wiper motion for topspin and forward movement of the arm from the shoulder for good extension is essential to hitting a great forehand. A forehand that uses mostly windshield wiper motion will create topspin but lack power, while a forehand that uses good extension without the windshield wiper motion will create power but lack the topspin to control the shot. You need both components of the swing to hit with controlled power.

B. POINT OF CONTACT

At contact, you must match the ball up correctly with the strings. To do this consistently, contact must occur in front of your body (*opposite bottom*). A contact point in front of your body allows you the time and space to build up to optimal racquet speed, and you can see the ball well. Moreover, it's here that your body is best positioned to have the physical strength to command the ball's impact. How far in front of the body will depend largely on the direction of your shot. Cross-court shots should be hit farther in front of the body than down-the-line ones.

C. EXTENSION

It is important to hit with good extension at contact. To do this, you must reach forward

Djokovic's windshield wiper motion sees his racquet rotate over 180 degrees following contact. He combines the use of the windshield wiper motion with good extension to hit his forehand with power and control.

Kei Nishikori makes contact in front of his body where his physical strength, swing momentum, and vision are best served.

with the racquet through contact, as if hitting through three balls lined up in a row. Here, the racquet face should remain steady at a slightly closed angle (*left*) — don't let it slip open or shake forward and close around the contours of the ball.

Remember, the reality of every tennis stroke is that it involves a compressible ball pushing into tightly wound strings on a racquet. Therefore, it is only by using good extension that you can effectively control the collision of the ball and hit with power, depth, and accuracy. An issue some players have is that they "lose" the collision, causing their racquet to stop short during the extension, and consequently, their forehand lacks these desirable qualities.

As you perform the extension, your wrist, forearm, and elbow will remain fairly steady as your shoulder drives the racquet forward. If this movement is done correctly, the racquet should face parallel to your target and stay on the right side of your body, creating good

Serena Williams displays good extension as her racquet remains on her right side and moves parallel to her target after contact.

Why is the windshield wiper motion an important technique to learn? It creates topspin, which produces air pressure above the ball that pushes it downward. Thus, topspin allows you to hit well above the net knowing the ball's dipping trajectory is going to bring it down into the court before the baseline. In coaching parlance, topspin gives a powerful baseline shot shape, and shape provides consistency. Topspin not only produces a favorable trajectory, but also opens up more acute cross-court angles and a higher and "heavier" ball for your opponent to defend against.

If you are unfamiliar with the racquet movement for a topspin forehand, try this exercise. Stand approximately one foot from the net in your forehand stance, match the middle of your racquet face up with the head band of the net, and gently "brush" up the net. Next, trap a ball with your strings against the headband of the net, and do the same motion while rolling the ball over the net. This exercise can help can help you gain a better understanding of how the ball's forward rotation (i.e. topspin) is achieved.

space between the racquet and the left shoulder (*above*).

The extension is easier to do well if your head and chest are still. Lifting your head and chest during extension will cause the racquet to veer left instead of extending straight towards your target. A good tip to keep your head and chest still is to look down at the ball through the back of your strings at contact. Keep in mind that the ball only stays on your strings for a few milliseconds, which is not long enough to register in your brain, so while you may not actually see the ball clearly on the strings, the point is that watching the ball helps keeps your chest still for a straighter racquet path and longer extension.

Additionally, at this stage of the swing, the moving of body parts to build kinetic chain power is almost over, and the emphasis shifts to keeping the body still to maximize racquet control. Even though modern swings are very explosive, elite players still keep their head and chest stationary at contact to help set the racquet face at the precise angle needed to hit their powerful shots in the court.

5. FOLLOW THROUGH

Following contact and extension, the racquet releases forward and fans across to the left to complete the windshield wiper motion. As the racquet fans across, the racquet face will close (*below*). The degree to which the racquet face closes will depend on the amount of topspin used as well as the ball's height. The racquet will close more on flatter shots and higher contact points and less on heavy topspin shots and lower contact points.

With the windshield wiper motion complete, the elbow bends and the racquet moves upward, to the left, and backwards to finish the stroke. As this occurs, the left arm continues to move left to clear a path for your body to finish the hip rotation.

A good follow through is an indication that your swing had solid contact, proper extension, and good racquet speed. And while a good follow through won't guarantee these stroke qualities, committing one to muscle memory will help them happen more consistently. I've found in my teaching that when students are conscious of following through fully, the extension part of their swing often improves too, adding velocity and depth to their shot.

The length and arc of the follow through will vary depending on the type of shot. There are three main types of follow through: elevated, horizontal, and reverse.

Following extension, Federer closes the racquet as it fans across to the left.

A flat hitter, Maria Sharapova often uses the elevated follow through.

A. ELEVATED FOLLOW THROUGH

The elevated follow through is typically used when hitting flat to moderate topspin ground-strokes. In this finish, the racquet ends behind your head with your knuckles stopping near your left ear and your elbow at shoulder height and pointing towards your target (*left*). For recreational players who typically use moderate topspin, the elevated follow through is the correct one to commit to muscle memory.

B. HORIZONTAL FOLLOW THROUGH

The horizontal follow through typically is used on higher balls or balls hit with moderate to heavy topspin (*below*).

Here, Murray's horizontal follow through indicates he likely used heavy topspin on this forehand.

Nadal uses the reverse follow through on most shots, but for other pros, this follow through is used only under certain circumstances.

COACH'S BOX:

Nadal uses the reverse follow through on most of his forehands, but this wasn't always the case. If you watch Nadal as a junior on video, you will see that he rarely used the reverse follow through on his forehand. However, he realized over a period of time — and after hitting thousands of balls — that his straight-arm technique and lean-back style resulted in the reverse follow through being the finish that worked best for *his* forehand. One of the talents of great players is their intuitive ability to figure out the technique that works best for them and commit to it.

C. REVERSE FOLLOW THROUGH

The reverse follow through is sometimes used by high-level players when rushed, running for a wide shot, or desiring extra topspin on their forehand. In the reverse follow through, the racquet swings almost vertically and releases above and then behind the head (*above*) instead of the traditional across the body finish. By ending this way, players can accelerate and hit an effective shot even though they may be hurrying through the stroke. The increased speed and spin of today's game has made the reverse follow through more popular because its later contact point allows a split second more time and its steep gradient assists spin.

RAFAEL NADAL'S HALL OF FAME CAREER can largely be attributed to his amazing heavy topspin forehand. Usually, when a player uses tremendous topspin, their shot's velocity suffers. However, Nadal's incredible racquet head speed allows him to have both explosive spin and power on his forehand.

In the first frame Nadal's forehand looks orthodox with his shoulders turning and his legs "digging" into the court to load up energy. In frame two, his racquet head is above the wrist and facing towards the ground in the power position, and his non-hitting arm is moving to the right to activate his core and rotate his hips. Here, Nadal's forehand begins to differentiate itself from most players, with his hitting arm becoming completely straight (versus slightly bent) at the end of the backswing. This technique stretches the arm muscles more and lengthens the swing path for greater racquet speed. In frame

4   5   6

three, he drops the racquet head below the ball as the racquet begins its low-to-high path to the ball. Between frames three and four, we can see the lag and explosive release of the racquet and how the racquet has rotated from a 5 o'clock to an 11 o'clock position. This 180 degree racquet rotation produces incredible topspin. In frame four, we see Nadal's straight-arm technique permits long extension, and his explosive release leads to a larger than average forward wrist movement following contact. The wrist is the closest part of the body to the racquet, and Nadal knows that moving it forward like this adds power to his stroke. Recreational players who don't enjoy 3200 rpms on their forehand like Rafa should move their wrist forward only slightly during this phase of the swing. Frames five and six show Nadal's signature reverse follow through with the racquet ending behind his head to finish his "buggy whip" motion.

III. Types of Forehands

NEXT, I WILL COVER THE TECHNIQUE and advantage of two important forehand shots, the inside-out and inside-in forehands. Then I will describe five other types of topspin forehands. Finally, I will conclude this section by discussing the slice forehand.

I. THE INSIDE-OUT AND INSIDE-IN FOREHAND

The game's two most feared shots from the baseline are the inside-out and inside-in forehands. If you have a strong forehand, these are shots you should use frequently; they represent one of the best chances to seize control of the point or force an error from your opponent.

In both, the player making the shot moves left into the backhand side of the court. From this position, a forehand hit cross court to the backhand side of a right-handed opponent is an "inside-out" forehand, while a forehand hit down the line is an "inside-in" forehand (*below*).

The inside-out and inside-in forehands have several advantages. **First**, the movement to the left side of the court adds momentum and power to the shot, and the body alignment on the forehand allows you to move left and still hit a well-balanced shot. **Second**, if your forehand is your strength and your opponent's weakness is their backhand, the inside-out forehand will help you set up a rally

pattern that pits your strength against their weakness. In this scenario, your opponent will feel pressure and may take risks that lead them to hit low percentage shots. **Third**, by dominating play from the middle of the court, you "shrink" the playing surface, leaving only a small space in the backhand corner for your opponent to hit their shot without damaging repercussions. Giving your opponent a small space to aim for will cause them to miss shots wide. **Fourth**, the inside-out forehand is hit over the lowest part of the net, into the longest court, and has the added positive effect of moving your opponent wider off the court than most other forehands will. **Fifth**, if the forehand is your strength, dominating play with the forehand will give you more confidence in your backhand. When you hit a majority of groundstrokes with your superior forehand, you no longer feel pressure to do something special with your backhand, knowing that there will be a forehand to unload on a shot or two ahead. This leads to a higher percentage shot selection on backhands and

Madison Keys enjoys moving left along the baseline and dominating play with her forehand.

overall a more patient and smarter crafting of the point.

2. OTHER TYPES OF TOPSPIN FOREHANDS

There are five main other types of topspin forehands. Players with the versatility to use different forehands gain a large advantage over those players who do not. Having options allows you to use the most effective tactical response for the specific circumstance. Sometimes it makes sense to drive the topspin forehand fast with little spin low over the net, while at other times the correct choice of shot is to hit the ball slower with heavy spin high over the net. Also, each opponent you face will have different weaknesses, and exposing these shortcomings is easier if you have different ways of hitting from the baseline.

There are five main types of topspin forehands.

A. THE ARC

This shot is hit from a few feet behind the baseline with good topspin three or four feet over the net and lands well inside the lines. It is typically used as a neutral or somewhat aggressive stroke to move your opponent around the court and put you on the offensive. The arc is the forehand used most frequently on clay courts.

B. THE DRIVE

The drive is hit from close to the baseline with moderate topspin one or two feet over the net and should land three to five feet inside the lines. This forehand's good speed and moderate topspin will leave your opponent scrambling. It is commonly used on hard courts when you have a good amount of time and balance to play your shot.

1   2   3

DESPITE HOW GOOD HIS BACKHAND IS, NOVAK DJOKOVIC OFTEN moves into the backhand side of the court to attack with his inside-out forehand. He has said, "The inside-out forehand is one of the most important shots in the game. I look for every opportunity to do it."[4]

In the first frame, Djokovic shuffles leftward in a semi-circle path to get into position for this inside-out forehand. He makes sure that he allows plenty of space to hit the ball so he can push forward into the shot. As he moves, he prepares his racquet and turns his shoulders in the unit turn position. This early preparation allows him to take a full wind-up and not rush the forward swing. In frames two and three, he places the racquet in the power position and grounds his feet, setting up a strong ground force reaction to initiate

4   5   6

the kinetic chain. In frame four, he unloads the energy by springing mostly off his left foot. We see how his hips have rotated from the frame before, allowing him to make contact in the most powerful location — in front of his body. In frame five, his right foot lifts in the air to balance out the body and his racquet closes after rotating upward to create topspin. It can be a little deceiving watching the pros play from a frontal view on television because it looks like the sideways windshield wiper motion dominates the forward swing, however from a side view, we can see how much they extend forward to master ball impact and drive the ball deep in the court. In the last frame, he follows through with his head upright, shoulders level, and his right elbow shoulder-high and pointing down the court to his target.

Agnieszka Radwanska's ability to mix up her forehand with different angles, spins, and speeds frustrates her opponents and gives her many strategic options.

C. THE LOOP

There will be occasions when your opponent has you pushed out wide and the loop shot can buy time to recover. This defensive shot is hit six to eight feet above the net from a position well behind the baseline. It is best to aim the loop forehand deep towards the middle of the court to reduce the angles available to your opponent.

D. THE ANGLE

The angle shot is hit with heavy topspin, one or two feet over the net and short in the court. It can pull your opponent wide off the court, leading to an opportunity to go on the offensive. The extra spin and control stemming from the new poly strings has made the angle forehand a more popular shot during baseline rallies in the modern era.

E. THE KILL

The kill shot is hit from inside the baseline with the incoming ball moving slowly and bouncing above the net. It is a power stroke hit toward the corners of the baseline with a limited amount of topspin. The inside-out and inside-in power forehands are examples of the kill shot where you are trying to end the point with a winner or unreturnable shot.

On the ATP Tour, you see players with varying degrees of versatility on their forehand. One of the strengths of Djokovic's game is the way he can arc, drive, loop, angle, and kill his forehand. He can do each of these forehands well, and importantly, he almost always makes the right choice of when to use each one. Sometimes when a talented player has many options, they can be prone to making the wrong shot choice.

One criticism of Nadal's game is that while he has one of the best arc and loop forehands the game has ever seen, his drive and kill forehands lack the velocity other top pros pos-

Murray uses the slice forehand, or "squash shot," to defend against this difficult, wide ball.

sess on their aggressive forehands. As a result, Nadal's career title tally is heavily lopsided with clay court victories (53 on clay courts and 16 on hard courts as of June 2017) even though most tournaments on the ATP tour are played on hard courts. On the other hand, the more forehand-versatile Djokovic has won 51 titles on hard courts versus 13 on clay - a statistic more representative of the ATP hard court-to-clay court tournament ratio.

3. SLICE FOREHAND

The forehand is predominantly a topspin shot, but it is also important to learn a slice forehand. Unlike most topspin forehands, the slice forehand can be hit well without the feet being grounded before the swing, and the compact nature of the swing allows you to hit an effective shot even if you are rushed. It is often needed when your opponent's shot is too low or short to hit comfortably with topspin. It can also be used strategically to force your opponent to hit their shot from a low, difficult height or to draw an opponent up to the net, forcing them out of their comfort zone at the baseline.

In desperate wide ball situations, the later contact of the slice forehand buys you more time to reach the shot. Also, the backspin of the slice forehand carries the ball farther in the air, so even when you are stretching or off balance, you can still hit the ball deep in the court. The past decade has seen the wide forehand slice shot, now dubbed the "squash shot," become more widely used due to the extra reach and time this shot permits (*above*). The squash shot has repurposed the stretching wide forehand from a defensive lob to an aggressive rally extender. In this era of stronger and fitter athletes, the extra court coverage this emergency stroke gives the players has made it an increasingly familiar defensive weapon.

The slice forehand is also a useful approach shot, particularly in doubles. The slower and lower bounce of the slice approach shot gives you time to set up for a good net position and causes an awkward, low contact point for your opponent's passing shot. The slice forehand is also used to block fast serves or to hit the ball low at a net player's feet when in trouble. Lastly, it can be used for lobs to defend the point or force your opponents to play difficult overheads deep in the court.

TECHNIQUE

The slice forehand is typically played with a neutral stance, but like the topspin forehand, a variety of stances are appropriate depending on the circumstances. Begin the swing with the continental grip and take the racquet back above the height of the ball with the racquet face open (*previous page, left*). The racquet ends the backswing pointing to the back fence with the racquet head above the wrist and the racquet butt cap pointing towards the ball.

The racquet moves forward with a downward arc and a slightly open racquet face (*previous page, center*). The strings make contact with the bottom half of the ball, causing the ball to spin backwards. The greater the backspin desired, the sharper the decline on the forward swing, and the more open the racquet face will be at contact.

The wrist should be firm and the elbow slightly bent during the forward swing before straightening slightly through contact. Keep the head and chest still and follow through with the arm extended below shoulder height (*previous page, right*). For a fuller explanation regarding the technique needed for strong slice groundstrokes, please refer to the slice backhand section in Chapter Eight.

IV. Groundstroke Practice

NOW THAT YOU UNDERSTAND the mechanics of the various forehand groundstrokes, and with instruction on the backhand to follow in the next chapter, it is time to commit these techniques to muscle memory through repetition. Groundstroke practice sessions should incorporate a combination of drills and point play. Drills will allow you to hit many balls in a

---

COACH'S BOX:

At the recreational level, it takes roughly 1.5 seconds for the ball to travel across the length of the court. When it comes to learning stroke technique, that is not enough time to use phrases to help you perform the stroke correctly; instead use imagery. Besides being quicker, imagery has been proven to be more effective. On topspin forehand and backhand groundstrokes and the serve, there are four key stages (power position, racquet lag, contact, and follow through) which I recommend committing to memory. You can print the photos I have at the end of chapters five, seven, and eight, or go online and download similar images of your favorite professional and file it away on your phone. Remember the saying "out of sight, out of mind" holds true in learning tennis. Use imagery to help cement good technique in all your strokes.

---

short amount of time, honing timing and technique, and point play will give you practice moving and reacting to all the different situations that may arise during a rally.

If you have an hour to practice groundstrokes, I recommend spending roughly 30 minutes drilling and 30 minutes playing points. Come prepared with drills that focus on improving your weaknesses and sharpening your strengths, as well as a variety of games that will keep your practice sessions fresh and interesting. Also, don't forget to do drills that practice offensive and defensive situations from the baseline; you need to able to play well in both phases to win consistently.

1. SHORT BALL RECOGNITION

Goal: Recognize short balls and take control of the point.

Using only half of the court at first, rally the ball cross-court with your practice partner. If the ball lands in the service box, players must hit down the line and play out the point using the full court. Play a game up to 11 points hitting cross-court forehands, and then repeat the game hitting cross-court backhands. Variation: Play a drop shot instead of hitting down the line when the ball lands in the service box and finish the point using the service line as the baseline.

2. FOREHAND TARGET PRACTICE

Goal: Hitting offensive forehands from a balanced position.

Set up three cones four to six feet apart in a triangle formation deep on the forehand side of both sides of the court. Rally using cross-court forehands with your practice partner. Players score one point if their shot lands in the triangle and two points if a cone is struck. First player to score 15 points wins the game. Variation: Set up cones deep in the backhand side of the court and both players hit inside-out forehands.

3. OFFENSE/DEFENSE

Goal: Learn to play offense and defense well.

Set up two cones on one side of the court about 12 to 14 feet apart in the middle of the baseline. You will hit aggressively using the whole court, while your practice partner defends, aiming their shots between the two cones. If your practice partner hits outside the cones they lose the point. For each point won, you score one point, while your practice partner scores two points. The first player to 15 points wins the game and then switch roles. You can adjust the width of the cones to make the game competitive or appropriate to your skill level.

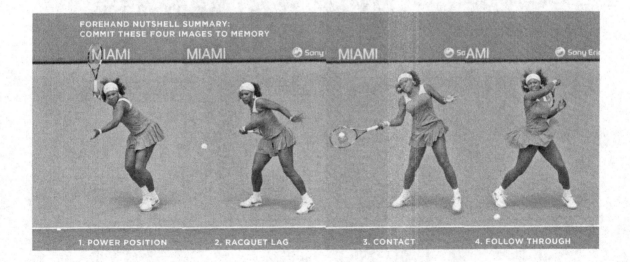

FOREHAND NUTSHELL SUMMARY:
COMMIT THESE FOUR IMAGES TO MEMORY

1. POWER POSITION   2. RACQUET LAG   3. CONTACT   4. FOLLOW THROUGH

Former World No. 1
Victoria Azarenka
launches into her
favorite ground-
stroke — the two-
handed backhand.

CHAPTER 8

Backhand

WHILE ALL STROKES HAVE EVOLVED in one way or another, probably no stroke has changed as much as the backhand. If you were to look at the singles draw sheets from Wimbledon fifty years ago, you would be hard pressed to find the names of even a handful of two-handed backhand players out of the 256 that entered the tournament. Today, it is names of one-handed backhand players that are scarce in the Wimbledon draw. Looking at the top 100 world rankings in 2016, there are just two or three women and about 20 men still using the one-handed backhand. The reason is simple; the game has become more powerful and players using a two-handed backhand are better equipped to handle this increased power.

Generally speaking, the higher the level of play, the more likely it is that the two-handed backhand is used. However, two-handed backhand players still need the use of the one-handed backhand sometimes for the added reach, finesse, and defense the shot provides. Notably, the one-handed backhand's less restrictive nature lends it to being the most common way of holding the racquet among recreational players.

This chapter covers the two-handed and one-handed topspin backhands, as well as the slice backhand. I begin by exploring the advantages and disadvantages of the two-handed versus the one-handed topspin backhand and suggest why the hybrid backhand may emerge as a new shot in the future. Then I discuss backhand technique, starting with the various stances. Next, I detail the upper body movements that will help you hit the three different types of backhands with power and control: the unit turn, backswing, forward swing to contact, contact, and follow through. The chapter concludes with a set of backhand drills.

I. The Advantages of the Two-Handed and One-Handed Backhand

THE TWO-HANDED TOPSPIN BACKHAND has several advantages over the one-handed version. The extra hand on the grip adds strength and stability. This is particularly useful when returning a serve or fast, high-bouncing topspin groundstrokes. The extra hand on the grip also keeps the swing more compact and regular, allows you to catch up to the ball if you are rushed, and enables you to hold your shot longer to better disguise your intentions. The two-handed backhand is also quicker to perform. You need more time to hit a good one-handed backhand topspin backhand given the larger backswing and earlier contact point required. Lastly, the two-handed backhand depends less on the stance. The open stances don't work particularly well on one-handed backhands, while on the two-handed backhand, you can use these stances for better balance, quicker positioning, and faster recovery.

Novak Djokovic and Andy Murray owe much of their success to their strong two-handed backhands. Whereas most players are limited to their forehand to take control of a baseline rally, Djokovic and Murray can also use their backhands to begin offensive shot patterns, especially with their down-the-line backhand. However, it is on the return of serve that their two-handed backhands probably have the most impact; both players have ranked near the top of the ATP return of serve statistics for almost a decade now. [1] The extra hand on the racquet allows them to effectively negate the force behind powerful serves and hit aggressive returns. In contrast, one-handed backhand players are often forced to chip or block the return and start the point in a less advantageous position.

Done correctly, the one-handed backhand is a beautiful shot and it does possess some advantages over the two-handed backhand. Since the slice backhand is a one-handed shot, one-handed backhand players usually have a stronger slice backhand because they develop more strength and coordination in their hitting

Two-handed backhand players like Nadal don't require the forward leg push for power like one-handed backhand players do.

As Richard Gasquet showcases, when done correctly the one-handed backhand is a beautiful shot.

1. THE HYBRID BACKHAND

The different advantages of the two-handed and one-handed backhand raises an interesting question: could the game evolve such that we see some players begin to use the two-handed backhand to return serve and then the one-handed backhand after the return? The introduction of a dual-purpose, or "hybrid" backhand, in the future does seem like a distinct possibility. For some players, the hybrid backhand might represent the best of both worlds — using the two-hander to handle the speed of the serve on the return and then the extra racquet speed and variety of the one-hander during the rally.

2. WHICH BACKHAND IS BEST FOR YOU?

Since both the one-handed and two-handed backhands have advantages, the question becomes determining which style suits you. It depends partly on age. Most juniors aren't going to be strong enough to hit a strong one-handed topspin backhand until their early teens. Therefore, the two-handed backhand is usually the shot first taught to kids.

Due to the longer development horizon, juniors who pursue the one-handed topspin backhand must be patient and have a clear long term vision of their future. Pete Sampras famously switched from a two-hander to a one-hander as a junior, recognizing that it would eventually suit the aggressive style of play he envisioned for himself. He lost some junior matches initially because of that change but certainly more than made up for it later with his seven Wimbledon singles titles. In contrast, former ATP player Paul McNamee switched from a one-hander to a two-hander at age 24. He saw his singles ranking soar soon afterwards and become the number one world

arm. The backhand volley, drop shot, and defensive lob are slice backhand derivatives, and therefore, are shots often performed better by one-handed backhand players. Also, one hand can swing faster than two; as a result, the one-handed backhand often can be hit with more topspin than the two-hander. And while the majority of touring pros hit a two-handed backhand, there are star players like Stan Wawrinka and Richard Gasquet who use the one-handed version and are considered amongst the best backhand players ever to play the game.

ranked doubles player.

You can take game style and physical characteristics into account, but ultimately the backhand you choose is a matter of what feels more natural and reliable. Some players feel less flexible and fluent with both hands on the racquet, while others feel they need two hands to hit a dependable topspin backhand. If you are new to the game, experiment using both styles and learn from experience what works best for you.

Regardless of what type of backhand you use, because the backhand has the hitting shoulder facing the incoming ball instead of behind the body as on the forehand, several parts of the swing are different from the forehand. **First,** the backhand backswing is shorter and the contact is made farther in front of the body. **Second**, the backhand typically requires the front foot stepping into the shot to achieve good power and thus, has different guidelines on the stances. **Third**, the backhand hip rotation is later and smaller, resulting in the racquet taking a longer, straighter path towards the target during extension. **Fourth**, because the backhand is a physically weaker swing it is usually a less aggressive shot than the forehand and often takes on a different strategic role.

II. Backhand Stances

I will explain backhand technique starting with the legs and then working up through the body. Like the forehand, a great backhand starts with good footwork and positioning the legs well in the best stance. You will need numerous stances for the various backhand shots, especially the closed and neutral stance, and to a lesser degree, the open stance.

Envisioning an aggressive net-rushing game style in the pros, Pete Sampras switched from a two-handed backhand to a one-handed backhand while still in the junior ranks.

I. THE CLOSED AND NEUTRAL STANCE

The most powerful leg positioning on the backhand is the closed stance. In the closed stance, the front leg takes a large diagonal step forward across the body at roughly a 45 degree angle (*opposite top*). There are four main reasons why the closed stance generates the most power. **First**, the larger step produces increased force. **Second**, the larger step widens the base and deepens the knee bend so you can create more energy pushing up from the ground. **Third**, the closed stance creates a good shoulder turn that allows for a strong uncoiling of the body later in the swing. **Fourth**, the closed stance aligns the hips in a good position to move the racquet forward in a powerful inside-outside path towards the ball. The neutral stance, where the step forward is

Nadal's closed stance produces a large, powerful step into the backhand.

Hitting in a neutral stance, Ana Ivanovic's cross-court backhand (*left*) sees her front foot less turned and back foot less behind the body than on her down-the-line backhand (*right*).

straighter in the direction of the net (*bottom*), is less powerful than the closed stance but is often needed on faster balls hit to the middle of the court.

TECHNIQUE

In both stances, the body weight that was loaded over your left foot at the end of the back-swing begins to transfer up the body as you step forward with your right foot and swing forward to meet the ball. The right foot should hit the ground a split second before contact to secure the forward momentum, push up from the ground, and stabilize the body to help the arm or arms control the racquet at ball impact.

Keep in mind, the step forward with the right foot into the shot should be more towards the net when hitting cross-court than when hitting down-the-line. This will help push your momentum towards your target. Also, the right foot on the cross-court backhand will point towards a 10 to 11 o'clock angle (*bottom left*) while on the down-the-line backhand, the right foot will point more around a nine to 10 o'clock angle (*bottom right*). These guidelines will help you attain optimal body weight transfer forward into the swing and align your hips well at contact.

The left foot will pivot in a controlled manner to the left during the forward swing. This will rotate the hips slightly and help move the kinetic energy up the body towards the racquet. The trick is not to pivot the left foot too much or too little. If the left foot pivots too much, the hips will open too soon and cause the arm or arms to bend too much at contact. If the left foot remains stationary, the hips will lock and reduce momentum into the shot.

Your balance at the end of the shot will indicate whether you hit the ball in the right position. At the end of the stroke, your weight should be solely on your right foot; after your left foot pivots to the left, your left heel should be raised up off the ground.

With the stroke complete, your left foot continues to move left and perform the recovery step. As mentioned in Chapter Seven when describing the neutral stance forehand, if you have moved quickly sideways prior to

Again, we can see how great strokes have similarities in technique, even as pre-swing movement can change body positioning and footwork. Compare Simona Halep and Murray's left leg positioning on their backhand swings (*frames three and seven*). Halep's sideways movement before the shot (*frame one*) produces an earlier recovery step (*frame four*) than Murray's more stationary backhand.

the stroke or are swinging the racquet aggressively, the recovery step will happen naturally during the follow through (*opposite top*). On backhands that require less movement before the swing or are more conservative, the recovery step will be later and more deliberate (*opposite bottom*). For recreational players who move and swing more slowly than the professionals, I prefer to see a higher level of body stability during the swing to better control the racquet at contact; therefore, the recovery step should be later and more deliberate.

2. OPEN STANCE

While the closed or neutral stance is ideal, it is not always possible during a heated point. Sometimes you need the semi-open or open stance backhand. While rarely used by one-handed players, the semi-open and open stance backhands are important strokes for two-handed players when rushed or on wider and higher balls when stepping forward into the shot is a difficult proposition.

TECHNIQUE

The keys to the open and semi-open stance backhands are a big shoulder turn and planting your left foot firmly and level with, or slightly behind, your right foot (*center left*). The left foot establishes a strong base to transfer power into the shot. Once your left foot hits the ground, your hips and shoulders will uncoil and your weight will shift across to your right foot as the racquet swings towards the ball. After the contact and extension, you continue to rotate and finish with your weight mostly on your right foot (*far right*).

With the backhand stances explained, let's turn to the five upper-body phases for two-handed, one-handed, and slice backhands. Since many of the same principles of the forehand discussed in Chapter Seven apply to the backhand, the five phases are presented in shorter form.

Serena Williams plants her left leg and then unloads on this open stance backhand.

III. The Five Phases of the Two-Handed Backhand

1. UNIT TURN

Start the two-handed backhand by pivoting with the left foot, lifting the heel of the right foot, and turning the shoulders (*below*). The elbows should be bent and relaxed with the racquet head pointed up at an approximately 45 degree angle above the wrists.

As you do this, prepare the grip. Most players wait with the left hand on the throat of the racquet and move it down to join the right hand on the grip during the unit turn. As outlined in Chapter Four, I recommend a continental grip with the right hand and an eastern to strong eastern grip with the left hand.

Murray begins his backhand with the unit turn.

COACH'S BOX:

In Chapter Four, we discussed the importance of grips and how they affect technique; on the two-handed backhand, this impact is particularly noteworthy. Regardless of your form, you will use many different stances over the course of a match, but you should use some more often than others depending on your grip.

On the two-handed backhand, the grip you use with the hitting hand will affect the amount of bend in your arms, which will in turn impact the contact point and stance. A weak continental grip will cause the arms to bend more and move the contact point less in front of the body (*below left*). In this case, the closed stance may be more comfortable. On the other hand, a strong continental grip will cause the arms to bend less and move the contact point further in front of the body (*below right*). In this case, the open stances may be more comfortable.

Simona Halep and Nadal use different backhand grips, resulting in different degrees of arm bend and stance preferences.

2. BACKSWING

Once the unit turn is done, use your arms and a continued shoulder turn to get the racquet to the end of the backswing. As you perform the backswing, remember to keep your arms and shoulders relaxed. The less tension in your shoulders the longer your backswing is likely to be and the more the racquet can lag and accelerate on the forward swing.

A full backswing should result in your chin resting near your right shoulder. Even though your shoulders are relaxed, your full backswing should place some tension in the back of your right shoulder to spring the racquet forward faster. The end of your backswing should be synchronized with loading weight on your back leg and moving your body into a crouched position ready to unleash the power stored in your body forward into the shot (*right*).

There are two main types of backswings on the backhand: the banana and the loop.

A. BANANA BACKSWING

The banana backswing starts with the hands going down past the waist and then backwards in a straight line before rising up slightly at the end of the backswing (*below*). The racquet ends the backswing slightly to the left, or "outside" of the body (*next page, right*), placing the wrists in a powerful position to lag the racquet when the hips rotate and perform the windshield wiper motion for additional racquet head speed and topspin.

Players who use the banana backswing typically use a strong continental or continental grip with their hitting hand. The power on this backhand is mostly generated by using the legs to push up from the ground and swinging the racquet more as a unit rather than primarily using the arms. It is the predominant backswing style on the ATP Tour and has the advantages of being compact, keeping the shoulders loose, and providing good topspin.

Using the banana backswing, Djokovic drops his hands below his waist before raising them again at the end of the backswing.

B. LOOP BACKSWING

The loop backswing starts with the hands going back in a circular fashion (*below left*) and ending further behind the body (*below right*), or "inside," than in the banana backswing. Also, as compared to the banana backswing, the arms bend more at contact and the wrists move more forward and less upwards, resulting in a flatter shot.

Players who use the loop backswing typically use a weak continental or continental grip with their hitting hand. The power on this backhand is generated more from the longer movement of the arms and hips rather than from moving the body as a unit and using the legs to push up from the ground. The loop backswing produces a powerful, flatter shot and is frequently used on the WTA.

Regardless of what style of backswing you use, at the end of the backswing the racquet should be just above waist-high and pointing slightly upward and towards the back fence (*right*). The edge of your racquet head

Djokovic keeps the racquet to the left, or "outside," to end his banana backswing in the power position.

In the loop backswing, Maria Sharapova takes the racquet back in a circular fashion (*left*) and "inside" (*right*) to end the backswing in the power position.

should be approximately perpendicular to the ground to simplify timing and help keep the arms loose. This is the backhand equivalent of the forehand's power position. With this position established, the racquet is in a powerful slot to transition from the backswing into the forward swing.

3. FORWARD SWING TO CONTACT

With the backswing complete, the forward swing starts by dropping the racquet down and the right foot ending its step forward by hitting the ground (*opposite, far left*). After the right foot hits the ground, the left shoulder and hips begin to rotate, releasing the energy stored in the legs and transferring it towards the torso, the arms, and ultimately to the racquet.

The hip rotation will allow the forearm muscles to stretch, leading the tip of the racquet to lag behind (*center left*). Then the right arm pulls the racquet butt cap forward towards the ball to lag the racquet for a second time.

After the right arm pulls the butt cap forward, the left arm starts to take over by turning the butt cap towards the body and releasing the racquet head forward to meet the ball (*center, and far right*). It is the left arm that creates most of the spin and racquet speed while the right arm's main responsibility is to help direct the shot.

The arms and wrists combine to move the racquet head in an inside-outside path towards the ball. If hitting topspin, the wrists move upward to "windshield wiper" the racquet and slightly forward as well to add power and square up the racquet at contact. As with the forehand, the swing needs to have the proper combination of the racquet head moving forward (for power) and upward (for topspin) in a single effort to produce a powerful and consistent shot.

Once the wrists move upward and forward before contact, they continue upward to create topspin, but their movement forward slows down an instant before contact to control ball impact and direct the shot.

4. CONTACT

With your head still and eyes looking down at

> **COACH'S BOX:**
>
> If you lack good extension on your two-handed backhand, practice hitting a weighted beach ball in the air from the service line. You'll find if you don't drive "through" the ball and extend fully, the beach ball won't travel the distance needed to cross the net.

Flavia Pennetta grounds her right foot to secure forward momentum and then accelerates a slightly closed racquet from low-to-high to drive through the ball.

the ball, make contact with the ball in front of your body. Keeping your head still as you rotate your shoulders through the shot steadies your chest and provides strength and stability to your arms (*left*). Unless the contact point is high, your shoulders should be fairly level at contact for good balance.

At contact, your right arm should be slightly more bent than your left arm. Slightly bent arms provide good leverage for the power created from the legs and hips. It also allows your left arm to straighten slightly and drive the racquet through the ball, helping you to hit with good extension (*right*). Arms that are too bent at contact will detrimentally shorten your

extension, while arms that are too straight will produce a contact point too far away from your body to effectively control the racquet.

Because the hitting shoulder is in the front on the backhand, the racquet takes a longer, straighter path towards the target following contact than on the forehand. If the mental image of the forehand imagines you hitting through three balls lined up in a row, the backhand increases that number to five to lengthen the hitting zone. To help you achieve this, imagine you are hitting down a bowling lane and the front pin is your target.

5. FOLLOW THROUGH
After hitting through the five imaginary balls,

Nadal keeps his head still and shoulders level as he makes contact in front of his body.

Immediately following contact, Kei Nishikori's left arm straightens and the racquet continues to move forward parallel to his target.

the follow through begins with the elbows bending as the racquet goes upward, to the right, backwards, and finally ends by wrapping around your right shoulder in a smooth and relaxed motion (*below*). Thus, the swing completes a full circuit with the left shoulder ending under the chin after beginning with than your right elbow under the chin at the end of the backswing.

On the flat to moderate topspin backhands, your should end the stroke with your left knuckles resting near your right ear, and your left elbow shoulder-high pointing towards your target and slightly higher than your right elbow. If you're hitting the ball with extra topspin, the racquet will finish lower, with the elbows closer to the body due to the rainbow arc of the racquet head as it fans across the body.

IV. The Five Phases

COACH'S BOX:

Imagine you are wearing a watch on your left wrist. If your two-handed backhand follow through is done correctly, you should be able to glance at your wrist and easily read your watch.

Victoria Azarenka follows through by wrapping her racquet over her right shoulder with her left elbow shoulder-high and pointing towards her target.

ANDY MURRAY HAS ONE OF BEST TWO-HANDED BACKHANDS the game has ever seen. It is a flat, fast, and extremely accurate shot that is very difficult to anticipate.

In the first frame, we see him set up in the perfect pose at the end of the backswing: chin above the shoulder, racquet edge pointing upward, with a wide stance for added strength and stability. He has his hitting hand in the continental grip, providing quick access to one of his favorite shots: the drop shot. In frame two, his hips rotate to lag and his wrists drop the racquet head to initiate the low-to-high swing. In frame three, he makes contact in front of his body and drives through the ball with his head still. In frame four, we see the result of Murray's pronounced use of his left arm to increase racquet speed. Some

two-handed backhand players use more left arm than others, and Murray certainly uses more than most. Here, we see how his right arm defers to his left as his left arm snaps the racquet forward to add power to his penetrating backhand. The dominance of his left arm permits him to keep his hips more steady and add disguise and deception to his shot. In frame five, Murray ends his leg drive and finishes the swing balanced with his weight fully over his right foot and left foot resting lightly on the toe. In frame six, the racquet finishes wrapped around his right shoulder with the left elbow pointing towards his target. His body ends in perfect position to perform the recovery step and return quickly to the middle of the baseline.

Federer tilts the racquet head up and keeps his elbows bent and relaxed during the unit turn.

of the One-Handed Topspin Backhand

1. UNIT TURN

The one-handed swing is longer than the two-handed swing, so it is important to start the unit turn earlier so the backswing is full and the forward swing fluent. The left hand holds the throat of the racquet, guides the racquet back, and helps turn the shoulders. The right hand holds the racquet lightly, allowing the left hand to turn the racquet into your preferred backhand grip.

The racquet head points upward with the hands around chest-high and the elbows bent and relaxed (*above*). It is important to point the racquet head upward during the unit turn because it increases racquet speed when it drops down later. Many of the top pros like to point the racquet head up at around 90 degrees during the unit turn, but for recreational players I prefer to see the racquet tilted up at around 45 degrees to simplify timing.

2. BACKSWING

After setting up in the unit turn, the racquet begins the backswing with your hands staying around chest-high and the elbows still bent (*opposite, top left*). The racquet should be slightly open in order to relax the arm and get the wrist in to a powerful position to accelerate the racquet on the forward swing. At the end of the backswing, the racquet face closes and loops down (*opposite, top right*).

Your shoulders should turn more than your hips during the backswing, and this full shoulder turn is largely dependent on taking a full

Stan Wawrinka turns his shoulders and begins to loop the racquet down at the end of his backswing.

As the racquet ends its loop down to begin the forward swing, the right foot hits the ground to secure forward momentum. Next, the hips rotate a small amount, causing the racquet to lag. Then the racquet butt cap is briefly pulled forward pointing towards the ball (*below center*) to lag the racquet some more and set it up in a powerful position to accelerate forward to meet the ball.

As the racquet moves forward to the contact point, the wrist moves forward as well to turn the butt cap towards the body, squaring up the racquet face to the target. The wrist also moves the racquet upward to brush the ball and produce topspin (*below right*). Keep in mind, unlike the topspin on the forehand, which is generated largely by the wrist and forearm, a backhand's topspin is generated mainly by the rising motion of the wrist and lifting of the arm.

The arm *straightens* as it moves the racquet forward. Here, it is important that the elbow stays low and passes close to the torso. The dreaded "flying elbow," whereby the elbow lifts and bends on the forward swing, will cause the racquet head to drop below the wrist, limiting

backswing. Good check points to ensure a full backswing are making sure your hands are past your hips and your chin is resting near your shoulder (*below left*). As mentioned with the two-handed backhand, if your backswing is full, you should feel some resistance in the back of your right shoulder; this resistance helps spring the racquet forward faster.

3. FORWARD SWING TO CONTACT

Stan Wawrinka grounds his right foot to secure forward momentum and then straightens his hitting arm and swings forward, keeping his head down and still.

racquet speed and topspin. If your elbow stays low, the racquet can take a powerful inside-to-outside swing (*below*), and the arm will be in a comfortable position to lift the racquet head to add topspin to your shot.

4. CONTACT

You should make contact with the ball approximately two feet in front of your right foot with your head still and hitting arm fully extended (*right*). After contact, the racquet head continues to rotate upward and extend forward facing parallel to your target and remaining on the left side of your body.

As your right arm moves forward after contact, your arm is going backward and remains behind the body in order to enhance balance and slow down and limit the hip rotation. The hips can rotate slightly, but any excessive movement of the hips will shorten extension and result in a shot that lacks power and control. The hip rotation is small, especially when striking a backhand down the line. On the cross

Richard Gasquet makes contact well in front of his body with his racquet moving forward parallel to his target.

Federer's low-and-close-to-the-body elbow positioning produces a powerful inside-to-outside swing and helps him add topspin to his backhand.

court backhand, the contact point is farther out in front of you and the hips will rotate more.

5. FOLLOW THROUGH

After the racquet extends parallel to the target, it closes and fans up and across to the right (*left*). Here, a straight right arm indicates good extension and racquet speed through contact. At the end of the stroke, your right hand should finish slightly above eye level with the butt cap facing towards the net and your left arm behind the body (*right*). The racquet should stop to the right of your head between a one o'clock and two o'clock position, depending on the direction and power of your backhand.

V. Slice Backhand

DESPITE THE DOMINANCE OF TOPSPIN

COACH'S BOX:

Every topspin groundstroke involves some "release" (or lag) for power as well as some "hold" for control at contact. A stiff swing that doesn't release will lack good acceleration, while an overzealous swing is an inconsistent one. Strong baseline players are able to use the right amount of each depending on their intentions and the situation. When hitting aggressively on a slow ball or using heavy topspin, their swing will involve more release, and when receiving a fast ball or using less topspin, their swing will be more deliberate. Evaluating the circumstances and finding the correct release/hold ratio on groundstrokes is a key factor in hitting with controlled aggression — a winning style of play at any level.

The best one-handed backhands are long, sweeping motions. Here, Federer finishes his one-handed backhand with his hitting arm high and fully extended.

IT IS RARE THAT A PLAYER HAS THE ONE-HANDED BACKHAND as their main weapon, but this is the case with Richard Gasquet. His one-handed backhand has tremendous power and spin, allowing him to dictate baseline rallies and bringing him a top ten world ranking.

Gasquet ends his backswing higher than most pros. This can complicate timing, but for players as skilled as Gasquet, it leads to greater racquet acceleration due to the racquet dropping faster into the beginning of the forward swing. In the first frame, his full backswing pulls his right shoulder back and correctly places his chin resting over his right shoulder. In the second frame, Gasquet's right foot hits the ground to secure the momentum attained from stepping forward. Notice how his right foot is positioned at a 45 degree angle to the net to place his hips in a perfect position for a cross-court backhand. His wide stance not only makes the forward step longer and more powerful, but also adds support to the torso, allowing the arms to swing with greater force. In the

third frame, his arm continues to straighten and stays close to the body. His racquet gathers more speed as it drops and begins its inside-to-outside path to the ball. In frame four, we see Gasquet's racquet head lag his hand before contact. From this point of the swing the shoulder will move the racquet forward, but it is primarily the movement of wrist and forearm that accelerate the racquet head with explosive speed towards contact. In frame five, Gasquet keeps the racquet on the left side of his body and extends the racquet forward to his target. Notice how his racquet has rotated up between frames four and five, adding topspin to his shot for better control. In frame six, Gasquet's racquet fans to the right with his arm fully extended as he performs the follow through. As his shoulder continues to uncoil, he keeps his hips stationary by moving his left arm backwards. It is only with the stroke completed that Gasquet looks up to see his shot and begin the recovery process.

in the modern power game, the slice backhand remains an essential shot. In today's game, many players are most comfortable when they are in a routine of hammering chest high topspin balls. The slice backhand can keep the ball low and out of an opponent's preferred strike zone, upsetting their rhythm by changing the speed and trajectory of the ball from previous topspin shots.

More importantly, unlike the topspin backhand, a good slice backhand can still be hit with the front leg doing a sideways step parallel to the baseline (*opposite*). This is why this shot is such an effective defensive shot; it can be hit well while moving sideways with little or no forward momentum. Additionally, on a wide, difficult shot, the later contact point of the slice backhand allows more time to hit the ball, and because the backspin gives the shot less pace, it also provides more time to recover.

A slice backhand is useful in many other situations. It can be utilized as an aggressive approach shot that creates a low skidding ball, forcing your opponent to attempt a difficult passing shot, or to draw your opponent forward inside the baseline to open the court for your next shot. It can also lead to well-disguised drop shots. After setting up in the regular slice backhand backswing, you can quickly change the arc of the forward swing to play a camouflaged drop shot. It is not just a versatile shot; it also requires less strength, timing, and set up time than the topspin backhand. This makes it an easier shot to execute in many ways. As a result, slice backhands are hit more often than topspin backhands at the recreational level.

Because the slice backhand is used a great deal, unlike the infrequently utilized slice forehand, a thorough explanation of the five phases of its swing is warranted. This shot has a

Feliciano Lopez sets up for his slice backhand by turning his shoulders and preparing the racquet.

great deal of uniformity with regard to style and there is little controversy in regards to recommended technique. For instance, players like Djokovic and Federer may have noticeable differences in their topspin forehand technique, but the differentiation in their slice backhands is more nuanced.

1. UNIT TURN

Begin the slice backhand by placing your right hand in the continental grip and your left hand on the throat of the racquet. Like any shot, the grip is key. If you use an eastern forehand grip, the racquet face will be too open and the shot will lack power. If you use the eastern backhand grip, your elbow will lift on the forward swing and cause your racquet head to drop too much at contact. After establishing the

Federer ends his slice backhand backswing with his arm slightly bent and racquet shoulder-high.

continental grip, turn your shoulders, open the racquet face, and place it around shoulder height (*opposite*).

2. BACKSWING

After setting up in the unit turn, take the racquet back and rotate your body so that your chest is facing towards the side fence and your head is looking over your right shoulder as you line up the shot. The racquet should be around shoulder height at the end of the backswing with your right arm bending slightly, forming a V-type shape. Your racquet face should be open, while the racquet itself should form an L-shape with the forearm and be roughly parallel to the baseline (*above*).

3. FORWARD SWING TO CONTACT

With the racquet face open and positioned above the contact at the end of the backswing (*left*), drive the racquet forward with the front of your shoulder while straightening your arm and keeping your wrist firm (*center*). If you are too close to the ball, your elbow will bend and the racquet head will drop below your wrist, causing a loss of power and control. Unless the ball is low, keep the racquet head above the wrist at contact and aim to hit slightly around the outside of the ball.

Unlike the low-to-high arc of the topspin backhand, the arc of the slice backhand swing mimics a hammer-like shape moving from high-to-low and back to high again (*below*). However, if you are trying to hit with greater spin, the racquet will start higher and the downswing will take a sharper angle. The height of the ball will also have an effect on the racquet path. The higher the ball, the sharper the decline; lower balls will have a more level swing path.

Besides the arc of the swing, there are two other significant differences to consider when comparing the forward swing on the slice backhand to the topspin backhand. **First**, in contrast to the topspin backhand, as the racquet moves forward, the power derived from the hip rotation and the stretching and contraction of arm muscles are needed much less. Here, the hips remain still and the wrist and forearm move very little as the arm goes forward to hit the ball. **Second**, the topspin backhand requires time after the foot hits the ground to unload energy upward from the legs into the swing. The slice backhand doesn't require the same unloading of energy, therefore, the forward step should be slightly later and make greater use of forward linear, rather than upward angular, momentum.

4. CONTACT

The racquet face that was open to begin the forward swing (*opposite left*) squares up to the ball, becoming almost perpendicular to the ground at contact (*right*). Opening the racquet too much at contact is a mistake I commonly see players make, causing them to pop the ball

Richard Gasquet's racquet follows a hammock-shaped path on this slice backhand.

Roberta Vinci drives the racquet forward with her shoulder by straightening her arm and keeping a firm wrist.

Djokovic squares up his racquet face for contact and moves his left arm backwards to assist balance.

up without much pace and control. It is important to understand that you don't have to force the backspin with a sharp swing down and a very open racquet face. The backspin will happen naturally with a gentle angle down and slightly open racquet face.

The contact point on the slice backhand will be less in front and farther away from the body than the contact point for the topspin backhand. The contact point will vary depending on the direction of the shot, but generally speaking, it should occur a foot or less in front of the right leg, compared to the approximately two feet in front when hitting a one-handed topspin backhand.

After contact, the racquet head opens and drops as it continues its high-to-low path forward (*above*). The left arm moves backwards

FEW PLAYERS HAVE EVER HIT THE SLICE BACKHAND with as much speed and spin as Roger Federer. His slice backhand has even more ball revolutions than his feared topspin forehand.[2] Use of this shot often leads to short balls that allow him to move forward and attack.

Federer defends this wide ball with a long, powerful stride parallel to the baseline. One of the big advantages of the slice backhand is that you can step sideways and still hit a great shot. In frame one, he sets up with his shoulders turned, elbows bent and relaxed, and the racquet open and shoulder-high. Notice how he maintains good balance by keeping his head upright, back straight, and shoulders level. In the second frame, the racquet begins its forward and downward movement to the ball. In the third frame, his foot hits the ground and he leans into the shot to add power to his swing. In

frame four, driving the racquet forward with his shoulder, he makes contact with his arm straight and hips perpendicular to the net. The racquet that was very open at the end of the backswing is now substantially less so. Federer hits his slice backhand with tremendous spin and therefore his racquet must rotate sharply. Between frames three and five, his racquet head has rotated down over 180 degrees; for recreational players, I recommend a smaller racquet rotation to simplify timing and improve shot depth and consistency. In frame five, the ball is gone but his eyes are still focused on the contact point; no one watches the ball better than the Swiss champ. Federer finishes the swing with his right and left hand in the same position on opposite sides of his body, enhancing balance and expediting the recovery process.

Grigor Dimitrov's racquet opens and continues to drop after contact.

for balance and helps you push the racquet towards your target. If your left hand comes forward, your hips will swivel and the racquet will pull too quickly across to the right. Your head should stay steady and should move only after driving through the ball, when it comes up to see the location of your shot.

5. FOLLOW THROUGH

There is a natural grace to the follow through as the arms lift along a perpendicular axis and end pointing in opposite directions. The racquet should finish shoulder-high and point outward towards your target (*below*). Due to the later contact and compact nature of

the slice backhand swing, your hips and back foot will stay fairly steady during the follow through. Your weight should be resting solely on your right foot, and after finishing the swing, step around with your left foot and begin the recovery.

VI. Backhand Practice

Grigor Dimitrov finishes his slice backhand with his racquet shoulder-high and pointing towards his target.

1. BACKHAND HOLD

Goal: Improve the down-the-line backhand to defend against the inside-out forehand.

Feed a ball to your practice partner from the baseline to the backhand side of the court. Your practice partner must return the ball with an inside-out forehand. Respond by hitting your backhand down the line, and then play out the point. The first player to 11 points wins the game, and then switch roles.

2. SPANISH DRILL

Goal: Learn to fight and succeed in long baseline rallies.

Begin with a deep feed to your practice partner then play out the point, counting how many times the ball crosses the net. When the point ends, the winner of the point gets as many points as the number of times the ball crossed the net. The longer the rally goes, the more intense the point will become. The first

player to 50, 75, or 100 points (depending on skill level) wins the game. If a player makes an error with their backhand, the other player scores an additional five points.

3. ZIG ZAG

Goal: Improve the ability to change stroke direction during a baseline rally.

From the baseline, hit only cross court while your practice partner hits only down the line. Play a game to 15 points where each of you must hit the ball into the correct half of the court or you lose the point. Then switch roles. Variation: If a player hits their ball into the wrong half of the court, the other player has the option to stop play and win one point or continue the point using the full court, with the winner receiving two points.

BACKHAND NUTSHELL SUMMARY:
COMMIT THESE FOUR IMAGES TO MEMORY

1. POWER POSITION   2. RACQUET LAG   3. CONTACT   4. FOLLOW THROUGH

Murray frequently uses the drop shot to draw his opponent out of position.

CHAPTER 9

Drop Shot and Lob

THERE ARE MANY TIMES DURING A MATCH when a regular topspin or slice groundstroke isn't the best response and a finesse shot like a drop shot or lob is the right play. Besides sometimes winning the point outright, these two shots can change an opponent's court positioning drastically and thus can have significant strategic implications. They can also tire an opponent out physically and even dent their spirit.

The drawback to the drop shot and lob is that if they are not played well or are played at the wrong time, you are likely to lose the point. Thus, they can make you look brilliant or foolish. The advice below will help you stay on the positive side of the drop shot and lob ledger to make these two shots a significant and successful part of your game.

I. Drop Shot

THE DROP SHOT IS A SOFT SHOT that lands close to the net and bounces low. The goal of the drop shot is either to make the ball bounce twice before your opponent can reach it or, if your opponent does run it down, to leave them off balance and vulnerable to a passing shot or lob.

Frequent use of the drop shot can wear your opponent down physically and mentally. If you see your opponent breathing heavily after an intense rally or becoming frustrated, look to use your drop shot. It is a shot that can both prey on an opponent's movement and emotions and also be used strategically to draw defensive baseline players out of their comfort zone and up to the net.

I. TECHNIQUE

The drop shot swing is similar to the slice groundstrokes in its use of the continental grip and body positioning. Like the slice groundstrokes, it can be hit in any stance, although the neutral or closed stance works best, especially if you are moving forward to play the drop shot (as is usually the case). However, there are technique differences: the backswing and follow through are shorter, the forward swing more downward, the racquet face opens more, and the step forward less

aggressive (*left*).

To play a drop shot, begin by setting up the racquet above the ball with an open face and then move the racquet forward and carve down and underneath the ball (*opposite*). This will cause the ball to spin backwards and stop quickly. After contact, follow through with your racquet face continuing to open and dropping below the wrist.

Using a light forward step and a short, downward swing, Federer plays this drop shot with heavy spin.

COACH'S BOX:

Somewhat paradoxically, even as tennis has become a more powerful game, the drop shot has become a more important shot for three reasons. **First**, players are standing increasingly farther behind the baseline to defend against the increased speed of modern groundstrokes, creating more opportunities to use the short part of the court for an effective drop shot. **Second**, because players are now moving so fast laterally to cover wide shots at the baseline, the short part of the court has become a more appealing area to find an advantage during the rally. **Third**, frequent use of the drop shot can change an opponent's court positioning and reduce their ability to cover the court — an important consideration against the speedy modern player. As Federer, who has used the drop shot more frequently later in his career, has said, "I just realized it was very hard to hit through the guys time and time again, because they track down everything. Maybe by using the drop shot more they have to play closer to the baseline; then it's easier to hit through them."[1]

Djokovic drop shots by rotating the racquet head down and sliding the strings underneath the ball.

2. DISGUISE

Keep in mind that deception is an important component of the drop shot. The more you can fool your opponents and delay their anticipation, the more successful your drop shot. Advanced players often disguise their drop shot by winding up like they are going to drive the ball and then quickly change their grip to play a drop shot. Recreational players may not be able to conceal a drop shot like this, but any trickery that makes a drop shot harder to read should be embraced. To maintain the element of surprise, it is also important not to overuse the drop shot; use it sporadically and when your opponent least expects it.

3. SHOT TRAJECTORY AND RESPONSE

The trajectory of the drop shot will vary depending on the height at which it was hit, but most drop shots should rise up initially before dropping down as the ball crosses the net. A higher trajectory gives the ball a better chance of stopping due to backspin, and greater net clearance makes it a higher percentage shot.

If you've played a good drop shot, move forward because your opponent's shot likely will be short. If they pop the ball up, you will be well-positioned to end the point quickly with a volley. If your drop shot is poor, however, move back and get ready to hustle and defend the point.

COACH'S BOX:

To learn the drop shot, I sometimes ask my students to play a game of "Catch and Release." With you and your practice partner on opposite baselines, have your partner hit a ball to you. Using the drop shot technique, tap the ball in the air a few feet in front of you (catch), let the ball bounce, and return the ball back to your partner (release), who does the same thing. This game helps players learn the "feel" of hitting the ball the short distance required on the drop shot.

4. WHEN TO DROP SHOT

Choosing the right time to play the drop shot is a key factor in its chances of success. Things to consider when deciding whether to play a drop shot include:

A. BALL HEIGHT

The drop shot is best hit when you receive a waist-to-chest high ball. It is hard to control a drop shot on a ball any higher or lower than this. Also, because time and disguise are important factors, you should hit the drop shot as the ball is rising or at its apex rather than on its way down. If you hit the ball on the way down, you allow your opponent more time to react and decrease your ability to disguise the shot.

B. BALANCE AND TIME

The drop shot is a skilled shot and requires a reasonable amount of balance and time to play well. Therefore, avoid playing drop shots when you are off-balance or receiving a fast ball.

C. COURT POSITIONING

Generally, it is best to hit the drop shot while positioned around the service line or closer to the net. If you play the drop shot from deep in the court, your opponent will have more time to run it down.

D. COURT SURFACE

On softer court surfaces, like clay, slice shots bounce lower and react more to backspin — favorable conditions for drop shots. In contrast,

Murray hits this drop shot with the recommended balance, ball height, and court positioning.

on harder court surfaces, drop shots bounce higher and grip the court less, making it more difficult to hit an effective drop shot.

II. Lob

THE LOB IS A SHOT HIT DEEP and high in the court. A deep lob will force your opponent to hit an off balance overhead or, better still, to let the ball bounce, allowing you to gain control of the point.

Besides presenting your opponent with a difficult overhead or a scramble to run the ball down, good lobbing has strategic advantages. It can lead to less aggressive net positioning from your opponents. If your opponent is concerned about having to defend against your lob, they may deepen their net position, thus reducing their volley angles, increasing the time you have to react to their shot and forcing them to hit more low, difficult volleys.

There are two types of lob: defensive and offensive.

1. DEFENSIVE LOB

The lob is often used in defensive situations when you are scrambling or unable to get balanced to set up for an aggressive groundstroke. The defensive lob can be hit with a short swing and therefore doesn't need a lot of time to execute if you are rushed or under pressure.

The stroke production on a defensive lob is similar to a slice groundstroke except that the racquet face is more open and the swing is shorter with a more upward plane (*below*).

Disguising the lob is important. If you were playing Djokovic, would you be able to tell a lob was coming at the time of the first frame?

The height required on a lob depends on the circumstances. If you are caught wide off the court, you may try to hit the lob very high in order to buy some recovery time (*below*). If you are well-positioned, your lob can be lower.

When hitting a defensive lob, the ball should reach its apex over your opponent's service line. Many players focus on lobbing the net player and this makes the high point of the lob occur over the middle of the service box, resulting in a comfortable overhead for your opponent. Instead, if the lob reaches its highest point over the service line, you will force your opponent to backpedal into a defensive situation. Also, try to aim the defensive lob over your opponent's backhand side because the backhand overhead is a very difficult shot.

The topspin lob requires a sharp upward lift and rotation of the racquet head.

2. OFFENSIVE LOB

If you have more time to set up, the lob can also be used offensively and hit with topspin, whereby once the ball clears the opponent at the net, it jumps towards the back fence after the bounce for a winning shot. Your goal with the topspin lob is to win the point outright, but if it lands shorter, its dipping trajectory can make it a difficult overhead for your opponent to hit.

Roberta Vinci opens the racquet face and hits a high lob to allow her time to recover.

The backswing on the topspin lob looks similar to a regular groundstroke, making it a shot that can be well disguised to fool your opponent. After the backswing, the racquet head drops well below the ball (*opposite, top left*) and then takes an almost vertical lift to create the necessary spin and height (*opposite, top right*). This sharp lift of the racquet results in your body weight being more evenly distributed during the swing and the contact point being less in front of the body compared to a regular groundstroke. The stroke ends with a shorter follow through, often finishing on the same side of the body where contact was made.

III. Drop Shot and Lob Practice

1. RALLY AND DROP SHOT

Goal: Learning to hit the drop shot at the right time during a rally.

Draw or mark a line six to eight feet inside the baseline across both sides of the court. With you and your practice partner standing on opposite baselines, start the point with a forehand feed and rally. Both players have the option to play a drop shot to score extra points, but only when positioned in front of the drawn line. The point ends once a drop shot is played. If a player's drop shot bounces twice before the service line, that player scores two points (or three points for three bounces). If the drop shot is an error or only bounces once before the service line, the other player scores two points. The first player to 21 points wins the game.

2. MINI TENNIS

Goal: To develop the good ball control needed for accurate drop shots.

Using the service line as the baseline, start with a forehand to your practice partner and play the point. All shots must be hit with slice and after the bounce. The first player to 15 points wins the game. Variation: Shrink the court to one service box for each player instead of two, or allow each player one or two volleys per point.

3. LOB AND OVERHEAD

Goal: Improve the lob and overhead.

Begin the game at the service line with your practice partner at the baseline. Using the half court to hit either cross court or down the line, your practice partner begins the point with a lob. Then, play out the point. The first player to 15 points wins the game and then switch roles. Variation: Have the net player stand in different locations to begin the point or require the baseline player to lob every other shot.

4. DRIVE, DRIVE, LOB

Goal: Improving aggressive groundstrokes to take control of the point following the lob.

Begin the game at the service line with your practice partner at the baseline. Using the half court to hit either cross court or down the line, start the point by feeding your practice partner, who must drive their first two shots and lob the third. The point begins only after the lob is played. After you overhead the lob, the whole singles court becomes available for both players. If your practice partner hits a winner or unreturnable shot off your overhead, they score two points. First player to 15 points wins the game, and then switch roles.

The quality of this Andy Roddick approach shot will largely determine his level of success at the net.

CHAPTER 10

Approach Shot

NOW THAT WE HAVE COVERED THE GROUNDSTROKES from the baseline, it is time to move forward and discuss playing the net position. Your success at the net is directly related to the strength of the shot you hit immediately before: the approach shot. This was on display at the 2015 ATP World Finals where Roger Federer's powerful serving allowed him to set up for his approach shots more inside the baseline than usual. This favorable positioning on the approach shot then allowed him to set up closer to the net for his volley, resulting in him hitting his first volley one foot closer to the net and five inches higher than his average. As a result, Federer controlled play from the front court lifting his winning percentage at net to as high as 75% in some of his matches during that tournament.[1]

In this chapter, I begin by going through the different types of approach shots. I then discuss the qualities of the approach shot that help you win at the net, the proper movement forward, and optimal court positioning following the approach shot. Next, I explain two other more immediate ways of attacking the net: the serve-and-volley and chip-and-charge plays. I then end the chapter with drills to improve your skills transitioning forward in the court.

Madison Keys drives her approach shot to the backhand corner.

I. Types of Approach Shots

THE APPROACH SHOT USUALLY IS HIT from several feet inside the baseline and placed deep in the opposite side of the court. If the ball is above your waist and you have some time to set up, a powerful flat or topspin approach shot is generally the best choice (*above*). In today's power game, this type of approach shot has become the predominant way to attack the net, however, there are several other types of approach shots to consider.

1. SLICE

The slice approach shot can be performed quickly, so it often makes sense when time is limited. Also, because the racquet is open, it is often used on low balls. The advantages of the slice approach shot are that the ball stays low, forcing your opponent to hit up on the passing shot, and its slower speed allows you more time to get closer to the net and set up good positioning for the volley.

2. THE SWINGING VOLLEY

The swinging volley (*see page 180*) is increasingly common in modern net play. It is typically used on high floating balls that would otherwise land near the middle of the court. The power of the swinging volley rushes opponents, making it difficult for them to hit accurate passing shots.

3. HIGH TOPSPIN

A high topspin shot hit deep to the corner can be an effective approach shot, especially at the recreational level. This shot allows you time to move close to the net for the volley and pushes your opponent deep behind the baseline into a defensive position.

4. DROP SHOT

The drop shot is not a "classic" approach shot but certainly is a stroke that can allow you move forward to the net and use your volley skills. A good drop shot will make your opponent scramble forward, leaving a large unprotected area of the court within which to place your volley.

Keep in mind, the court surface is important when choosing the most effective type of approach shot. On faster surfaces, where attacking the net is a strategic focus, the quick set-up of the slice approach shot allows you to move forward to volley more often. In contrast, on slower clay courts, where the ball bounces high more frequently, the high topspin approach shot can be a productive choice. Remember the court surface will also affect the amount of time your opponent has to prepare for their passing shot. Therefore, you must be more selective with your approach shots on slower clay courts than when playing on faster hard courts.

II. Approach Shot Qualities

FIRST, HITTING THE BALL DEEP towards the baseline is a high priority when playing an approach shot (unless you are using a drop shot). The deeper you hit the approach shot, the less time your opponent will have to line up their passing shot following the bounce of the ball. **Second**, the approach shot is usually best directed to the weaker groundstroke of your opponent. **Third**, it often makes sense to hit the approach shot to the side that forces your opponent to run the greatest distance. This will not only force your opponent to hit their passing shot off balance, but also open up the other side of the court for a winning volley. **Fourth**, if your opponent is hurting you with angled passing shots, an approach shot hit deep towards the middle of the court can be an effective tactic. By hitting towards the middle of the court, you limit the angles available to your opponent and almost guarantee a play on your volley following the approach shot.

III. Approach Shot Movement

YOUR MOVEMENT TO THE BALL will be an integral part of your approach shot's success. A strong first step is key to moving well, so prior to the approach shot you should be leaning slightly forward and looking for opportunities to attack the net. If your first steps are explosive, you will have more time to help ensure good positioning for your approach shot.

After making a strong first move, on most approach shots your body will need to decelerate as you prepare to swing. However, as with any groundstroke, the approach shot involves dynamic, variable footwork. Off a high ball, you may have time to stop, load the legs in a semi-open stance, and hit an aggressive topspin approach shot. In contrast, on a topspin approach shot off a ball with a shorter

COACH'S BOX:

If you have the time, measure your steps as you move forward and establish the same stance on your approach shot as you would use if hitting a groundstroke from the baseline. For example, on the forehand approach shot, if the ball is low, use the neutral stance. If the ball is higher, an open-type stance will work better. Too often players tighten up when they move forward and their footwork suffers. Spend time during practice working specifically on the approach shot to learn the footwork and build confidence. This will help you avoid hitting the approach shot in an unfamiliar stance that lacks the balance and hip alignment necessary to execute a strong one.

location and lower height, the front leg will step forward, plant, and then hop during the follow through (*below*). Moving through the approach shot this way will get you closer to the net for your volley.

When hitting a slice approach shot, the correct movement is to glide through the shot with your feet remaining close to the ground and the body low and balanced. The slice shot needs little ground force reaction, so you can move forward during the swing more than if you were hitting a topspin approach shot. The carioca step is often used on the slice approach shot, particularly on the backhand side. This step sees the back foot moving behind and in front of the front foot during the swing (*right*). Using this footwork allows you to turn your body fully and make contact with good positioning and balance.

Tomáš Berdych uses the carioca step to keep his body sideways during contact on this slice approach shot.

On this approach shot, Djokovic uses the forward hop step and then moves his back foot over and in front to speed his movement to the net.

IV. Court Positioning

AFTER FINISHING ANY APPROACH SHOT, it's important to move forward quickly. The closer you set up at the net, the easier and more aggressive your volley can be. While moving forward, track the ball, favoring the side to which you hit the approach shot. For example, if you hit the approach shot towards

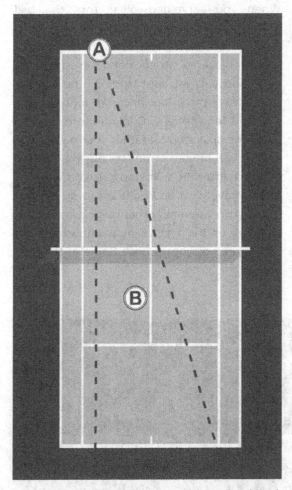

When attacking the net you should favor the side of the court from where your opponent is hitting their passing shot. Above, by being positioned slightly to the left of the center line, we see that Player B is in the midpoint of Player A's passing shot angles.

the deuce side singles line, you should do your split step a couple of feet left of the center line (*left*). This will position you at the midpoint of the down-the-line and cross-court passing shot angles.

Most approach shots should be hit down the line because then you are on the correct side of the court to split the angles of your opponent's possible passing shots. Cross-court approach shots can be dangerous because of the extra distance you'll need to cover to reach the midpoint of your opponent's passing shot angles.

Once you have done your split step and established good positioning at the net, get your mind and body ready for action and try to anticipate your opponent's passing shot attempt by reading their body alignment and taking into account their favorite shots. Always be on the balls of your feet and have an aggressive presence at the net. Let your opponents know that you enjoy being there and that you are ready to quickly pounce on any misdirected lobs or passing shots.

V. Other Ways of Attacking the Net

THE SERVE-AND-VOLLEY and the chip-and-charge allow you to attack the net more immediately than the approach shot. Using these two tactics makes your game more versatile and gives you additional options to expose your opponent's weaknesses and utilize your strengths.

I. SERVE-AND-VOLLEY

The serve-and-volley play, whereby a player serves and immediately runs forward to volley, was once the dominant serving tactic on the ATP. This is not the case anymore. In the 2001 Wimbledon men's final, the players served and volleyed 243 times.[2] In contrast, there were not 150 serve and volleys in all the men's Wimbledon finals combined from 2004-2013.[3] The main reason for the change is that new equipment has improved the quality of returns of serve and passing shots, making the serve and volley a surprise tactic rather than the staple it had been in the past.

With that said, the serve-and-volley can be a successful part of your game plan. If volleys are a strength in your game, or if your ground-strokes don't match up favorably with your opponent, then coming forward after a strong serve to knock off an easy volley can give you an advantage in the match.

Additionally, mixing in some serve-and-volley plays can place doubt in your opponent's mind as to the best type of return of serve. When a server comes to the net, the best returns are low and wide; however, when a server stays on the baseline, the best returns are higher and deeper. These are two opposite returns, and if you vary up your play, you can confuse your opponent and force more mistakes. If you always stay on the baseline after the serve, you allow your opponent to return high over the net without immediate negative consequences. By serving and volleying occasionally, you will force your opponent to hit lower and riskier returns.

A. MOVEMENT AND FIRST VOLLEY PLACEMENT

When you serve-and-volley, toss the ball slightly farther in front of you on the serve. This will produce good forward momentum for your movement to the net. After you hit the serve and your left foot lands on the ground, push off with that foot and step forward with the right leg (*far left*). Continue to move forward and split step to gather your balance an instant before your opponent hits their return (*center*). After the split step, push off your left leg to move right and right leg to go left (*far right*). Also, remember that because court positioning on the first volley is important, fast serves are not always best. Some of the best

After Taylor Dent serves, he moves forward, split steps, and pushes off his right leg to move left and volley.

serve-and-volley players of the past, like Patrick Rafter and Stefan Edberg, used spin serves rather than powerful flat serves. This allowed them to get closer to the net on the first volley.

The placement of your serve and first volley should be coordinated. Placing your serve wide opens up the other side of the court for your first volley. Alternatively, serving down the "T" often makes the short angled volley towards where the service line meets the singles line a smart choice. If you find yourself off balance or rushed on the volley after a strong return, play the volley deep towards the middle of the court in order to limit your opponent's angles on their next shot and allow yourself time to recover and set up for a second volley. If you are balanced, move forward to meet the ball and hit the volley with authority to the open court or to the wing of your opponent's weaker groundstroke.

2. CHIP-AND-CHARGE

The chip-and-charge, in which you rush the net immediately after returning a serve, is another good way to quickly attack the net. This type of return is difficult to execute against big serving opponents, but for most recreational players, it can be a frequently used or effective surprise tactic.

Begin the chip-and-charge play by positioning yourself three or four feet inside the baseline and setting the racquet in the continental grip. As your opponent tosses the ball, start moving forward and hit the return early using a volley-type swing technique. Glide through the swing and then hustle forward quickly and split step at the midpoint of your opponent's passing shot angles.

VI. Approach Shot Practice

1. APPROACH AND VOLLEY

Goal: Learn to transition well from the baseline to the net.

Feed a short ball to your practice partner positioned on the baseline. They hit the feed as an approach shot and move forward to volley. Play out the point down the line in the half court. Repeat until one player reaches 11 points and then switch roles. Variation: After the first volley is hit, the whole court becomes available to play out the rest of the point.

2. SWINGING VOLLEY

Goal: To hone your technique and timing on the swinging volley.

Feed a high ball to your practice partner, who moves forward from the baseline, hits a swinging volley, and continues forward to volley. Play out the point. First player to 15 wins the game and then switch roles.

3. CHIP AND CHARGE

Goal: To practice the return of serve and immediately attack the net.

Serve to your practice partner and they hit the return and immediately move forward to volley. Your practice partner wins two points if they win the point after receiving a first serve, and one point if they take the point following a second serve. First player to 15 wins the game and then switch roles. Variation: Allow one serve only or designate a side of the court the return must be hit into.

Djokovic is an example of
a player who learned to
approach the net more as his
professional career progressed.

CHAPTER 11

Volleys

RECENTLY, THE VOLLEY HAS SEEN A SMALL RESURGENCE on the professional tour. More frequently, players are serving and volleying or moving forward to volley opportunistically during a rally to finish the point. There are three main reasons for this increase in net play. **First**, greater firepower from the baseline has resulted in more short balls that players can attack and use to set up at net in a commanding position. **Second**, playing the net well involves a high degree of agility and speed, and the modern tennis player is the most athletic the game has ever seen. **Third**, given the growing physicality of the game, the pros are more eager to use their net game to keep the points shorter and reduce their level of fatigue at the end of long matches. Many experts believe that as players become even more aggressive from the baseline and the rallies more grueling, coming to the net to volley will become an increasingly important strategy in the future.

A strong volley is especially important at the recreational level because most competitors play doubles. In doubles, when your partner is serving or receiving serve — roughly half the points played — you are usually positioned near the net hitting volleys. If, in addition, you immediately move up to the net position after you serve or return, then volleys may represent well over half your shots. And although hitting from the baseline is the most popular style of play in singles, being able to approach the net gives singles players more strategic options. For example, if you don't rally as well from the baseline as your opponent, rushing the net might tilt the odds in your favor and help you win. Also, effectively attacking the

Gaël Monfils displays the athleticism sometimes needed to cover the net well.

net often will induce errors from opponents by forcing them to hit deeper to keep you away from the net and lower and faster once you are set up at net.

Once you are set up at net, the rally becomes an adrenalized do-or-die situation where winning or losing the point can happen in an instant. Your attitude must reflect this, and your play at the net should be feisty and assertive. Also, contact on the volley occurs at many different heights with very little time to position oneself, so you often have to improvise by bending and lunging to cover the court (*above*) and attain the balance needed to hit a good volley. While it is an exciting and athletic shot, it is also an aggressive one. Volleys are hit in the "green light" area of the court, that is, the place to hit winners. This aggressiveness can make it great fun. To me, there are few occasions on the court more

enjoyable than stringing together a series of strong groundstrokes and finishing the point off with a winning volley.

In this chapter, before explaining the specifics of swing technique on the forehand and backhand volley as well as the swinging volley, drop volley, half volley, and overhead, I will first discuss the other important aspects of the volley: grip, ready position, footwork, contact and grip tension.

I. Important Aspects of the Volley

1. GRIP

The continental grip should be used on both the forehand and backhand volley for several reasons. **First**, if using the continental grip, you will not not be caught between grip changes during quick exchanges at net. **Second**, the continental grip naturally opens the racquet face to produce the "cradling" effect needed to harness the impact of the ball and comfortably lift the ball on low volleys. **Third**, it helps produce backspin for superior control on finesse volleys. **Fourth**, it puts the wrist in a position that allows you to hit wide, difficult volleys back in the court in a way that that wouldn't be possible using other grips.

The exception to using the continental grip on volleys is on high or slow balls. There you should use an eastern grip. The eastern grip is a more powerful hand positioning, making it easier to hit a winning volley on slow balls or ones above the shoulder. Higher balls move slowly, allowing time to make the small change from the continental grip to an eastern forehand or eastern backhand grip.

2. READY POSITION

The ready position for the volley is a little different than the ready position at the baseline. The racquet should be slightly higher and farther in front of the body. Remember not to squeeze the grip too tightly. Being agile is important at the net, and when your arm and shoulder muscles are tight, it is more difficult to move the body and racquet quickly.

Additionally, compared to your ready position at the baseline, your body should be in a lower crouched position, achieved by bending the knees and widening the stance (*right*). This lower body position drops your center of gravity and facilitates fast movement. Watch the best volleyers at net. They cover the court with cat-like movements, staying low to the ground in a crouched position that allows them to move quickly and volley with superior balance. The lower body position also puts your line of vision closer to the height of the

In her ready position at net, Ekaterina Makarova lowers her body, establishes a wide stance, and keeps her hands up and well in front of her body.

incoming ball, improving your ability to read the ball's trajectory.

The split step also plays a major role in the ready position at net where time is precious. It is only by performing the split step that you can get an explosive first step, and because you are often moving forward aggressively from the baseline to volley, the split step is necessary to stop the forward momentum and move quickly in various directions.

3. FOOTWORK

The arms move very little on the volley. The volley is said to be "hit with the legs," meaning that the legs play a crucial role in providing the power, balance, and court positioning for winning at the net.

Federer pushes forward with his legs to add power to this volley.

A. POWER

In the volley, increased power can be created by pushing off with your back leg while stepping forward with your front leg, allowing your body weight to move smoothly through the shot. In 2014, shortly after Roger Federer switched to new coach Stefan Edberg, his volleys improved. Edberg, a tremendous volleyer himself, coached Federer to rely less on his hands and to add power to his volleys by pushing more forcefully with his legs (*above*).

Your legs can also lower your body to increase power on your volley. Bending your knees allows you to tilt the racquet head up more and places the wrist and elbow in a physically stronger position. With this physiological fact in mind, if the ball is waist high, you should crouch down and tilt the racquet head above the wrist at around a 10 o'clock angle. By lowering your body, you can turn a stomach-high volley into an easier chest-high one. On a waist-to-knee-high ball, crouch down and aim to keep the racquet head horizontal at contact (*opposite*). If the incoming ball is below the knees, crouch to lower the body; however, because bending your knees deeply enough to keep the racquet head above the wrist would take too much time, it is fine to drop the racquet head to around an eight o'clock angle on very low balls.

Serena Williams crouches down to help her racquet head stay horizontal on this volley.

B. BALANCE

Using your legs to establish correct positioning to the ball will help you hit a balanced shot; being positioned too far to the left, right, forward, or back of the ball will adversely affect balance and hurt the shot.

If you have to hit a low volley, you should lengthen your forward step and widen your stance to keep your center of gravity between your feet and your body balanced. Bending at the knees — not at the waist — is also vital for balance on lower balls, because it keeps your shoulders more even and head upright (*next page*). If you don't bend your knees, your shoulders and head will tilt and cause your body to lurch.

C. COURT POSITIONING

On the volley, it is important you move forward quickly, meet the ball as close to the net as possible, and attain good court positioning. Doing this will lead to four positive

developments. It will: **First,** give your opponent less time to respond to your shot. **Second,** make the angles available for your volley more acute. **Third,** allow you to hit the ball at a higher contact point. **Fourth,** place pressure on your opponent to hit their passing shot lower, forcing more errors.

I sometimes see players freeze their legs when playing volleys. Consequently, they hit their volleys with less than optimal power, balance, and court positioning. To keep this from happening, you first must always do your spilt step and then the following footwork sequence: pivot your outside foot in the direction you need to move, then move forward to make contact as close to the net as possible, and finally, step with the inside foot at the right time and in the correct direction. Let's discuss in greater detail.

I. PIVOT THE OUTSIDE FOOT

The first foot movement after the split step is typically done with your outside foot, which

By bending his knees, Marin Cilic keeps his head upright and shoulders level to better control his racquet.

will pivot from being perpendicular to the net to almost parallel to the net. On the forehand volley, the right foot pivots to the right (*opposite left*) and, if time permits, moves a half-step to the right. This initial pivot and step with the right foot gets the knees pointing in the direction you want to move. For the same reasons, the first foot movement on the backhand volley following the split step is the left foot pivoting to the left.

II. MOVE FORWARD

The footwork after the initial pivot will depend on the speed of the incoming ball. If the ball is slow, there may be several steps forward following the pivot, whereas on fast balls there may be only time for the pivot.

III. STEP WITH THE INSIDE FOOT

After pivoting with your outside foot and moving forward, time your volley swing with your inside foot stepping forward into the shot. Your left foot will step forward when hitting a forehand volley, and your right foot does so when hitting a backhand volley (*above*).

Your front foot will hit the ground at different times and with varying levels of aggressiveness based largely on the speed of the incoming ball. On most balls, your foot lands an instant after you make contact — your weight will transfer through the shot best if your foot is slightly airborne at contact. Remember to avoid stopping suddenly after hitting the ball because it will jolt the upper body forward and affect your balance. Instead, try to glide into the volley like a car easing towards a stop sign rather than a car slamming on the brakes in an emergency.

To gain more power with your legs on slow balls, your front foot should hit the ground later and more aggressively. When receiving a slow ball, take several steps forward to meet the ball, then push hard with your back foot, lift the front foot in the air during the backswing, and move through the shot (*right*). After your front foot hits the ground, your back foot will kick back behind you for balance.

Because the location of the ball is always different, the direction of your front foot step will vary. Your footwork needs to be light and flexible. There are three main forward steps on the volley that I will describe using a clock face:

The Straight Step: The straight step should be used on incoming balls that are comfortably two or three feet to the side of the body. On

Following the split step, Federer pivots his right leg to assist fast movement to the right to play a forehand volley.

Stan Wawrinka hits the ground forcefully after contact to aggressively volley a slow ball.

THE STRAIGHT STEP

THE LUNGE STEP

THE AWAY STEP

this volley, the left foot steps between noon and one o'clock on the forehand and the right foot between noon and 11 o'clock on the backhand (*left*). If you have time, move your feet to get into this stance, as it helps to turn the shoulders and place your legs in good position to push forward into the shot.

COACH'S BOX:

A common problem I see around the courts is players getting "stuck" at the net in doubles, hurting the power, balance, and court positioning on their volleys. To help my students "flow" on their volleys, I instruct them to imagine they are standing on the sand of their favorite beach on a hot day when playing at the net. Nobody likes to keep their feet on the ground for long on hot sand. I find this image helps players stay in motion during the rally and improves their net play. When the point is over, your mind can switch your feet's location from the sand to the cool ocean water.

The Lunge Step: The lunge step is used on wider balls. On this volley, the left foot steps between two and three o'clock on the forehand and the right foot between nine and 10 o'clock on the backhand (*center*). When using the lunge step, strong legs and superior balance are needed to stay low and maintain control over your center of gravity. A low center of gravity will help you stop and recover quickly for the next shot.

The Away Step: Sometimes the ball will be hit quickly right at your body and there's only time for your front foot to step away from the ball and finish the shot in a semi-open stance. Under these circumstances, your left foot will step between nine and 10 o'clock on the forehand and the right foot between one and two o'clock on the backhand (*right*). This move away from the ball will provide you with space and give your arms enough room to comfortably swing the racquet with your shoulders level and body in balance.

4. CONTACT

Once you've moved your feet to establish good power, balance, and positioning, make

Stefan Edberg makes contact in front of
his body on this backhand volley.

solid contact with the ball in front of the body
(*above*). When and where you make contact
with the ball is a critical element of the volley.
If you hit the ball too late, you will be hitting in
a physically weak spot, whereas if you connect
too early, you will lose control. Making contact
too close or too far away from the body is
equally detrimental.

5. GRIP TENSION

How firmly should you hold the racquet at contact? You will often hear coaches advising players to squeeze the grip and "punch" the volley.
This is good advice sometimes, but not all the
time. Punch is the right word in the sense that
the volley is often a short, sharp motion, but
it shouldn't always be taken literally. There will

be times when receiving a fast shot that you
want the ball to leave your racquet at a slower
speed that what it arrived, or others that call
for playing a softer, shorter volley. In these situations, the right technique is to "absorb" the
ball rather than punching through. "Punching"
the ball is more appropriate when you are aggressively hitting a slower incoming ball and
your aim is to increase the speed of the ball.

There are three main types of ball impact
on the volley: hammer, catch, and brake. For
each of these, the grip is manipulated differently. Generally speaking, on a slow or high
ball you will "hammer" the impact with a
strong grip (*next page, top*); on the moderate
speed or low ball you will "catch" the impact
with a steady grip (*next page, bottom*); and
on a fast ball you will "brake" on impact using
an absorbing grip.

In doubles, you will use these three types
of volleys frequently and often in repetitive
ways. For example, when poaching aggressively at the net, you will "hammer" the volley. When hitting a low volley, you will "catch"
the volley and aim the shot conservatively to
a safe area of the court. Or, when the ball is
rifled at you at the net position, your racquet
should "brake" at contact to absorb the high
speed of the ball. Good doubles players are
able to manipulate the racquet face in these
different ways and adjust grip tension and
swing length to best play a wide variety of
shots.

The principles discussed above regarding
grip, ready position, footwork, and grip tension apply to both the forehand and backhand
volley, but because the hitting shoulder lags
on forehand and leads on the backhand, there
are differences in form. In the next two sections I explain the forehand and backhand volley technique.

Maria Sharapova lengthens her backswing and "hammers" the contact on this high, slow ball.

In contrast, on this low ball, she shortens her backswing and "catches" the contact.

Sania Mirza's forehand volley sees her open and set the racquet head above the ball and move it forward on a gentle high-to-low gradient.

II. The Forehand Volley

ON THE FOREHAND VOLLEY, your first re-action is to move your hands and shoulders as a unit to the right to assist your shoulder turn and help guide your racquet head to the correct place. On most forehand volleys, your shoulders should turn to approximately 45 degrees to the net and your racquet head should set up slightly above and behind the flight of the incoming ball (*above*). Keep in mind, while groundstroke swings often circle and arc, the volley is a much quicker shot that requires the racquet to move in a straight line during the set-up and swing.

The volley set-up involves a short back-swing. You can get all the power required on the volley with a compact swing, and your accuracy and consistency will be better when adhering to a disciplined short motion. Of course, the length of the backswing will vary depending on the situation, but on most volleys it is around one to two feet. If the ball you are volleying was hit to you at a slow speed, your backswing will be longer (*opposite, top*). If the ball was low or fast, it can be shorter (*opposite, bottom*). As the racquet moves into the end of the backswing, your arm and racquet should be forming a U-shape (*below*) whereby the forearm represents the base of the U with the upper arm and racquet forming the two sides of the U. The U-shape prepara-tion helps keep the swing compact and the racquet in your field of vision. If you lose sight of the racquet, you will also lose the U-shape in your arm and take too big of a backswing.

Aisam-ul-Haq Qureshi prepares with his racquet and arm forming a U-shape.

To remind my students of the correct wrist positioning on the volley, I sometimes ask them to choke up on the racquet and observe the position of their grip after hitting the ball. The grip should end a good distance away from forearm.

When setting up your arm and racquet in the U-shape, remember to keep your elbow close to your body and in front of your shoulder. This naturally lays your wrist back and places the racquet butt cap slightly in front of the strings (*below*). By having the butt cap in front of the strings, you create a powerful fulcrum effect whereby a small movement of your hand produces a much larger movement of the racquet head. This creates fast racquet speed, helps ensure the contact happens in front of the body, and produces a comfortable wrist position to move the racquet head towards your target for greater accuracy.

A common issue at the recreational level is that players move their elbow to the right during the set-up, placing the elbow behind the shoulder. This incorrect elbow positioning diminishes the fulcrum effect and increases the

Nadal lays his wrist back to create a position of leverage on this forehand volley.

chances of producing a late contact point and a swing path that goes across the body instead of towards the target.

With the backswing complete, to hit the ball, move your elbow forward, keep your wrist firm, and drive the racquet forward and down at a gentle high-to-low angle. The swing path of the racquet goes slightly down as well as right-to-left (or outside-to-inside), moving the butt cap down towards your body. On a typical chest-high ball, the racquet head will set up at an approximately 45 degree angle and rotate down to horizontal at contact. If the ball is particularly fast, high, or low, or if you are positioned close to the net, the racquet head will rotate less.

Drive with the shoulder to retain the U-shape on the forward swing. This will keep your elbow slightly bent, optimizing the physical strength needed to stabilize the racquet for the collision of the ball. Because the ball is hit in the air, the volley has the most intense ball impact of any shot. For this reason, it is important to "attain and retain" your arm shape on the forehand volley and play the shot using the body as a unit.

As you make contact, keep your head stationary and turned sideways facing towards the right net post with your eyes watching the back of the strings. Turning your head this way will not only help you align your hips correctly, but also assist concentration, increasing the likelihood that you will hit the ball cleanly. Also, lean forward slightly as you hit the ball; pushing your chest in a similar direction as the racquet will add power to your shot.

After contact, your palm should go forward facing towards your target (*left*). Unless you are receiving a very slow incoming ball, avoid swinging across the body and finish with the racquet on the same side of the body as the swing began.

After contact, Sorana Cirstea finishes the volley with her palm facing her target.

COACH'S BOX:

As mentioned earlier in the chapter, doubles dominates recreational play and the ability to volley well is key in doubles. It is important to note that the volley's simple, short racquet technique is the foundation for many crucial doubles shots, including the drop shot, lob, and all of the slice forehand shots that are used when rushed for time or attempting to keep the ball low at the opponent's feet. Indeed, if you can learn the correct racquet and elbow positioning on the forehand volley, you will execute many shots well and play a substantial part of doubles (and a small part of singles) skillfully.

III. The Backhand Volley

THE BACKHAND VOLLEY FOLLOWS many of the same principles as the forehand volley, but there are four main differences in technique. **First**, the hitting shoulder should stay more stationary and the hitting arm straighten more often. This results in a slightly longer swing. **Second**, because of the way the muscles in the arm align with the racquet, the backhand volley uses a slightly more open racquet face and increased backswing. The open racquet face will produce a slightly larger decline on the forward swing than is typical on the forehand volley. It is important to recognize this differ-

ence in the decline between the two volleys; if you apply the same arc of swing on both shots, you could produce too level of a swing on the backhand volley or too sharp of a decline on the forehand volley. **Third**, the shoulders should turn more. **Fourth**, the contact point should occur farther in front of the body.

The first move of the upper body on the backhand volley is to turn the shoulders slightly more than perpendicular to the net with your right arm slightly bent and the left hand cradling the throat of the racquet (*below*). The racquet head should be open and set up slightly above and behind the flight of the incoming ball. The length of your backswing will vary, but on most backhand volleys

COACH'S BOX:

For recreational players who have difficulty with their one-handed backhand volley, a two-handed backhand volley may be a viable option. The extra hand on the racquet can remedy grip issues, keep the swing compact, and stabilize the racquet better at ball impact. If trying this option, I recommend hitting the ball with two hands on the grip and then releasing the left hand immediately following contact as former world number one player Martina Hingis does below.

Stefan Edberg sets up for this backhand volley by turning his shoulders and cradling the throat of the racquet with his left hand.

Federer sets his racquet head up above the ball with his elbow slightly bent (*left*). His elbow straightens as his racquet moves forward to meet the ball, and his left arm moves backwards for balance and to keep his racquet on a straight path to his target (*right*).

the racquet head should be lined up with the left shoulder. At the end of the backswing, the arm and the racquet should form a U-shape, and the forearm and racquet should form an L-shape (*above left*).

With the backswing compete, drive the racquet forward and down with your shoulder and a firm wrist. Your right arm — which was slightly bent during the backswing — should straighten, and your left arm moves backwards (*above right*) in order to maintain balance and keep the racquet on a straight path towards your target.

On a typical chest-high ball, the racquet head will set up at an approximately 75 degree angle and rotate down to horizontal at contact. If the ball is particularly fast, high, or low, or if you are positioned close to the net, the racquet head will rotate less. The racquet face that was open on the backswing should

Kei Nishikori turns his head to look through the back of the strings at contact.

become almost perpendicular at contact. Naturally, the openness of the racquet at contact will vary depending on the height of the ball and shot intentions.

After contact, your head should be turned towards the left net post with your eyes still looking at the contact point (*previous page, bottom*). Finish with the racquet on your hitting side and well in front of your body. Finishing this way indicates you powered through the ball by driving with your shoulder and that contact correctly occurred in front of you.

IV. The Swinging Volley

THE SWINGING VOLLEY uses a swing similar to that of a regular groundstroke, but instead of hitting the ball after the bounce, you hit it in the air. It is typically hit from the middle part of the court after receiving a high, slow moving ball. For recreational players, due to the slower pace of game and frequent lobbing, there can be many opportunities to use this powerful stroke.

The first step on the swinging volley is to quickly recognize the high ball and set up in your stance, shoulders turned, and body positioned with good posture and balance. Your goal should be to position yourself to hit the ball around chest height (*center*). Hitting the ball below your waist or above the head on the swinging volley is a risky proposition.

Remember to play the swinging volley with a controlled swing and keep your body fairly level through the shot. The ball is hit in the air, so there is inherent power. Thus, this is a shot that can be hit with tremendous speed without swinging with great force or driving aggressively with the legs. Because it is a powerful shot, there is no need to aim for a small target — anywhere outside your opponent's immediate reach should be a winner or unreturnable shot.

Recreational players should hit the swinging volley while grounded, but for Murray, being airborne is no problem. Here, he uses his athleticism to play this swinging volley at a more comfortable height.

V. The Drop Volley

DUE TO THE IMPROVEMENT of passing shots in recent years, the drop volley has become a much more common shot on the professional tour. The art of hitting a series of volleys and moving the opponent around the court from side to side is rarely seen anymore. Instead, finishing the point more quickly at the net has become a priority and increased the need to develop a good drop volley. The pros are typically coming forward to volley only when they have control of the point and their opponent is several feet behind the baseline. This leaves the short part of the court exposed — a perfect occasion to play the drop volley.

The drop volley is a soft shot that lands close to the net and bounces low. As with the drop shot, choosing the right ball for a drop volley is crucial. The best time to play the drop volley is when the ball is waist high or lower and you have a reasonable amount of time and good balance. It is more effective on clay courts where the backspin will grip the softer surface and stop the ball's forward progression more as compared to hard courts.

It's best to disguise this shot, so prepare for the drop volley as if you were going to hit a regular volley. Then, using a relaxed grip to absorb the pace of the incoming shot, carve the racquet down sharply with an open racquet face to meet the ball. The control needed on a drop volley necessitates a technique in which the racquet moves very little before and after contact. For this reason, the wrist is the primary body link on this shot, with the arm moving only slightly.

On cross-court drop volleys, you should keep your racquet head up and hit around the outside part of the ball (*below*). By hitting around the outside of the ball, you can accelerate the racquet and the ball will still only travel a short distance. On down-the-line drop volleys, you should drop the racquet head down and hit the inside of the ball (*next page*).

Sam Querrey carves around the outside of the ball on this cross-court drop volley.

Federer makes contact on the inside part of the ball on this down-the-line drop volley.

VI. The Half Volley

THE HALF VOLLEY IS ONE of the more difficult shots and usually one that you don't hit by choice. You are forced to hit a half volley when the ball lands near your feet and is too short to volley but too deep for a regular groundstroke.

It is a shot you typically play while moving forward to the net and is done just as the ball is coming up off the bounce. Your stance will usually be closed but not always. As on any shot, maintain good balance by bending your knees and adjusting the width of your stance appropriately. If using the closed stance, then your lead foot should point towards the net. This opens up the front knee slightly and provides space for the hands to maneuver to the

Taylor Dent places his racquet behind the expected bounce of the ball and uses a short, low-to-high swing to play this half volley.

quick bounce of the ball.

As the ball approaches, move your hand into an eastern grip and position your racquet head low to the ground near the spot where you expect the ball to bounce (*opposite left*). Your racquet should start roughly two feet behind the contact point. Because the ball is hit just after the bounce, it has a good amount of energy behind it and a short swing is best to control the shot. From there you want to swing forward with a slightly low-to-high arc and your racquet face perpendicular to the ground (*opposite, center and right*). Stay in a crouched position with your head still until after you have made contact.

VII. The Overhead

THE OVERHEAD SWING IS SIMILAR to the serve and is played in response to an opponent's lob. It can be one of the most rewarding shots because it usually represents a situation where you have your opponent on the ropes and you can finish the point with a decisive winner. It may look like an easy shot, but because the lob drops from a considerable height, it takes a great deal of concentration and practice to do well.

1. FOOTWORK

A strong overhead begins with a well-timed split step and anticipation. If you see your opponent lean back and open their racquet face, start preparing mentally for a lob and have your feet ready to skip back for an overhead. Begin your footwork by turning your body and pivoting both feet to the right, preparing yourself to skip backwards in a sideways position. Too many recreational players don't turn to initiate the overhead and thus can only backped-

Nadal loads his weight on his back leg before transferring it forward to add power to his overhead swing.

al for the lob. This results in slower movement going backwards and a less powerful shoulder rotation when its time to swing at the ball.

After turning and pivoting your feet, if the lob is deep in the court, your left foot should do a backward cross over step, finishing behind and to the right of the right foot. If the lob is shorter, your left foot will move backwards and almost meet your right foot.

Remember, the main danger on the overhead is not being able to reach the lob, and it is much easier to move forward into the swing than to back up at the last second. Therefore, make an aggressive backward first move; once the lob is nearing its apex, you will know better where the ball will come down and can adjust your footwork accordingly.

Following a strong first movement, begin skipping back sideways from the net in the serving stance. Your footwork should get you into a position that allows your hitting arm to be fully extended and in front of the body at contact. Like a bad ball toss on the serve, bad positioning on the overhead will lead to poor balance and stifled arm extension.

The most powerful overheads occur when you can firmly plant your back foot and push forward into the court (*previous page*). Unlike the serve, the legs should remain bent and grounded through contact to keep the body level and assist timing. On a short lob, your weight shifts from your back foot to your front foot as it steps forward, while on a deep lob you may need to use the "scissor kick" whereby your back foot plants and your front foot rotates backwards as you swing up at the ball (*far right*).

2. THE UPPER BODY

As soon you pivot your feet to begin the overhead, you turn your shoulders and move your hands to around eye-level (*far left*); the overhead doesn't require a long backswing like you might use on the serve. Your hands should stay at eye level during the movement phase; lifting your hands too high will slow down your movement and having your hands too low will slow down your preparation and rush the swing.

Once you have arrived at the correct location to swing, plant your back leg and reach up with your left arm towards the ball to help measure the shot. As you do this, your right arm loops the racquet down your back and accelerates up to the ball, much like a serve (*center left*). You then extend your right arm, straightening it upwards to hit the ball (*center right*) making sure to pronate your wrist (*far right*). The overhead can be a "nervy" shot so make sure you keep your head up at contact and focus on the ball hitting the strings. The swing finishes with the racquet moving down and to the left, and the left arm that was folded into the chest at contact falls to the left side.

Andy Roddick turns and prepares his racquet, pushes off his back leg, and then uses the scissor kick to maintain balance through this overhead return of a deep lob.

VIII. Volley Practice

ONCE THE BALL GETS PAST you at the net, the point is over. Therefore, make the split step mandatory and move around in a lively way whenever you practice your volleys. Include incentives that keep your practice intensity high. For example, establish penalties like push-ups if you or your practice partner fail to touch the ball on passing shots and lobs. Also, set up targets around the court to help you focus and evaluate your volleying strengths and weaknesses. You should use not only drills that have structure and improve your skills through repetition, but also games that involve random ball locations and simulate the unpredictability of an opponent's passing shots in a match.

Two-on-one drilling is a great way to practice all the shots, but I find it especially beneficial for improving volleys. **First**, the two players on one side of the court are usually hitting with good balance, leading to longer rallies and more volleys struck. **Second**, the player alone on the other side of the court gets an intense workout. This player can go "all out" knowing there are frequent rotations and an easier time playing on the other side of the court is coming soon. Playing the net is an urgent situation and giving maximum effort is the right way to practice it. **Third**, there are many different two-on-one formations that lead to players defending against a wide variety of shots; these shots must be learned to become a strong volleyer.

1. TWO-ON-ONE SHORT AND DEEP DRILL
Goal: Improve ball control on drop volleys.

This drill sets up with Player A positioned at the net on one side of the court, while on the other side of the court, Player B is positioned at the deuce side service line and Player C at the ad side baseline. Player A starts the rally with a feed to player C at the baseline. Player A then alternates hitting drop volleys to Player B, and then volleying deep to Player C at the baseline. Players rotate positions every two or three minutes.

2. SIDE-TO-SIDE, UP-AND-BACK
Goal: Improve accuracy on the volley while moving in different directions around the court.

With your partner remaining stationary at the service line, rally with volleys as you move sideways back and forth along the service line to the doubles alleys. Switch roles every 30 seconds for three to five minutes. Then rather than moving left and right, have one player stationary at the "T" while the other player moves forwards and backwards along the center line. Switch roles every 30 seconds for three to five minutes. Variation: Do this drill with both players either mirroring or moving in an opposite direction of each other across the service line or up and back along the center line.

3. NO BOUNCE
Goal: Establish an attacking mind set when playing the net and learn to volley well from difficult positions.

While positioned at the net, have your practice partner at the baseline try to land the ball on your side of the court using lobs, drop shots or driving groundstrokes. You should use only the half court, choosing to hit cross court or down the line. Switch roles when your partner gets the ball to land on the court five times. Variation: Have your partner hit from the service line rather than the baseline.

Angelique Kerber is one of several number one world ranked professionals who play or played with their non-dominant arm. This fact (among others) raises an interesting question: if the forehand is a physically stronger motion compared to the backhand, could replacing the backhand with a left-handed forehand be a common method of play in the future?

CHAPTER 12

Future Strokes

THE PREVIOUS CHAPTERS DISCUSSED TENNIS' PRESENT, detailing the various strokes and methods used as the game is played today. But how will tennis look in the future? What currently commonplace shots may be modified? What entirely new ones might enter the game? Sports are not static. This is particularly so in the increasingly powerful game of tennis. In fact, the rallies on the professional tour are now so fast that the game sometimes resembles table tennis more than it does the tennis of long ago. As the game has sped up, methods of play have been modified, even though initially these changes were often resisted. In this chapter, I will outline three strokes that could produce superior results as the game continues to evolve: the overlapping dual forehand (ODF), the reverse serve (RS), and the volleyball serve (VS).

I. Learning from Tennis History

"All truth passes through three stages. First, it is ridiculed. Second, it is violently opposed. Third, it is accepted as being self-evident."
- German philosopher Arthur Schopenhauer

TENNIS HAS SEEN MANY stroke innovations, such as the two-handed backhand and the "flamingo" and "squat" versions of that stroke, the open stance groundstrokes, the inside forehand, the reverse forehand, the swinging volley, and the "jump" serve — all strokes discussed earlier in the book. Some of these strokes evolved because new equipment increased the speed and spin of the ball,

Jo-Wilfried Tsonga's flamingo backhand and Agnieszka Radwanska's squat backhand are relatively new shots to the game.

while others resulted from player's improved athleticism and size. Off court training methods are far superior to yesteryear, and WTA players above six feet tall are now common, while ATP players below that height are seen less and less. Some changes were born out of necessity, while others were just good ideas that previously were not examined fully due to our natural reluctance to enter the less safe domain of new ideas. Interestingly many of these changes only became cemented or "accepted" after their consistent and successful use by a top professional. It seems we often need proof from excellence before we decide that different is indeed better. Let's discuss how these stroke innovations occurred.

Before the two-handed backhand became popular, tennis legend Jack Kramer wrote, "The use of two hands not only weakens your

stroke but also robs you of confidence and gives your opponent a psychological advantage." [1] However, Kramer was proven wrong because the game sped up and having a second hand on the backhand grip proved helpful for absorbing the more powerful strokes. In the 1970s, after two-handed backhand players Bjorn Borg and Jimmy Connors dominated the professional tour, it became the main way to hit the backhand.

The two-handed backhand shot itself has evolved with the game. For instance, the flamingo two-handed backhand entered the sport in the 1990s, emerging as the use of increased topspin made higher balls more common. This shot sees a player jump up with the front foot and hit the ball while the body is in mid-air in a flamingo-type pose (*left*). By adding the jump, players raise their body to obtain a more comfortable contact point on higher balls, thereby approximating the swing that would occur on a waist-high ball. More recently, the pros adopted another new two-handed backhand groundstroke named the squat backhand. Used on shots hit fast and deep, the squat backhand sees players swinging with both knees almost touching the ground (*opposite right*), again to position the body at a height that makes the contact point more comfortable. Watching their students hit either of these backhands would have raised a coach's blood pressure in the not too distant past.

Bjorn Borg often receives credit for speeding up the forehand revolution as well. When he began winning major titles with his open stance forehand some experts told him that his forehand's lack of forward weight trans-

fer would result in great stress on his shoulder and injury to his arm. His arm was fine, he went on to win 11 majors, and the open stance forehand fast became a standard technique. The same occurred later with the open stance backhand, with the Williams sisters helping that shot evolve from being frowned upon to required (*below*).

They say necessity is the mother of all invention and this proverb holds true with the origins of the inside forehand and swinging volley. The inside forehand became a recognized shot in the late 1980s when the sage coaching of Nick Bollettieri teamed up first with Jimmy Arias and later (and more importantly) with Jim Courier. Bollettieri met Courier when the player was a talented junior equipped with an unorthodox backhand. Bollettieri worked around this weakness, smartly devising a game plan in which Courier avoided his backhand and hit as many forehands as possible, especially inside-out forehands. Courier's world number one ranking shined a spotlight on this stroke and it quickly became the most devastating baseline shot in the game.

On the swinging volley, it was again Nick Bollettieri — this time teaming with Andre Agassi — who is largely credited with kick starting a new shot's influence on the game. After identifying the swinging volley's potential and considering the discrepancy between Agassi's outstanding groundstrokes and less natural volleys, Bollettieri advised Agassi to use the groundstroke swing on his volleys as much as possible. Agassi's great timing made his swinging volley a feared shot and the stroke caught on. In the past, the volley was always taught as a short motion, where over-swinging and follow through were considered bad form. Juniors are now trained that when they are inside the baseline and the ball

Venus Williams helped the open stance backhand become a common shot.

Players of the past did not elevate high above the ground on the serve as Samantha Stosur does here.

is slow and above the net, the swinging volley is the correct shot to use. The advantage of the the swinging volley is clear: the ball can be hit with much greater speed than with a traditional volley.

The reverse forehand is another more recent addition to the tennis player's repertoire. Rarely seen in the past, it is now frequently used to cope with the increased speed of the ball and to facilitate the sharp vertical lift of the racquet required for added topspin on certain shots. When Rafael Nadal first made this stroke popular, many pundits considered it a fad and expressed concern that it would increase mishits on groundstrokes. Now, it is the concern, rather than the reverse follow through technique, that has faded away.

Serve technique has also changed, literally taking to the air. In the wooden racquet era, most players' feet barely left the ground on the

serve, and the back foot moved forward ahead of the front foot during the follow through. The common serving strategy back then was to serve and volley, and this type of footwork gave the server a quicker start for the forward move to the net. Today, when the serve is more commonly followed by a rally from the baseline, players execute the serve by elevating many inches off the ground at contact and move into the court with the front foot leading and the back foot lagging behind (*above*). Thus, the emphasis has changed from mostly forward power with some vertical lift to mostly vertical lift with some forward power.

Even elements of the game like doubles serving formations and movement have transformed. It is only in the last 20 years that the "I" formation (*see page 246*) has become a well-used doubles strategy, and touring pros are now doing something that only ankle surgeons would have recommended in the past: sliding into shots on hard courts.

I could continue with more examples, but my point is that there have been many changes in tennis, some of which were resisted for years. So the question becomes, are there any shots that will one day make us wonder why they didn't become commonplace earlier? Having thought deeply about the game and its evolution — and using the template of biomechanics coupled with my lifelong experiences of coaching and playing — I believe there are three strokes that could help players in the years ahead: the overlapping dual forehand (ODF), the reverse serve (RS), and the volleyball serve (VS).

Of course, these strokes are not for everyone. Tennis is too individualistic and idiosyncratic to ever have just one style of play. But perhaps the ODF, RS, and VS could become established techniques just as the strokes mentioned above are today. At the very least, they are ideas that are interesting to contemplate and explore. Let's examine these three shots in depth, beginning with the ODF.

II. The Overlapping Dual Forehand

WHAT MAY FOR SOME become a superior way of playing groundstrokes is using the ODF and a style of play I call "Ambitennis." In this stroke, or style of play, players use an overlapping grip technique paired with a forehand swing that uses both the right arm and the left arm, thus eliminating the backhand (*below*).

Why adopt this stroke? Mainly because of the forehand's superior physical qualities (*see page 194*) over the backhand. At the professional and recreational levels, the forehand is typically stronger than the backhand. For most of you, when the ball comes to your forehand, your mind lifts in anticipation of an offensive situation about to unfold. When the ball comes to your backhand, your offensive expectations are lowered. If you, like most players, favor your forehand, Ambitennis could have you looking forward to every ball crossing the net.

The ODF, demonstrated by Kirill Azovtsev, takes advantage of the forehand's superior strength, timing, and reach from both sides of the court.

Has the dual forehand been used before? Yes, in fact there have been a handful of professional players in the past, like 1955 Wimbledon singles runner-up Beverly Baker Fletz, who used the dual forehand method. However, none of these players combined it with my recommended overlapping grip technique (*opposite left*). In the past, dual forehand players set up with both hands on the grip and hit their left-handed forehand using one of two grip methods: moving the left hand down a few inches on the grip, which takes time, or leaving the left hand in place and choking up on the grip, which restricts power. In contrast, the overlapping grip sees the left hand move down the grip very little if at all, making it a quick and powerful way to hold the racquet for dual forehand players.

Margaret Court won the most Grand Slam singles titles in history playing with her non-dominant hand.

1. THE STORY OF NADAL AND OTHERS

Before discussing the advantages of Ambitennis, I'd like to address the main argument against it: that players can't hit the forehand well with their non-dominant hand. This argument doesn't hold, however, when you consider the number of players who have become champions using their non-dominant hand.

The story of Rafael Nadal is a powerfully persuading case in point: Rafa is naturally right-handed. As a young kid, he played with both hands gripping the racquet on the forehand and backhand. Recognizing the limitations of that style of play, his coach asked him to change and hit his forehand with only his left hand and his backhand with both hands on the racquet. Ironically, it is his forehand — the shot with no right hand in it — that is his strongest shot and one of the greatest forehands ever.

Beside Nadal, there are many other famous examples of tennis champions playing with their non-dominant hand. Margaret Court (*above*), who has won the major singles titles in history, played right-handed even though she was naturally left-handed. Former world number one players Carlos Moya and Maria Sharapova are also left-handed but play right-handed. ATP former top-ten player Jurgen Melzer and world number one Angelique Kerber, like Nadal, are right-handed and play left-handed. And the list goes on. These examples demonstrate that a player can be successful — even legendary — while hitting their forehand with the "opposite" arm.

2. OVERLAPPING DUAL FOREHAND GRIP

The way you hold the racquet while waiting in the ready position is a key component of a successful dual forehand. In the ODF, you wait in the ready position with your right hand in your preferred forehand grip. Then, place your

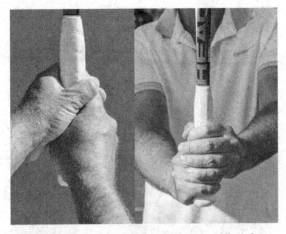

The ODF grip sees the left middle, ring, and pinky fingers overlap the right hand.

left hand angled in your preferred left-handed forehand grip almost halfway above your right hand with your left middle, ring, and pinky fingers placed on top, or overlapping, your right middle and ring fingers (*above*). All your fingers are touching the grip except for your left middle, ring, and pinky fingers. Both hands should be placed together as closely as possible to position the left hand low on the grip.

When using the ODF, there is no turning of the hitting hand on the grip to the right or to the left as is currently done when changing from a forehand to backhand. Instead, because both hands are already angled in the forehand grip, one hand simply releases off the grip to play the shot. After the non-hitting hand releases, moving it up towards the throat of the racquet to conduct a strong unit turn is recommended but not mandatory. The length of hand movement here is similar to the length that two-handed backhand players move their non-hitting hand down from the throat of the racquet to the grip to hit their backhand.

3. ADVANTAGES OF THE OVERLAPPING DUAL FOREHAND

Although there are genetic and neurological reasons for playing with your dominant arm, the physical advantages of the forehand over the backhand along with other rationales make the case for using the ODF an interesting one nonetheless. Let me explain why.

A. THE FOREHAND PROVIDES INCREASED POWER.

There is a significant difference in physical strength between the forehand and one-handed backhand. First, the forehand has the hit-

The forehand's powerful upward angular momentum often causes Federer to lift off the ground.

ting shoulder lagging the front shoulder and uses the stronger "pull" motion across the body, while the backhand has the hitting shoulder facing the ball and uses the weaker "push" motion of the arm away from the body. In addition, the forehand swing uses the stronger pectorals, anterior deltoids, and biceps, in contrast to the backhand swing, which uses the weaker trapezius, posterior and middle deltoids, and triceps. When compared to the one-handed or two-handed backhand, the forehand also makes greater use of the big muscles of the lower body and core than the backhand. On the forehand, the legs push more aggressively from the ground, creating more upward angular momentum (*previous page, right*), and the hips rotate faster and longer compared to the backhand. Lastly, because the forehand is hit with the back shoulder, the forehand backswing is longer than the backhand backswing, allowing it to build up greater swing momentum to accelerate the racquet.

B. THE FOREHAND TAKES LESS TIME TO EXECUTE.

When uncoiling to hit a topspin forehand you have the benefit of having the hitting shoulder behind the body, whereas when hitting a backhand your hitting shoulder is in front of the body. This means you have more time to play a forehand versus a backhand; with time becoming more precious in this era of power tennis, this is a very important consideration.

Moreover, a good backhand typically requires the power created from the forward step into the shot. This is not necessary on the forehand. A forehand can be hit very well or even better without the forward step and hit with a quickly arranged semi-open or open stance instead. It is true that the backhand can be hit with an open stance, but there is a rea-

Nadal bends his wrist forward and flicks the ball back into the court; this shot would not have been possible with the backhand.

son why the closed stance is used much more often on the backhand than the open stance; the open stance is inferior. At the higher levels, open stance forehands outnumber closed stance forehands in a similar way that closed stance backhands outnumber open stance backhands.

C. THE FOREHAND PROVIDES EXTRA COURT COVERAGE.

In difficult defensive situations, it is well known that once the ball gets behind you on the backhand, the shot becomes almost impossible to hit back in the court. However, if the ball gets behind you on the forehand, you can bend your wrist forward with some strength and flick an effective shot back in the court (*above*). Therefore, having the ability to use the forehand motion from both sides of the body increases your court coverage significantly. This allows you to extend some rallies that would not be possible if playing in the traditional manner.

D. AMBITENNIS PROVIDES A STRONG AND FAST CHANGING GRIP.

On the forehand, most of your palm and four fingers are behind the grip at ball impact, while on the one-handed backhand, it is only

---

COACH'S BOX:

It is interesting to note that because Nadal is so right-hand dominant on his two-handed backhand (because he is naturally right-handed), he can use the open stance two-handed backhand more frequently, almost like a right-handed forehand (*below*), and therefore, take some advantage of the ODF benefit of time. Federer made an interesting observation about Nadal's game after losing to him at the 2008 French Open saying, "He plays like two forehands from the baseline because he has an open stance on both sides. I can't do that, so I lose a meter or two here and there from the baseline. So he's got a huge advantage in this aspect, you know." [1]

---

the thumb and a small part of the palm. Having a bigger part of the palm and more fingers behind the grip allows you to better handle the collision of the ball and control the shot.

When using a two-handed backhand, you have a strong grip, but there is an issue of time, with the left hand moving down from the throat of the racquet to join the right hand on the grip. Additionally, you have the problems associated with correctly positioning two hands, rather than only one, on the grip. With the ODF, both hands are always set in the forehand grip and all that is required is to release one hand off the grip.

This advantage of quickly setting the grip is especially significant on a crucial shot: the return of serve. It is partly the grip change that makes the return of serve challenging, especially when you are up against a fast serve. The grip change on the return of serve leads to over-anticipation to the direction of the serve and favoring one stroke to the detriment of the other stroke. Players with a one-handed backhand definitely have issues with grip changes, but even two-handed backhand players have to change grips between the forehand and backhand. Ambitennis players have fewer grip issues on the return of serve since both hands are already in the forehand grip and therefore can quickly handle all types of serves whether hit to the left or right side of the body. Plus, you have the ODF advantages of additional power, time, and reach to help you play a strong return.

E. AMBITENNIS HELPS NEUTRALIZE AN OPPONENT'S TACTIC OF HITTING WIDE OR HIGH TO GAIN AN ADVANTAGE IN THE POINT.

Because the forehand is hit with the back shoulder, it permits a good wind up when rushed on a wide ball. This is not the case with the backhand. In fact, the running forehand can be a dangerous weapon, while the running backhand is usually a defensive shot. Thus, because the ODF gives you the ability to be aggressive on wide balls from both sides of the court using a forehand swing (*below*), it negates the common tactic of taking control of the point by hitting wide to the backhand. Additionally, while the high forehand is not an easy stroke, it is certainly much easier than the high backhand. Therefore, Ambitennis helps you thwart an opponent's tactic of hitting high topspin shots to your backhand to gain the upper hand. By neutralizing these two tactics, your opponents will have to find new shot patterns that are unfamiliar and underdeveloped and, consequently, less effective.

Unlike the wide backhand, the wide forehand can be a dangerous shot.

F. AMBITENNIS SIMPLIFIES MECHANICS.

Currently, players switch hundreds of times every match from the forehand motion to the backhand motion. These two swings require not only different upper body mechanics, but also different stances and contact points. This can be challenging to do quickly and successfully during a long match or even an extended rally. It is a well-known tactic in tennis to hit several balls to one wing and then hit to the other wing, knowing that the change in mechanics required between the two groundstrokes will sometimes lead to a weak shot or error from your opponent. Ambitennis, on the other hand, uses the same forehand pull motion on both sides, simplifying the upper body mechanics, producing greater uniformity of stances and contact points, and making the switch between swings easier.

G. AMBITENNIS IMPROVES SHOT SELECTION.

There is a usually a different tactical approach taken on the forehand versus the backhand. The forehand is generally the aggressive stroke and the backhand the more conservative one. This difference can make shot selection problematic because it brings into question exactly how aggressive to be on the forehand and how conservative to be on the backhand. This can lead to overly ambitious errors or missed opportunities. With Ambitennis the level of aggression is more even on both the right and left sides of the court, making for more coherent decision making on how to hit the ball.

H. AMBITENNIS IMPROVES COURT POSITIONING.

Moving to the left of center in the court to dictate play with your forehand or protect your backhand exposes the right side of the court and risks losing court positioning (*opposite*).

Moving left to play a forehand opens up the right side of the court for your opponent to exploit.

If you move left of the center to hit your forehand, you need to hit a strong shot, otherwise you may pay heavily for leaving two-thirds or more of the court open. Also, constantly moving left to hit your forehand or avoid your backhand expends a lot of energy. Over the course of a long match, this can prove costly.

Furthermore, because the backhand has less reach and requires more time, players must position themselves left of the midpoint of their opponents' angles. This positioning makes the opponent's down-the-line backhand and cross-court forehand particularly damaging shots. ODF players, on the other hand, can position themselves in the midpoint of their opponents' angles and be less troubled by these two shots.

I. AMBITENNIS REDUCES BODY POSITIONING ISSUES.

If you have misjudged the location, speed, or spin of the ball on the backhand, you are almost guaranteed a weak shot. The strength and power of the backhand usually depend on an accurate launching forward with the front foot in a closed stance; therefore, there is very little margin for error on body positioning. Additionally, on the two-handed backhand, because there are two hands on the racquet, any misjudgment of the ball will lurch your upper body in different directions and cause a loss of power and racquet control.

In contrast, the forehand often uses an open stance and is a one-handed shot. This means you can usually still hit an effective, if not ideal, shot even if you have slightly misjudged the ball. Also, the forehand uses the non-hitting hand in front of the body to help measure the shot and secure good positioning.

J. AMBITENNIS DECREASES RISK OF INJURIES AND INCREASES MENTAL STIMULATION.

The constant swinging of the racquet by the hitting arm and the impact force incurred at contact in those swings can overdevelop and fatigue muscles as well as wear down the joints in that arm. This can lead to injuries. Ambitennis reduces the likelihood of such injuries, as

Studies have shown that learning a new way of playing a sport has positive effects on the brain.

the impact of swing repetition does not fall all on one arm.

Additionally, research suggests that using your non-dominant hand stimulates the mind and helps the brain to better integrate its two hemispheres. We are "cross-wired," meaning that playing the forehand with the left hand gives the mind greater access to the brain's right hemispheric functions, such as intuition and creativity. The right side of the brain is more responsible for three dimensional perception — an important factor in good hand-eye coordination and successful tennis. Furthermore, neurological studies have shown that learning a new motor skill, like the ODF, increases the myelination of neurons in the motor cortex.[2] The myelination process insulates the brain cells so that the messages between neurons can move more quickly, improving brain performance. Even if the mental improvement is subtle, any improvement that does occur is a wonderful side benefit of Ambitennis.

4. THE OVERLAPPING DUAL FOREHAND VERSUS THE TWO-HANDED BACKHAND

It is interesting to note that the two-handed backhand is often described as being essentially a left-handed forehand. Certainly, the left arm contributes much more to the power and spin of the two-handed backhand than the right arm. And, while the hip rotation is later and the swing more compact on the two-handed backhand compared to the left-handed forehand, the left arm follows a similar path on both shots.

In comparing the ODF to the two-handed backhand, there are four advantages of the ODF over the two-handed backhand that can be added to the general benefits discussed above. **First**, the ODF is less restrictive. Some players find the two-handed backhand awkward. Such players have difficulty taking a full rhythmic swing and accelerating the racquet fluently with two hands on the racquet. With the ODF, only one hand is on the racquet at contact, avoiding these issues. **Second,** the ODF provides greater topspin. One arm can swing faster than two and this means more topspin. **Third,** the ODF requires less energy. Swinging the racquet with two arms on the backhand expends more energy. **Fourth,** the ODF allows you to handle low balls better. On a low ball, the two-handed backhand player may be forced to take the left hand off the racquet and hit a defensive one-handed backhand slice shot; on the same ball the ODF player may be able to hit an offensive topspin shot with the left-handed forehand.

5. HOW TO PRACTICE THE OVERLAPPING DUAL FOREHAND

The key to learning a motor skill well, especially a new one, is to slow things down and increase the difficulty gradually, step by step. If you try to learn the ODF by hitting baseline to baseline with regular tennis balls, you will learn much more slowly than if you follow the progressions I recommend below.

A. OFF-COURT TRAINING

Before you go to the courts to work on your ODF, you can familiarize yourself with the grip at home. Keep a racquet near your TV or computer and practice flipping your hands in and out of the overlapping grip. Obviously, becoming fast at releasing and replacing your hands on the grip is an important component of Ambitennis.

Shadow swings will also help your ODF and they can be done at home too. Shadow swings

COACH'S BOX:

As Nick Bollettieri wrote in *Tennis Magazine*, Andre Agassi (*below*) would often spend time hitting left-handed forehands during practice to help his two-handed backhand. "He would do this every day. This forces you to accelerate your top hand and make it your dominant hand at contact." A wonderful feature of the ODF is that, even if you eventually decide to play with a two-handed backhand, practicing a left-handed forehand will make your two-handed backhand a stronger and more technically sound stroke.

are highly effective for reinforcing muscle memory of correct technique, as well as developing the strength needed to swing the racquet with control and power. It is a great way to groove your lefty forehand and learn the different footwork, stances, and swing paths

ON-COURT ODF TRAINING PROGRESSIONS

1. ABBREVIATED SWING

2. POWER POSITION

3. AND 4. FOOTWORK AND SWING

efficiently, all without needing a court or a hitting partner.

Set aside 15 minutes a day to do the following ODF shadow swing session: start by using the three main forehand stances — neutral, semi-open and open. Complete about 100 left-handed forehand swings using the three stances roughly the same number of times in a random sequence. Following these 100 swings, play 25 random imaginary points of various lengths where you are swinging both offensively and defensively and moving in different directions around the court. Begin five points where you are serving and the next five points where you are receiving serve. Follow that sequence until the 25 points are finished. Be sure to include some right-handed forehand swings during these imaginary points to practice moving your hands in and out of the overlapping grip.

B. ON-COURT TRAINING

While doing the grip change and shadow swing training at home, you can start practicing Ambitennis on the court by using low-compression balls. Named QuickStart balls in the United States, these balls are lighter and move more slowly than regular balls, making them easier to hit. Importantly, they lead to longer rallies and greater repetition. These balls come in different sizes and weights, so begin by using the slower balls and move up gradually to the faster balls.

Begin by having a practice partner feed you QuickStart balls from a basket. Start on the service line and spend around a total of 15 minutes doing left-handed forehand swings in the four following feed progressions.

1. ABBREVIATED SWING: First, familiarize yourself with correctly balancing the racquet at contact. Standing on the service line, establish the neutral stance and begin with the racquet aligned with your back foot (*above left*). Using this abbreviated backswing, swing at the ball with your left-handed forehand and follow through fully. During this stage of the progression you are focusing on learning the contact point slightly in front of the front foot and keeping the angle of the racquet face steady through the contact zone. Use this abbreviated backswing to hit the ball for 25 shots.

2. POWER POSITION: Next, begin the swing in the power position (*opposite center*) and hit 25 shots slowly. Use a low-to-high swing and brush up the ball with a moderate amount of topspin.

3. FULL SWING: Now use a full swing starting from the ready position. Hit 25 shots slowly with moderate topspin and hold the swing at the end of the stroke to ensure you follow through fully with good balance. Remember to always return back to the ready position and place your hands in the overlapping grip after each stroke.

4. FOOTWORK AND FULL SWING: Lastly, introduce some footwork and different stances. Bounce on your feet while waiting for the feed, step out to the left with the left foot, take two or three small adjustment steps, and step forward with the right foot as you swing using the neutral stance for 25 shots. Then have your practice partner feed the ball higher and down the middle and hit 25 shots using the semi-open stance (*opposite right*). Then have your practice partner feed the ball wide and hit 25 open stance shots for a total of 75 full swings with variable footwork. At this stage, it is a good idea to set up targets on the court to help improve accuracy and concentration.

After working on your ODF with feeds, rally slowly with your righty and lefty forehand using QuickStart balls. Stand five feet behind the service line and rally using the service line as the baseline. This smaller court allows you to focus on using the correct leg and arm movement of the lefty forehand swing. By using the full court too early in the learning process, the focus on the correct swing can be lost in the complications that arise from moving and hitting long distances. As you rally, focus on the upper body fundamentals discussed previously in Chapter Seven (unit turn, backswing, forward swing to contact, contact, and follow through) and transfer those principles from the right side to the left.

Spend approximately 10 minutes rallying from five feet behind the service line, 10 minutes rallying positioned 10 feet behind the service line, and 10 minutes rallying from the baseline for a total of 30 minutes of rally practice. Hit most of the balls slowly to best learn the correct contact point and body balance.

If you can be disciplined and follow this one hour training routine that includes 15 minutes of shadow swings, 15 minutes of feeds, and 30 minutes of rallying, you will reach your Ambitennis goals more quickly. Keep in mind, hitting against a wall or using a ball machine can provide helpful repetition too. Naturally, the use of these progressions will change over time as you become more and more familiar with the ODF. Once you reach a reasonably comfortable level with your ODF, you can end the shadow swings, use of QuickStart balls, and the feeding progression and start your practice sessions by rallying with regular balls.

6. OVERLAPPING DUAL FOREHAND CONCLUSION

The physical advantages of the forehand over the backhand make a compelling case for the ODF in the modern game. As players become more athletic — making the increased use of the left hand more possible and wise — and the game continues to speed up, the tennis community may greater appreciate the increased power, time, reach, and other advantages of the forehand swing and view the current perspective that the game can only be played with a forehand and backhand as an antiquated one. The game is finely balanced and sometimes small improvements lead to tectonic shifts in how it is played. The upgrade in racquet strings in the 1990s almost wiped out ATP serve and volley tennis in the 2000s. What kind of impact will slightly faster and stronger athletes and a marginally quicker

game have on baseline play?

As mentioned earlier, I suppose the main question is how skilled we can become with our non-dominant hand. Studies done on handedness run into a "chicken-or-egg" question in regards to skill and preference. Does a person's handedness happen because one

As modern players become increasingly athletic and the game becomes faster, maybe the use of the ODF will become more advantageous and justifiable.

COACH'S BOX:

Everyone needs the mental components of motivation and confidence to make changes in life or start something new like Ambitennis. Your motivation can stem from making the connection between the ODF and the joy of reaching shots previously out of reach, attacking second serves more aggressively, or defeating an old nemesis for the first time. Your confidence in the ODF can come from understanding the forehand's kinesthetic superiority when compared to the backhand. Besides motivation and confidence, you will also need patience and perseverance to overcome the hurdles you will encounter along the way. Spend time visualizing Ambitennis success in your mind and remember that your goals are more attainable if you write them down on a weekly basis and include three things you need to do to help make it happen. This structured approach will deepen your focus and provide resiliency to the process of achieving your Ambitennis ambitions.

hand is more skilled, or is that hand more skilled because it is preferred and, therefore, used more? It seems likely that handedness begins to some extent as a preference rather than as a notable skill difference. Certainly, the tremendous success attained by players like Nadal, Court, Moya, Sharapova, Melzer, Kerber, and others support this belief.

Scientists don't categorize us as exclusively right-handed or left-handed, but instead place us along a handedness spectrum. Along this spectrum, there is a small percentage of the population at the ends of the spectrum who are very right-handed or very left-handed. For those towards the middle of the handedness spectrum, maybe Ambitennis is the right choice. Conceivably in the not too distant future, we may be able to measure handedness in children through genetics, and from that information, the children that fall towards the middle of the spectrum might be encouraged to learn the ODF method, while the children that fall towards the ends of the spectrum are not.

III. The Reverse Serve

1. ADVANTAGES OF THE REVERSE SERVE

Many of the most successful doubles teams in history — Mike and Bob Bryan, Todd Woodbridge and Mark Woodforde, Martina Navratilova and Pam Shriver, and John McEnroe and Peter Fleming — have one important trait in common: they are a right handed/left-handed combination. Why is this combination so advantageous? For one, players competing against such a doubles combination must make the adjustment of returning a serve that cures right and then, on the very next returning game, a serve that curves left, in each case crossing the net at a different angle.

A good spin serve in singles is always a weapon and is particularly effective at the beginning of a match. But once the returner has seen the serve for several games, they begin to read the spin and time their returns progressively better. However, if you are able to hit righty *and* lefty spin serves, you can disrupt your opponent's rhythm and make returning

Right-handed and left-handed doubles combinations like the Bryan brothers make it difficult for opponents to find a rhythm returning serve.

serve frustrating all match long.

In addition to disrupting your opponent's rhythm by adding an unpredictable dimension to your serve, there are three other reasons why being able serve with both righty and lefty spin can make your service games easier to win.

A. ONLY AROUND 10% OF PLAYERS ARE LEFT-HANDED. [3]

The lefty serve is an enigma to many players because left-handed people represent a small part of the population, and thus, the chance to compete against them is infrequent. The ball's flight, spin, and bounce run counter to what players are used to returning the vast majority of the time.

B. YOU CAN GAIN COURT POSITIONING ADVANTAGE EVERY TIME YOU SERVE.

If you can curve your serve right or left you can move your opponent off the court serv-ing to both the deuce and ad side, instead of being limited to just the deuce side as is tra-ditionally the case. This skill gains importance when considering the advantage gained serv-ing on the ad side, which is the side on which many important game points are held — 30-15, 15-30, 40-30, 30-40, ad-in, and ad-out.

C. YOU CAN ATTACK YOUR OPPONENT'S BACKHAND MORE EASILY.

The rightward curve of the lefty spin makes it easier to place your serve to a right-hand-ed opponent's backhand, often their weaker groundstroke.

The benefits of being able to serve with both the right-handed and left-handed spin are clear, but how do you acquire the advantage of the left-handed spin if you are right-handed, or the right-handed spin if you are left-handed? It's by developing the reverse serve (RS).

2. THE REVERSE SERVE TECHNIQUE FOR ADVANCED PLAYERS

For advanced players, the RS begins with the continental grip. There is no need to use a different grip from your regular serve or change your ball toss to the left and lose the element of surprise. By disguising the serve, you leave your opponent without time to shift their return of serve positioning to cover the RS's ball curve.

Advanced players should keep the ball toss in the same alignment as a flat serve, but shift the toss approximately a foot further in front than usual. Remember your opponent can see right to left variations in the toss but not slight changes forward. Interestingly, because the toss is in the same direction as the flat serve, the RS may be easier to disguise than the traditional slice serve, which is hit with a ball toss slightly to the right.

On the reverse serve, the leading edge of the racquet moves towards the left net post through contact.

The RS begins the same way as a regular serve (*next page, top left*). Then, once you enter the trophy position, move the grip slightly to the weak continental or eastern grip position (*next page, top right*). This grip adjustment allows the racquet face to break more easily around the left side of the ball. Next, drop the racquet down your back and swing up at the ball with the leading edge of the racquet moving towards the left net post (*below*). Brush the strings around the left side of the ball. The serve finishes with the hips rotating fully, and due to the racquet's leftward movement, the RS moves the server more to the left during the follow through. This places the server in good position to use their forehand on the third shot of the rally (*next page, bottom right*).

The RS creates the same spin as the left-handed serve by brushing the strings from right to left across the ball, instead of the usual left to right direction of right-handed spin serves. The type of serve you wish to hit will determine what part of the ball the strings brush over. If you wish to hit a reverse slice serve, the strings will brush around the 10 o'clock edge of the ball. If the reverse slice-topspin is your goal, the strings will impact the middle of the ball and then brush over the 11 o'clock part of the ball.

Although using the weak continental grip slightly reduces the wrist pronation compared to the flat serve, the RS does have a bigger wrist pronation than the slice serve. In fact, because the wrist pronation on the RS is more similar to the flat serve than the slice serve, I actually serve my RS several miles an hour faster than my regular slice serve. I also find the RS is easier on my arm, especially on my elbow. This is because the wrist pronation of the RS stretches the forearm muscles, taking pressure off the elbow, while the slice serve

The RS begins the same way as a regular flat serve. In the third frame, Kirill moves his hitting hand out of the continental grip and into the eastern forehand grip. In the fourth frame, his left arm moves left earlier and faster than it would on a flat serve to open up a path for the racquet to travel left. Between frames four and five, we see the racquet move up and to the left before making contact with the 10 o'clock part of the ball. In the sixth frame, the leading racquet edge continues its movement towards the left net post following contact. In the final frame, Kirill follows through and will end more to the left on the court than in the regular serves. This places him in good position to use his forehand to dominate the baseline rally.

places more strain on the elbow with its smaller wrist pronation.

The RS is not without its imperfections. Two negatives of the RS as compared to the traditional serves are that the hand alignment on the grip to the forearm is not as strong at contact, and the contact point is slightly lower and more in front of the body than ideal. But these are minor drawbacks when matched against the benefits of occasionally surprising your opponents with a menacing left-handed type curve on your serve.

3. THE REVERSE SERVE TECHNIQUE FOR RECREATIONAL PLAYERS

The RS instruction above applies to recreational players, except to make it easier to perform,

there are differences in the grip and the ball toss. Recreational players should begin the RS in the eastern forehand grip and the ball toss should be approximately a foot more to the left and a foot further in front than a flat serve ball toss. Because the toss is in a different position, an additional advantage of the RS is that the negative impact of the sun being in your eyes during the ball toss can be avoided on both sides of the court by serving the RS from one side and a traditional type serve from the other.

4. REVERSE SERVE CONCLUSION

There are other sports where athletes routinely curve the ball both right and left. The action that most correlates to the service motion in tennis is the baseball pitch. Like the serve, pitching requires high speed and precision, and involves mixing up the type of deliveries with different wrist movements to keep the opponent off rhythm. In pitching, you have the slider, which makes the ball move right to left much like a slice serve in tennis, and the screw-ball, which makes the ball break left to right much like a RS. If a pitcher can throw a ball 60 feet over a plate that is 17 inches wide with a variety of wrist motions, I see little reason why a tennis player can't learn to hit the RS over a three foot net into the 283 square-foot service box. Also, keep in mind that the serve is the one shot in tennis that you have 100% control over. This characteristic of the serve makes it easier to learn a variety of racquet movements and assortment of spins.

Almost anyone who has played a high level of tennis has experimented with the RS. It is not a new idea. I have coaching friends who, without practicing it conscientiously at all, can ace me with their RS. Knowing its effective-ness, it is perplexing to me why the RS hasn't become a well-recognized occasional serve used to surprise opponents. But then again, as explained earlier in the chapter, there are several shots that are common today that took time to evolve and become established — maybe I shouldn't be so surprised.

IV. The Volleyball Serve

WHY DO HIGH JUMPERS take a long run up before planting and elevating over the bar? It's because the forward momentum of the run up allows them to jump higher. It is for this rea-son that I believe the volleyball serve (VS) may some day be part of the tennis lexicon.

You begin the VS by establishing your regu-lar serving stance but standing 12 to 18 inches behind the behind the baseline (*opposite left*). After initiating your backswing, step forward with your left foot 12 to 18 inches before per-forming a regular pinpoint serve (*opposite center and right*). This step forward with the left foot not only increases racquet speed but also produces a longer and higher lift off the ground.

This stronger lift upwards improves the serve in two important ways: it raises your contact height and and shortens the court. As dis-cussed in Chapter Five, a higher contact point

Federer finishes his serve well above the ground. The volleyball serve helps players elevate higher, improving the ball's trajectory into the service box.

I start the VS in my regular serving stance but a little over a foot behind the baseline (*left*). Next, I step forward with my left foot during the backswing (*center*) and then enter the trophy position (*right*) with extra forward momentum to increase the contact height and power on my serve.

improves the ball trajectory into the service box by increasing the margin for error above the net and inside the service line. There's a reason why 6'11" Ivo Karlovic has served the most aces ever on the ATP Tour. The longer jump also shortens the court, stealing reaction time away from your opponent. If you have ever received serve from a practice partner standing slightly inside the baseline, you know how much a split second of reduced time can adversely affect your return of serve.

V. Another Serving Option

THERE IS ANOTHER SERVING STANCE option that may enhance your serve. It makes use of the different advantages offered by the platform and pinpoint serves (*see pages 40-*

41) to help all servers in different ways.

In any strong serve, you push your body both upward and forward. The leg drive of the platform stance is better than the pinpoint stance on the upward push, whereas the pinpoint stance has stronger forward momentum. The platform stance is more stable, but less vigorous in other ways, whereas the pinpoint stance has a more powerful hip movement and surge of energy but requires superior body control.

These advantages and disadvantages can help or hurt your ability to hit effective first and second serves. The explosive power of the pinpoint stance is particularly useful on the first serve, but the second serve demands consistency with less emphasis on speed. This is why the stability of the platform stance often makes it a good choice for the second serve. Not only is there a difference in purpose be-

Moving the back foot forward, but leaving a gap between the feet, can add power to a platform server's first serve and consistency to a pinpoint server's second serve.

tween the first and second serve, but the ball toss is also different. The ball toss on the second serve is less in front of the body than the first serve, and therefore, both serves warrant a slightly different leg stance.

Is there a technique that can solve the dilemma of stance on the serve? Moving the back foot foot forward during the backswing and leaving a small gap between the feet at the trophy position could be helpful (*above*). This technique combines positive elements of the pinpoint stance (forward momentum and hip movement) together with positive elements of the platform stance (leg drive and stability). These qualities can improve a platform server's *first* serve, and a pinpoint server's *second* serve.

VI. Conclusion

THROUGHOUT THE HISTORY OF TENNIS, players and coaches have created innovative techniques that were initially met with resistance before being embraced as superior methods. The ODF, RS, and VS are not currently taught, but just as tennis has adopted many changes in technique in the past, these strokes too may become familiar to us in the future. The hybrid backhand mentioned in Chapter Eight, that is, using the two-handed backhand on the return of serve and the one-handed backhand during the rally, is another shot that may take hold as well. Certainly, tennis is now more athletic, aggressive, and scientific than it has ever been, and the tennis community is more open to these alternative ideas than in the past.

I say, be bold and remember the great players who ignored the skeptics, pioneered new strokes, and reaped great rewards. Just as Courier established the inside forehand, Agassi the swinging volley, the Williams sisters the open stance backhand, and Nadal, the reverse forehand, the ODF, RS, and VS may need to be adopted by a highly ranked touring professional before gaining wide acceptance. But even if these strokes are a decade or more away from being taught, you don't have to wait — you can be a trailblazer and start today.

COACH'S BOX:

There are many examples in sports where the traditional has given way to change, even though at the time it was a controversial decision. The case of Seattle Seahawks football punter Jon Ryan illustrates both the resistance to and benefits of a new idea. At the beginning of the 2013 season, after seven years in the NFL, Ryan altered his style of punting, adopting what he calls the "Aussie style approach" in short punt situations and began kicking the ball using end-over-end spin instead using the traditional "torpedo" spin. This change made his punts more accurate and resulted in only 28.4% of Ryan's punts being returned that year, the second best percentage in the league.[4]

Olympic sports have also changed their technique for the better — and sometimes radically — like for example in high jumping. Dick Fosbury was initially ridiculed when he changed the way of high jumping by inventing the "Fosbury Flop." The Fosbury Flop uses a head-first, back-to-bar method of high jumping that he pioneered and used to win the 1968 Olympic gold medal. Fosbury wasn't given a chance to win, but his courageous adoption

of a new idea gave him an edge to capture the gold medal that year. He said, "I guess it did look weird at first, but it felt so natural that, like all good ideas, you just wonder why no one thought of it before me."[5] It is a testimony to society's unwillingness to change and take risks, as well as its general belief that time tested techniques must be optimal and, therefore, rarely challenged. To spectators in 1968, the Fosbury Flop was bizarre, but looking back, it is his competitors using the scissors jump that look odd.

Here at the U.S. Open, like all the
Grand Slams, the singles tournament
is the marquee event for tennis fans.
A closely contested professional
singles match highlights not only the
players' fitness and skills, but also their
personalities and minds, making for
a true physical and cerebral drama.

CHAPTER 13

Singles

PROFESSIONAL PLAYERS SPEND A GREAT DEAL OF TIME watching and researching their peers, looking for any chink in their armor. Their coaches mine the large amounts of data now available, scouting their next opponent and looking for the slightest informational edge to help their player. For example, maybe the data shows that their next opponent likes to serve wide on the ad side break points. The extra split second of time that information provides on the return may increase their player's chances of breaking serve. In a close match, a small tactical advantage like this can be the difference between winning and losing.

On the professional tour, opponent tendencies are often nuanced and deficiencies subtle. But at the recreational level, these characteristics are easier to identify and successful recreational players know how to exploit them. During rallies, they chose the right shot given the circumstances, and in between points, they contemplate the most effective tactics to improve their chances of victory. Drawing the correct conclusions at these junctures requires not only a thorough knowledge of tennis, but also an awareness of your strengths and weaknesses and being observant to those same qualities in your opponent.

In this chapter, I will explain these various tactical components of the game to help you win. I begin with advice on how to skillfully move through the four phases of play, attain optimal court positioning, establish winning shot patterns, and increase your opponents' mistakes while limiting your own. I then provide game plans on how to defeat defensive and aggressive opponents. Next, I help you ask the right questions and give direction on how to make strategic adjustments during a match. I finish the chapter with some suggestions for drills to spark your singles practice sessions.

I. The Four Phases of Play

PLAYING SMART TACTICAL TENNIS means making the right shot choices during the "four phases of play" that occur during a rally: the offensive, building, neutral, and defensive phases.

On some points, a strong serve or powerful return will see you begin the rally in the offensive phase, where you will hopefully stay. On the other hand, if you are receiving a fast serve you may start the point in the defensive phase and then attempt to transition to a more favorable one. For most recreational players, whose serve and return usually is not dominant, most points begin in the neutral phase and then proceed up and down the phases from there.

During a rally you might start in the offensive phase and then your opponent hits a great defensive shot and the complexion of the point changes. When that happens, you must reset and not blindly continue playing offensively just because you once had control of the point. To shift sensibly between the phases, you sometimes need to be patient and resolute. At other times, you need to be alert and ready to pounce.

It is important to be aware of how the point is progressing through the phases to know the appropriate height, speed, and spin to use on your shot. Because different shots are needed in different phases, players with versatility in their strokes have the advantage in moving fluently between the phases over those who do not. For example, players that lack power on their forehand may get stuck in the neutral or building phase, or a player without a quality slice forehand may have a hard time moving from the defensive phase to the neutral one. Also, because many factors influence the way you transition through the four phases, includ-ing the way you mesh with your opponent, court positioning, and court surface, having different stroke options can help you use the most effective tactical response to these factors in each phase.

Naturally, because everyone plays different-ly, all the phases have exceptions and "gray" areas. For example, an aggressive player like Serena Williams moves through the phases very differently than a counter-puncher like Caroline Wozniacki. Also, a player with a solid all-round game and no obvious weapons or weaknesses should construct points more pa-tiently than a player with greater variability in

Serena Williams is a player who seeks to enter the offensive phase quickly during a rally. Here, she is in her element pouncing on a high ball in front of the service line.

stroke abilities. To move through the phases successfully, you need to analyze your game and adhere to the level of aggression and length of point that best helps you win.

Here are more detailed descriptions of each phase and suggestions to consider as you move through them on the court.

1. OFFENSIVE PHASE

The offensive phase occurs when you have ample time to set up your shot, good ball height, and favorable court position. The offensive phase from the baseline usually happens on slower, shorter balls that bounce above the waist, where you use a faster, flatter groundstroke. Good examples of offensive phase shots are a powerful inside-out or in-

side-in forehand hit from in front of the baseline. Other examples are when a scrambling opponent sets you up for a winning volley or a big serve that leads to a weak return and a promising attack situation.

All these circumstances represent offensive phase scenarios that you should look for and capitalize on. It is important to take advantage of these "green light" situations when they arise because the opportunity may not happen again during the rally. An offensive opportunity squandered may reverse itself and eventually end with your opponent taking command.

A common mistake players make is attempting an aggressive shot when they are not actually in the offensive phase. Don't at-

The inside-out forehand is a shot often used by players in the offensive phase of a rally.

tempt an aggressive shot if you don't have the offensive phase ingredients of ample time, good ball height, and favorable court positioning. Hitting an offensive shot when you lack any one of these elements is low percentage tennis. **First**, limited time usually results in a lack of racquet control caused by being rushed. **Second**, low balls must be treated with respect because of the height of the net and the limited effect gravity has on a two ounce tennis ball. **Third**, attempting a winning shot from a deep court position makes little sense because your opponent has plenty of time to react to your shot. Smart offensive tennis requires discipline; the trick is not to force it unnecessarily. If you build the point well, the offensive phase will present itself in good time, and when it does, lock onto it.

2. BUILDING PHASE

The building phase of a point occurs when you are moving your opponent around the court, forcing them off balance and setting up the rally for the offensive phase. Your ideal mindset here can be described in two words: controlled aggression.

It depends on your skill level and the court surface, but a typical building phase shot is characterized by hitting the ball two to three feet above the net and three to five feet inside the lines while positioned near the baseline. The most common way to build a point in this phase is by hitting with power or depth, but it can also be achieved with slower shots, like a short, cross-court topspin angle, or even a drop shot.

A player with strong building shots can exhaust their opponent by running them from side to side of the court. One of the defining aspects of Nadal's heavy topspin game is the high percentage way he plays his building

During the neutral phase, mix up the spin, speed, and height of your shots to upset your opponent's timing.

shots and fatigues his opponent. His shots have the net clearance of a safe neutral shot but the speed and spin of an offensive building shot. This unique combination of qualities in his baseline shots demoralizes opponents and contributes greatly to his success.

3. NEUTRAL PHASE

The neutral phase occurs when neither player has an advantage and usually represents a large part of baseline play at any level. This phase is distinguished by shots hit with good net clearance with both players hitting from a similar court position.

A typical neutral phase shot is hit deep towards the middle of the court. This type of shot will cut down your errors and allow you to rally well with the hopes of hitting more offensively later in the point. While hitting towards the middle of the court, you can use variations in spin, speed, or height to disrupt your opponent's timing, leading to a weak shot from them that allows you to transition from the neutral phase into building an attack.

One of the keys to playing well in the neutral phase is finding the correct rallying speed. Often, I see players practicing at a rallying speed that's too fast and then playing their matches at a rallying speed much slower than their practice. Obviously, this defeats the purpose of practice. It takes concentration and discipline to practice the rallying speed that you will use in the match.

Every player's rallying speed in the neutral phase will be slightly different depending on their skills. I tell my students the right neutral shot "speed limit" is determined by the velocity at which the player can hit ten consecutive shots in the court with confidence. Remember, playing consistently results in playing victoriously. Players who are sometimes derided and called "pushers" know their skill level and are actually playing intelligently. They rally in the neutral phase at the right speed in accordance with their skills: that's smart tennis.

4. DEFENSIVE PHASE

The defensive phase is the least appealing phase of a point, but it is an important part of the game. The defensive phase occurs when you are rushed, off balance, or positioned deep behind the baseline. Your goal with the defensive shot is to buy time, neutralize the point, and then hopefully build up to an offensive situation.

The lob, high topspin groundstroke, and slice groundstroke on a wide baseline shot are good examples of defensive strokes. These strokes all have slower ball speeds to provide you time to return to the middle of the baseline. The slice "squash shot" (*see page 109*) done on wide balls has gained in popularity

> ### COACH'S BOX:
>
> **Playing defensive shots well requires being agile and athletic enough to control the racquet when you're in trouble. The improved athleticism of the players on the professional tour has corresponded with a marked improvement in their defensive skills. Modern professionals are stretching and contorting their bodies to allow them to extend points in ways rarely seen in the past. Consequently, the ability to play quality defensive shots has seen a big jump in its influence on a player's likelihood of winning a match. In fact, it could be argued that players like Andy Murray owe as much of their success to superb defensive skills as their talent for crushing winners.**

as the defensive shot of choice at the higher levels of the game because of the faster speed it creates compared to other defensive options. The introduction of the swinging volley has made the slow, loopy shot a less attractive defensive option for the professionals, but it is still a viable tactic at the recreational level.

Hitting deep down the middle also can help turn the tables when you're facing a defensive situation. Hitting deep will force your opponent to hit from behind the baseline, allowing you time to recover, and hitting down the middle will reduce the angles for your opponent to run you around the court. If you have gotten the point back to neutral after being in a defensive situation, don't be in a rush to get to the offensive phase. You may be out of sorts from playing defensive shots and need a shot or two in the neutral phase to regain your composure and rhythm.

II. Court Positioning

HOW QUICKLY YOU MOVE TO THE BEST location on the court during the different phases is an important part of the game. You must be flexible with your court positioning and move forward when you can, backward when needed, and right or left to best cover the angles.

If you are able to move forward and play closer to the baseline than your opponent, they will be covering more ground and have less time to prepare for their shot. Often this will result in the rally tilting in your favor simply because of where you are standing on the court.

You should move forward several steps following a strong groundstroke, especially if your opponent is going to be rushed or off balance playing their shot (*below*). By moving forward a couple of steps, you will get a jump start on your next shot and give your opponent less time to recover. Recognize that you will stand closer to the baseline in a more aggressive court position on hard courts than on the slower clay courts.

Everyone loves to play offense, but there will be times when defense is required and you should move backwards away from the baseline. For example, if you hit a weak short ball and your opponent is about to unload on a forehand, moving back will buy you an extra split second of time to defend the court and extend the point. Or, if your opponent hits a high ball, instead of staying forward and hitting the ball on the rise above your shoulder, it is often the smart play to move back from the baseline and allow the ball to drop to a comfortable height and hit a high topspin ball back to your opponent (*opposite bottom*).

Court positioning is also important during a baseline rally where neither player has a distinct advantage and the ball is moving laterally around the court. If you are hitting cross court to your opponent, position yourself slightly on the same side as you are hitting. This will place you in the midpoint of your opponent's angles. For example, after hitting a cross-court backhand that pulls your opponent left of the singles line, you should position yourself three or four feet left of the

If you see your opponent scrambling, move forward.

center hash mark (*next page*). If you hit the backhand down the line, you should move quickly a couple of feet to the right side of the center hash mark to be positioned in the mid-point of your opponent's possible cross-court or down-the-line shot. Interestingly, when looking at a match from a bird's eye view, it becomes obvious how tennis is game of geometry and the importance of placing oneself in the middle of angles becomes clearer.

1. COURT POSITIONING AND TACTICS

Court positioning also plays an important tactical role in your matches. If you have a game plan that emphasizes getting to the net, then you may position yourself closer to the baseline to enhance your chances of coming forward to volley. You can serve from different positions to make use of your weapons or make it easier to angle your serve to your opponent's weakness. For example, by serving a few feet to the right of the center hash mark on the ad side, you will get a better angle to

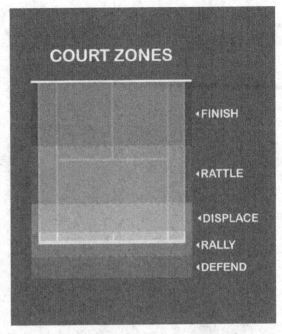

The purpose of your shot will vary depending on your court positioning. There are five main zones. 1. Finish — hit winners, 2. Rattle — hit to rush your opponent, 3. Displace — hit to move your opponent away from the middle of the baseline, 4. Rally — hit with patience, and 5. Defend — hit to buy time.

Federer backs up to make use of his powerful forehand and hit the ball at a more comfortable height.

The player at the opposite baseline is correctly positioned left-of-center at the midpoint of his opponent's angles.

aim your serve to the right hander's backhand as well as opening more of the court to your forehand. Your positioning on the return of serve can also have a powerful effect on your strategy. You can position yourself several feet inside the baseline and go for an outright winner on the return or come forward to attack the net immediately following the return. Or, if you believe your chances of winning the point are better by engaging your opponent in a long rally, you can return serve from well behind the baseline to allow yourself more time to return serve and neutralize the serving advantage.

Court positioning can sometimes take precedence over hitting to an opponent's weak-

ness. For example, serving out wide on the deuce side to a player's forehand may open up the court and allow you to control court position, even though your opponent's forehand may be their strength. Serving towards the center line to the backhand on the deuce side may be a play to their weaker stroke but do little to hurt your opponent's court positioning. Furthermore, sometimes it is tactically savvy to hit aggressively to your opponent's strength and weaken their court positioning, thereby opening up the court to then hit to your opponent's weakness on the next shot. For example, hitting a cross-court forehand return of serve from the deuce side to your opponent's forehand will enhance your ability to attack their backhand on your next shot. Throughout the match, you must constantly evaluate the best shot, weighing your opponent's weakness versus court positioning. This can change during the course of a match as a stroke may improve or deteriorate, or fatigue might make the court positioning factor a stronger consideration.

III. Shot Patterns

YOUR REPERTOIRE OF SHOT PATTERNS is a major strategic building block — that is, predetermined, high percentage sequences of shots. Champion players have shot patterns that make the best use of their strongest strokes. For instance, Federer uses his slice backhand to keep the ball low and move his opponent inside the baseline and then uses his forehand weapon to hit deep to the open corner. One of Djokovic's many talents is his ability to change the direction of cross-court shots by driving the ball down the line and get his opponent scrambling. Murray's superior groundstroke finesse allows him to play more short slices to pull opponents forward to the net and force them to defend his precise passing shots. Federer's slice backhand, Djokovic's stroke change of direction, and Murray's finesse are all personalized weapons which they have developed into distinctive winning shot patterns.

A player's level of success is greatly influenced by how their favorite shot patterns match up with their opponent. For instance, consider the pairing of Nadal's cross-court forehand to Federer's one-handed backhand: Nadal's high topspin creates an awkward contact point for Federer's one-handed backhand, often forcing him to hit a defensive slice and allowing Nadal to take control of the point. However, the match up of Nadal's cross-court

forehand to Djokovic's two-handed backhand works in reverse. The high bounce of Nadal's topspin creates a contact point that Djokovic enjoys. Djokovic can take Nadal's cross-court forehand and power his backhand down the line, causing the Spaniard to play a rushed backhand of his own and lose control of the point. Indeed at any level of singles, you can find examples of a player who defeats one opponent consistently and loses to another opponent consistently, but when those two opponents play each other, the results are even; such is the impact of shot patterns on the out-

Djokovic's success against Nadal can be partly attributed to the fact that Nadal's cross-court forehand often results in a chest-high contact point on his backhand — a contact height Djokovic enjoys.

An Analysis of 702 shots (87% Backhands)

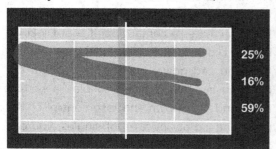

25%

16%

59%

An Analysis of 309 shots (100% Forehands)

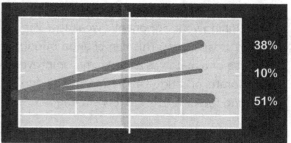

38%

10%

51%

Nishikori shot charts: In the first shot chart (*left*) we can deduce that Nishikori favors the cross-court backhand. In the second shot chart (*right*) we see he likes to hit his forehand down the line. This shot often "funnels" the rally back to his favorite shot pattern: the cross-court backhand rally. [1]

come of a match.

Professional players now have access to in-depth shot charts that provide highly useful information on their next opponent's shot patterns. Analyzing the shot charts, it becomes clear what shot patterns the pros think work best for them. Above are two shot charts of Kei Nishikori's play over a period of six months in 2014-15. Looking at his chart, it is clear that Nishikori believes the backhand cross-court pattern works in his favor (*above left*). He also embraces the down-the-line forehand (*above right*). Nishikori knows the likely response from his opponent to his down-the-line forehand is a cross-court backhand, which gives Nishikori the option of establishing his favorite shot pattern — the cross-court backhand rally.

You too should analyze your game and establish successful, repetitive shot patterns that revolve around maximizing your best shots. Keep in mind that occasionally, winning a match might mean using a sequence that is not your favorite shot pattern; however, because it troubles your opponent it might be a smart shot sequence for that particular match. Irrespective of whether a specific shot pattern is used frequently or not, the point is, as

in chess, you should think a shot or two ahead during the rally and hit your shots with purpose and a sequence in mind.

THE CROSS-COURT SHOT PATTERN AND HITTING DOWN-THE-LINE

Most shot patterns in tennis involve some cross-court hitting from the baseline. Hitting cross-court is the primary direction in a baseline rally due to the benefits of better court positioning, a lower net, a longer court, and a swing path that produces a bigger hip rotation for added power.

Early in the match, learn which cross-court rally (forehand or backhand) favors your strength or attacks your opponent's weakness and then quickly figure out the type of serve, return of serve, or sequence of shots that steer the rally into that cross-court scenario. Once you are involved in a favorable cross-court rally, do your best to stay in it. If the reverse is true, then you should be looking to change the pattern by hitting down-the-line. Using the inside-in or inside-out forehand, approach shot, or even a drop shot are other ways to break an unfavorable cross-court shot pattern.

Because of its shorter distance, the down-the-line groundstroke can be an effective offensive shot when positioned inside the baseline.

Generally speaking, it makes sense to hit down the line when you are positioned reasonably close to the baseline and have ample time to set up for the shot (*above*). The down-the-line shot has the advantage of shorter distance and, therefore, less time for your opponent to defend the shot. However, you must choose when to play a down the line shot judiciously. One that's poorly hit can open the door for your opponent to hit cross court — a diagonal shot that can force long lateral movement — and turn the point against you. On most occasions, if you are deep behind the baseline or rushed, play your shot safely cross court, and if you are inside the baseline and have time, hit your shot aggressively down the line.

IV. Mistake Management

YOUR STRATEGIC FOCUS should always be to play in a manner that keeps your errors to a minimum. The ratio of errors to winners for most recreational players is greater than three to one. Therefore, improving your skills or shot selection to decrease errors will have a much larger impact on your chances of victory than increasing winners at the same rate. Most players know this, but even so, when they come to me for advice, one of their first questions often is, "How do I hit more winners?" There's no question hitting winners is fun, but they usually don't have an impact on the outcome of most matches.

I. REDUCING YOUR ERRORS

At the recreational level, the defensive players that do the best job at limiting their errors often have the greatest success. They win because they concentrate on the correct side of the point ledger and therefore play with the power of numbers on their side. Below are seven ways to reduce your errors.

A. PLAY WITH GOOD NET CLEARANCE BY VISUALIZING YOUR TARGET

The net is enemy number one for tennis players so hit your baseline shots with "shape" and well above the net. Hitting low over the net will not only result in more errors into the net, but also less depth on your shots and a more comfortable height for your opponent to play their strokes.

To help your shot clear the net, it is important to visualize its trajectory as you are setting up for the swing. You should always have a target in mind for the trajectory of your shot, in addition to its speed and depth. In my experience, too many players are vague in their shot intentions, and consequently, their shots lack the height to clear the net consistently. Remember, the body performs better when the mind provides a clear purpose; accomplish this and your aim will be more likely to be true.

> **COACH'S BOX:**
>
> It is important to be aware that psychologically, because you can see *through* the net, it seems less threatening. Consequently, you may become less conscious of the real impediment posed by the net. Studies have shown that when the net is covered with blankets, players hit into the net substantially less. Next time you play, imagine the net is not a net but a brick wall. This will help reinforce the importance of clearing the net by a good margin and reduce your errors.

B. HIT WELL INSIDE THE SINGLES SIDELINES, ESPECIALLY IF YOU ARE NOT CONTROLLING THE POINT

Aiming your shot close to the singles sidelines during the neutral or defensive phase usually won't change the dynamic of the point, but it will increase the chances of making a mistake. The risk/reward trade-off is not worth it. Not only that, but it can also give your opponents more angles to work with and allow them to move you more easily around the court from side to side. In most situations, it is only during the building or offensive phase that aiming your shot closer to the singles sidelines makes strategic sense.

C. MAINTAIN QUALITY FOOTWORK AND GOOD FOOT SPEED

Mistakes often result from being too close or far away from the ball during the swing. By using the correct steps before the swing, you will obtain proper spacing to the ball and swing with the balance needed for consistent contact. Also, good foot speed will allow you more time to set up for your shot and ground your feet for improved racquet control.

D. USE OF SPIN

Topspin gives you the ability to hit with good net clearance and backspin improves consistency by increasing ball control.

E. BE SELF-AWARE

Some errors occur because players try shots that are not high percentage options given their skills and ability. Don't depend on divine intervention as you attempt to hit a running forehand six inches inside the line at 80 miles an hour, like the one you saw Djokovic do on television the night before. Be realistic about your capabilities and play shots you know you can perform reliably.

F. DEVELOP SUPERIOR MENTAL TOUGHNESS AND PHYSICAL FITNESS

You sometimes see players get upset, lose concentration, and play frustrated low per-

Powerful running forehands that skim the net are best left to the pros.

centage tennis. Train yourself to stay in a positive emotional state and play high percentage tennis every point. Also, if you are not physically fit, you are more likely to play a risky shot in an attempt to end the point quickly; this often results in an error.

G. BE PATIENT

Some players hit several shots and feel like they need to do something special because their shot "quota" has been met. Raise your shot tolerance and pick your spots to be aggressive wisely.

2. INDUCING OPPONENT ERRORS

While a main focus of any game plan is to limit your own errors, you should also look for ways to induce your opponent to make more errors. Remember most of the points you win in a match are going to be from your opponent's forced and unforced errors (roughly half forced and a quarter unforced), so always be looking for openings that make hitting the ball difficult for them. Below are six ways to induce more errors from your opponent.

A. USE DIFFERENT SPEEDS AND SPINS

Don't let your opponent establish a confident rhythm by sending them a ball that consistently arrives at a similar speed and spin. By giving your opponent different shot speeds, they have to adjust their body movement and and swing velocity to create power, and varying the spin on your shot can cause opponent misfires by changing the speed, flight trajectory, and height of the bounce. Tennis is an exact game. Upsetting the timing of your opponent's swing by even a tenth of a second can lead to an error or a weak shot that you can attack.

After defending this difficult corner shot, Angelique Kerber is likely to find herself behind in the point.

B. VARY THE HEIGHT OF SHOT

Most players like a waist-high contact point. Instead, force your opponents to hit shots at an uncomfortable height above the shoulders or below their knees.

C. UTILIZE CORNER SHOTS

By hitting towards a baseline corner, you are able to move your opponents from side to side, forcing them to hit off balance and increasing the likelihood of them making an error.

D. COVER THE COURT WELL

Returning ball after ball with good court coverage and hustle will frustrate opponents and lead them to make poor decisions on shot choices. Superior foot speed will often lead to more mistakes from your opponents as they aim closer and closer to the lines to try to win the point.

E. BE CONSISTENT

If you are consistent and show your opponent a dogged determination to keep the ball in play, you will often succeed in coaxing your opponent into an error. After engaging and winning several long rallies, you will often find your opponent becomes eager to pull the trigger on a risky shot and makes a mistake.

F. HIT DEEP

Hitting deep gives your opponents less time to set up for their shot off the ball's bounce, increasing the likelihood they'll mistime the shot or rush their swing. Remember the three keys to superior shot depth - hit "through" the ball and use good extension through contact, give your shot good shape by hitting well above the net, and visualize a deep target in the court.

V. Game Plans

TENNIS IS A BEAUTIFULLY DESIGNED GAME. The size of the court, the height of the net, and the weight of the ball results in no one "right" way to play. You have many strategic options available to you and learning to develop a winning game plan during matches means processing the choices and selecting the right one (or two).

A smart game plan can sometimes lead you

COACH'S BOX:

Some players fail to hit deep because depth perception tricks them, making the space behind the service line seem smaller than it really is. For example, if you are standing on the baseline and looking to the opposite side of the court at one ball placed on the service line and another ball placed on the baseline, it would appear there is little room between the two balls. But if you were to view those same two balls from the side you would see the two balls are actually 18 feet apart. Don't let the depth perception "illusion" dissuade you from hitting the ball deeper and higher over the net.

Hitting deep is such an important factor to winning baseline rallies that I never get upset with my students if they hit a shot with the appropriate speed, height, and spin for the circumstances, but the ball lands a foot beyond the baseline. If the goal is to hit four or five feet inside the baseline, which of the following two shots is more accurate: the shot lands that lands 15 feet inside the baseline or the shot that lands one foot past the baseline? One could argue the latter is closer to the goal.

---

to victories over more skilled opponents. It was definitely an important factor in my best win on the professional tour. I was a successful U.S. college player, but found the leap to the pros a big one. The opponent I defeated was Paul Kilderry, a gifted professional player who went on to win several ATP doubles titles and earn a spot on the Australian Davis Cup Team. During the warm-up with Kilderry, it became obvious to me that this was a guy I didn't want to get into extended baseline rallies with. His groundstrokes were powerful, deep, accurate, and superior to mine. I decided in the warm-up that on my return of serve and during the rally following my serve, I was going to slice my forehand and backhand short and low in the court and move forward to volley as much as possible. It was an unusual strategy, not the "right" way to play, but it did make use of one my strengths (slice groundstrokes) and expose one of his few weaknesses (short, low balls). In front of a team of national selectors and a group of my surprised peers, I won a tightly contested first set. The second set was easier as I served well and his level of frustration continued to rise as the prospect of losing became a reality. My game plan, combined with the good fortune of my having a terrific day and him a bad one (an influential element of the game and good reason why you should always go into a match against a higher ranked opponent with a positive attitude) led to one of my most satisfying wins. The key takeaway here is, in any match up, there will be ways to exploit your opponent's weaknesses or better utilize your strengths to give yourself an advantage; sometimes small adjustments or insights will be the deciding factor in winning the match.

Choosing and employing the game plan that gives you that advantage comes largely from being observant of your opponent's likes and dislikes, in addition to cultivating a deep understanding of oneself. In fact, the first step in developing a smart game plan should be to sit down with a pen and paper and write out your strengths and weaknesses. It is only through self-awareness that you can know how to play your matches intelligently.

It is important to note, if you can execute a game plan that gives you a small edge, you should be in good shape. Statistically, in a match that lasts 100 points, winning 55 points

A small edge can be huge in tennis. Nadal won "only" 56.7% of the points he played en route to winning eight French Opens.

of these points will allow you to win the majority of the time. For example, when Nadal dominated the French Open from 2005-2014, winning the title eight times in nine years and compiling an incredible 59-1 record, what do you suppose was his winning percentage of points played? 60, 65, 70%? No, Nadal won "just" 56.7% of the points he played. [2] Another revealing statistic shows how fine the margins are between winning and losing in tennis. Between 2014 and 2015, Djokovic raised his percentage of points won in matches by just one percent. In 2014, he won 61 matches. In 2015, he won 82 matches (and an extra seven million dollars). [3]

With the margins in tennis often being so fine, game plans are crucial, but so are winning the so-called "big" points. All points are worth the same value and therefore all are important, but because certain points have a larger scoring and psychological impact than others, some carry more weight. For example, if you are ahead 4-3, 30-40 receiving serve and win that point, you are ahead 5-3 and serving for the set. Lose it, and you may soon be facing 4-4 and an even match. Break points, tiebreak points, 30-30, and deuce points at the end of a close set are decisive junctures that the pros point to from the locker room as having decided a close match. I also believe the 15-30 stage of a game is particularly important. If you are receiving serve at 15-30 and win that point, you have double break point; lose it, and the game is tied.

Through statistics, we can see the influence that "big points" can have on a professional match. During the 2016 U.S. Open men's final between Stan Wawrinka and Novak Djokovic, Wawrinka won 6 of 10 of his break points while Djokovic won just 3 of 17. Even though the point tally was almost identical (144 to

143 in Wawrinka's favor) Wawrinka won 30% more games (25 to 19) on his way to victory in a well-fought but reasonably comfortable four set match.[4] So when a big point arrives in your matches, remind yourself to raise your focus and intensity and execute your game plan to the very best of your ability.

Most players you compete against will fall in the middle of the aggressive play spectrum. Therefore, as discussed earlier in the chapter, your strategic focus is moving through the four phases wisely, making the right court positioning moves, establishing successful shot patterns, and reducing and inducing mistakes. However, you will also compete against players

Winning a much higher percentage of break points than Djokovic helped Stan Wawrinka win the 2016 U.S. Open.

who are particularly defensive or particularly aggressive. Against such players, the focus remains largely the same but there are several other strategic tips to consider that can help you develop a winning game plan.

1. DEFEATING A DEFENSIVE PLAYER

Anyone who has played a decent amount of competitive tennis has run into the defensive player. This type of player doesn't possess power but wins by keeping the ball safely in the court and playing very consistent tennis. These players can be a dread to play, and it can be tempting to try thumping the ball past them. However, this is low percentage tennis and unlikely to lead you to victory. You must be appropriately patient and understand that you may have to work the point harder than usual before receiving the right ball to dispatch.

Psychologically, some competitors find it hard to understand how they are unable to easily defeat players who hit the ball without power. Defensive players often rely on this frustration to help them win the match. It is part of their strategy. They feed off negative energy, so if you can suppress pessimistic emotions, you will deny them their desired mental edge. The right approach is to acknowledge that even though these players have few weapons, they can be difficult opponents to defeat and deserve respect. You should be mentally prepared and appreciate the fact that you are likely to be engaged in a competitive battle.

Below are five tactics to consider for your game plan when playing a defensive player.

A. USE DROP SHOTS

Defensive players feel at home when planted at the baseline. Therefore, bringing them forward with frequent drop shots to make them play the net can make them uneasy and ineffective. Additionally, the slower speed of their shot makes it easier to set up a good drop shot more often, even if it means hitting from a position deeper in the court than usual for you.

B. FORCE SIDE-TO-SIDE MOVEMENT

Defensive players don't hit with pace and this allows you the time to place your shots accurately towards the baseline corners. Corner shots will get them moving from side to side across the court and test their endurance. This tactic may not reap big rewards early in the match, but as the match progresses it can pay handsome dividends. Don't always be in a rush to end the point if you have them running side-to-side. If they lack superior fitness and don't possess the power to bail themselves out of a defensive situation, you can safely run them around for a few more shots to exhaust them a little more before finishing the point.

Also, keep in mind that defensive players

Attacking the net can be an effective tactic against a defensive player.

typically pride themselves in recovering quickly to the middle of the baseline after returning a corner shot. Such players are good candidates to "wrong foot," that is, hitting the ball back to the same corner from where they are recovering. Their fast recovery can make it difficult to stop quickly and change directions to return a ball hit in the same corner twice in a row.

C. ATTACK THE NET

Defensive players don't like to be hurried, so if you can use your net game, you are forcing them out of their rhythm and preferred tempo of play. They typically don't hit the ball hard, so there is a high probability you will have a play on their passing shot. Here, the swinging volley can be a very useful shot. Using the swing volley to attack their high groundstrokes will force them to hit lower and faster and result in more mistakes.

D. USE SPIN AND ANGLES

Against defensive players, don't be seduced by the allure of trying to hit flat winners all the time. Their ball will lack pace, and using topspin and backspin is a key way of controlling your shots and playing with consistency. The slower speed of this player's shot may be difficult to generate power from, but it makes for a comfortable speed to play angled cross-court topspin shots to open up the court. Well-executed building shots such as these will lead you to many winning offensive situations.

E. CHANGE COURT POSITION

As mentioned, playing more drop shots and attacking the net are key strategies, so playing closer to or even inside the baseline can make strategic sense as it increases the effectiveness of these two strategies.

2. DEFEATING A POWER PLAYER

Tennis has become faster and more aggressive, and power hitters, players who seek to keep the point short by hitting deep and fast, have become more common than ever before.

These players thrive on pace. If you hit with pace, you will line the ball up in their favorite strike zone, making it comfortable for them to replay with equal (or more) velocity. For example, Serena Williams, an offensive player, accumulated an 18 match winning streak against five-time Grand Slam champion Maria Sharapova partly because she enjoys the regularity of Maria's flat, fast strokes. On the other hand, when Serena played Monica Niculescu at the 2015 BNP Paribas Open, it was evident how much Serena dislikes the slower paced ball. Niculescu's slow slice forehand caused Serena to rack up 48 errors as she struggled to beat the 68th ranked player in the world.[5]

Below are six tactics to consider when up against a power player.

Monica Niculescu's slow slice forehand has been known to trouble the power hitters on the WTA Tour.

A. USE DIFFERENT SPINS AND SPEEDS

Power hitters enjoy an incoming shot that is waist high with good speed and little spin. Make life difficult for them by feeding them plenty of high, slow topspin shots. This forces them to generate their own pace, and the higher bounce will get the ball out of their ideal contact height.

Slice shots can be effective too. The backspin of a slice shot produces a slower, lower bounce and forces the power hitters out of their preferred speed and strike zone. The low bounce means they must arc the ball into the court, reducing their ability to hit hard. Also, the slice groundstroke is easier to control and hit accurately very deep or very short in the court. This moves them up and back when playing shots and limits the time available to establish the necessary balance for a powerful shot.

The type of forehand grip your power hitting opponent uses will play a role in what spin to use more frequently. For example, if they use a western grip, then you should use slice shots more often. The low bounce of slice shots creates an awkward height for such opponents since the western grip hand position is better suited to higher bouncing balls. On the other hand, if your opponent uses an eastern grip, which is suited to a lower bounce, then the high topspin shot should be hit more often.

B. ATTACK THE STRENGTH FIRST

Sometimes the easiest way to attack a power player's weakness is by attacking their strength first. For example, assuming the forehand is your opponent's power shot, aggres-

Power players often like to move left to hit forehands, leaving an open court for the down-the-line backhand.

sively hitting your forehand cross court will open up the right side of the court to attack your opponent's backhand.

C. HIT THE DOWN-THE-LINE BACKHAND

Power hitters often try to dominate play by moving to the left side of the court to hit big inside forehand to their opponents' backhand (*above*). A good down-the-line backhand in response to an inside forehand will force your opponents to move quickly to the right and play a rushed stroke.

D. ATTACK THE NET

Power hitters typically don't use a lot of top-spin. Therefore, they are less skilled at dipping the ball at a net player's feet or hitting a sharply angled cross-court passing shot. Also, they usually don't lob frequently, allowing you to move forward aggressively and obtain good net positioning.

E. BE TENACIOUS

Remember a tennis match is a long jog, not a sprint, so don't be discouraged if a power player hits a series of flashy winners. Being tenacious and unflappable will often frustrate them and tempt them to try riskier shots, tilting the odds in your favor.

F. CHANGE COURT POSITIONING

Moving further back from the baseline allows you more time to defend power shots and lengthen the point. Power hitters don't play a high percentage brand of tennis, so with every ball you return, the probability that they will make an error increases more than when playing other opponents.

VI. Strategic Questions and Adjustments

SOMETIMES YOU WILL KNOW your opponent and can establish a game plan before the match. But often you will not know your opponent and need to develop a strategy quickly during the match. To do this well, you must ask and answer specific strategic questions. Even if you know your opponent, the court surface, weather conditions, and other intangibles can lead to unpredictability and these questions will need to be asked and answered.

Champion players ask these same questions in an effort to gain an advantage shot by shot, point by point, and match by match. Recently, I was watching a televised Federer-Djokovic match, and the commentator suggested that Federer would have more success by attacking the net more frequently. I thought to myself that there was little doubt that Roger is contemplating all his strategic choices, including attacking the net. I'm sure he was asking questions to himself regarding the speed of the court, the quality of Djokovic's passing shots, and his court positioning for approach shots, as well as many other factors throughout the match. Only after taking all these things into consideration would he make a determination of when and how best to attack the net.

Federer's adaptability to match circumstances and determining whether attacking the net was the right tactic was clearly evident during two matches he played at the 2015 ATP World Tour Finals. In two victories in matches of almost identical length, he came to the net nine times against Djokovic and 32 against Wawrinka.[6] During an interview after the Wawrinka match, he said he planned to attack

Federer versus Djokovic is a match between two very observant champion players with a keen sensitivity to all the objective variables (e.g. court speed and weather conditions) and subjective variables (e.g. confidence and timing) a tennis match brings.

the net but was prepared to make mid-match strategy adjustments depending on the success he had employing his net rushing tactic. We can all learn from Federer and be observant of our opponent's level and style of play to come up with the best strategy to win on *that* day.

Recreational players are sometimes too self-conscious and thus unaware of the signs and signals their opponent is sending about their abilities. If you are observant, you will notice that your opponent is telegraphing information that you can use to win. For example, during the warm-up take notice to see if your opponent is moving to the right or left to play their forehand and backhand. I've found that players are often nervous in the warm-up and like to hit their preferred groundstroke as much as possible. If you see your opponent warm up their volleys with a forehand-type grip, you can almost be guaranteed that player will stand too far to the left on the court to protect their backhand, and opportunities to hit through open spaces to the right are going to present themselves during the match. If you see your opponent lacks the ability to put good spin on their serve, be extra aggressive on your return. There's a good chance their serve will break down, especially their second serve, in a pressure situation. You should train yourself to be observant to the happenings on the court and remember it for present and future proceedings.

1. STRATEGIC QUESTIONS TO ANSWER

To determine the best strategy quickly, questions about your opponent's game need to be answered early in the match. Here are 16 questions to ask yourself as you dissect your opponent's game and establish your strategy:

1. What are your opponent's groundstroke strengths and weaknesses?
2. What are the typical depths, heights, speeds, and spins of your opponent's forehands and backhands?
3. How does your opponent respond to different depths, heights, speeds, and spins of your shots?
4. Where and how does your opponent prefer to hit their forehand and backhand?
5. Does your opponent prefer to hit their forehand moving to the right or left?
6. Do the forehand or backhand cross-court rallies work in your favor?
7. If the forehand or backhand cross-court rally doesn't work in your favor, how should you look to change that rally?
8. Does your opponent lose patience five, 10, or 15 shots into the rally?
9. What is your opponent's foot speed for reaching wide balls and drop shots?
10. Where does your opponent stand on the court for the return of serve, volleys, and during the baseline rally?
11. Where should you stand to serve and return serve and during a baseline rally?
12. Where and how does your opponent like to serve their first and second serve?
13. Where does your opponent like to return your first serve and second serve?
14. How well does your opponent lob?
15. What is your opponent's ability at net?
16. What is your opponent's level of mental toughness and physical fitness?

2. STRATEGIC ADJUSTMENTS

As the match progresses, you will be able to answer these questions with increased confidence and develop a full profile of your opponent's abilities. From this profile try to establish and then place firmly in your mind one or two tactics you think will be particularly effective — keep it simple. The clearer you are with your strategy, the better your decision-making will be in the course of a rally, resulting in smarter shot selection. On the other hand, strategy indecisiveness will lead to missed opportunities and overly ambitious mistakes.

After the first set, assess the situation again and make adjustments to the strategy if necessary. If you are winning, stay focused and consistent with the shot patterns and level of aggression that gave you the lead. For instance, think of Nadal's straight set victory over Federer at the Australian Open in 2014, which saw him serve 92% of his first serves to

Federer's backhand.[7] Rafa saw the winning results of that tactic and stayed with it. Attacking an opponent's weak stroke repeatedly will usually go one of two ways. The stroke will crumble, or the repetition will help it, so be observant and decide during the match whether it is best to stay relentless or mix up your shots more.

If you are losing, slow the pace of the match

Nadal stayed with a winning serving tactic in defeating Federer at the 2014 Australian Open.

COACH'S BOX:

It takes many competitive matches over a considerable period of time to become strategically astute and make the right decisions on the court. Take, for example, two well-known strategies in tennis: the battering ram and the punisher. The battering ram strategy involves hitting to an opponent's weakness time and time again — a good tactic when the opponent has an obvious weakness. The punisher strategy refers to the tactic of relentlessly moving an opponent around the court from side to side and up and back a good tactic against a player who moves poorly or lacks endurance.

Deciding which of the two strategies to employ and to what degree to use it against each opponent takes a good amount of match experience. Against the same opponent, you may use the battering ram on a fast court surface and the punisher on a slow court surface or vice versa. You may even use both strategies over the course of the same match; the battering ram early, and then if repetition is starting to groove the weakness or the opponent is becoming tired, you may end the match focused on executing shots that force the opponent to move the most.

down by taking a little more time between points and employ a different tactic that might turn the match around. That might mean raising the level of aggression and aiming faster shots more towards the lines. This style of play paid off for Federer when he defeated Nadal to win the 2017 Australian Open. He told himself, "Be free in your shots. Go for it. The brave will be rewarded here."[8] He swung freely, particularly on the backhand side, and the short aggressive rallies worked in his favor. Or the opposite style of play and hitting the ball higher and down the middle may be the smart tactical choice. Sometimes you may have the right strategy but not the right execution, and what is needed is greater focus and intensity rather than a change of strategy.

Because these strategic decisions often

aren't obvious, experience is important. Compete as much as possible to hone your decision-making. It is only with accrued match experience that you will be able to quickly assess opponents' strengths and weaknesses, understand your own strengths and weaknesses better, and deduce what strategy will work best for you in response to all the match variables. Play practice matches against a variety of playing styles, including aggressive net rushers, all-court players, and defensive baseline players. Mixing up your style of opponent will help you learn what shot patterns work best and how your skills match up against different types of players. Also, play practice matches against better, equal, and less skilled players than yourself. You can gain tactical knowledge by competing against players of varying abilities. Lastly, one's memory can be temporary, so keep a logbook and write down your experiences after each match and review and draw from them in the future.

VII. Singles Practice

TO PRACTICE WELL FOR SINGLES, you need to do what the professionals do: that is, practice with little difference from your level of intensity in matches. Professionals are fully committed to applying themselves on every shot because they know that the way they practice translates into how they will play in matches.

U.S. Open doubles champion Bethanie Mattek-Sands subscribes to this maxim; it was something I observed in her game when she was just 12 years old. Early in my career, I was part of a coaching team working with some of the best juniors in the world, of which Mattek-Sands was one. There were many parts

of her game that impressed, but what stood out most to me was the professional way she practiced. She always came to practice prepared and with purpose, and during practice, she applied tremendous focus and effort on every shot. I remember thinking that this girl, equipped with these strong practice habits to go along with her natural ability, had a good chance at succeeding on the professional tour, and she did. In contrast to Bethanie, I often see recreational players practicing in second or third gear. If you practice with low intensity, that is what your body and mind will be familiar with and you will be unprepared for a tough competitive match.

Also, wise tennis players use the experience of recent matches and come prepared for practice. They plan their practice to im-

Nadal once said, "The glory is not winning here or winning there, the glory is enjoying practicing.... trying to be a better player than before." [9]

prove the areas of their game that may have let them down during the last tournament. For example, if your forehand was a liability in a recent match, do forehand-focused drills that will help your rhythm and confidence return in that shot.

1. DEPTH GAME

Goal: Hitting the ball deep during the baseline rally to keep your opponent on the defensive.

Draw a line or place markers six or seven feet inside the baseline. Feed the ball to your practice partner and begin the rally. First player to hit 21 times beyond the line wins the game. Move the line or markers forward to three or four feet inside the baseline and play a second game. Add a variation by drawing a line or placing markers four or five feet parallel to the singles line to configure two corners and shots that land in one of the corners score two points instead of one.

Adding portable lines to your practice court can train your mind to target your strokes and improve the depth and accuracy of your baseline game.

2. OFFENSE/DEFENSE

Goal: Learn to take control of the point when the opportunity arises and defend the point when necessary.

Your practice partner scores a point when they end the point successfully before five shots, whereas you score a point when you extend the rally to at least five shots to win the point. First player to 11 points wins and then switch roles.

3. MOMENTUM

Goal: Create the pressure that resembles what is experienced in a match.

Each player serves five points at a time and the first to 21 points wins the game. The scoring multiplies with each point won. On the second consecutive point you win two points, on the third consecutive you win three points, and so on.

4. VOLLEYBALL

Goal: Reinforce the importance of the serve and its impact on your chances of winning the match.

You must serve to score points and the first player to win 11 points wins the game. Receiver must win two points in a row to win the serve back.

Doubles play can be fast and exciting. Venus Williams' (*foreground left*) body language says "Watch out!" as she lines up this easy forehand volley.

CHAPTER 14

Doubles

F OR RECREATIONAL PLAYERS, doubles is the most popular form of tennis. Doubles is beloved for many reasons. As compared to singles, it is played at a faster and more exciting pace. It involves more finesse, reflexes, and net play than singles, and because the doubles court is nine feet wider, it opens up greater angles and leads to more variety and creativity in shot making. Doubles is a game that can be played at an older age because there is just a little over half of a singles court to cover. Therefore, it allows prolonged participation in the sport. It is also more social because there is a lot of talking between partners, and because it isn't one on one, it is often considered less threatening and more fun to play.

With four players on the court, each with different strengths and weaknesses, there are also more tactical options to consider than when playing singles. In this chapter, I focus on the core tactical principles to help you play your best doubles. I begin by explaining the role of each of the four players and various formations and strategies available to each player. Next, I provide instruction on how to attain optimal court positioning, poaching, and how to elect the right shot given the circumstances. Then I discuss game plans, communication, how to choose the ideal partner to complement your game, and finish the chapter with tips for doubles practice.

I. The Role of Each Player

A SET OF DOUBLES IS PLAYED in four game rotations; at the end of each game, players change their role and, therefore, their responsibilities. The more you and your partner do each of your "jobs" well, the more likely you will perform as a cohesive and successful team. In each role, it is important that you know what tactics and shots work best and what court positioning options can be used to tilt the point in your favor. In this section, I will discuss the four roles: the server, the server's partner, the receiver, and the receiver's partner.

1. THE SERVER

Winning service games on a regular basis is paramount to the success of a doubles team. By using the advantage of being first to strike the ball and serving well, you should be able to make breaking serve difficult for your opponents and stay ahead or even in the set.

There are five main considerations for the server in doubles.

A. SETTING UP YOUR PARTNER AT NET TO THEIR GREATEST ADVANTAGE

The best way to do this is to serve down the center line towards the "T." This serve limits the angles available for your opponent to pass your net partner down the line, allowing them

Setting up their partner at net should be a main consideration of the server.

Mixing up the placement and spin on the serve will keep your opponents off rhythm and help you hold serve.

to move towards the middle of the court and exert a greater influence on the point.

The serve at the returner's body is another effective option to set up your partner at net. By "handcuffing" the returner, they will not be able to swing freely and likely offer easy balls for your net partner to pounce upon. Keep in mind that because there are two opponents defending the court in doubles, gaining positional advantage from serving wide is less important as compared to singles; thus, the serve at the body should be used more frequently.

The wide serve can also be effective; however, it does have negative impacts. It forces the server's partner to cover the alley, leaving them less able to intercept balls hit in the middle of the court. Additionally, the partner's movement to the alley forces the server to cover a larger portion of the court. However, if you can hit the wide serve fast and force your opponent to hit late on the return, you can set up your partner at net with an easy volley.

B. ENSURING HIGH FIRST SERVE PERCENTAGE

While achieving a high first serve percentage is important in singles, it is even more crucial in doubles because the difference between the first and second serve winning percentage is usually larger. The desired first serve percentage for doubles is 75 to 80% opposed to 60 to 65% in singles.

In order to achieve a high first serve percentage, aim for a bigger target towards the middle of the service box and use spin serves more frequently. If you have a strong second serve, you can afford to go for bigger first serves, with the goal of winning points from missed returns. If your second serve isn't a strength, it is advisable to slow down your first serve and increase your focus on placement and consistency.

C. MIXING IT UP

The server should keep the returner off rhythm by mixing up the serve with different placements and spins. Serve wide, down the "T," or directly at the returner's body. These different locations will reduce your opponent's ability to anticipate and get a jump start on their return. As discussed in Chapter Five, you also have four different spin serves (flat, slice, slice-topspin, and kick). These spins will change the trajectory and speed of your serve and hopefully produce some mistimed returns.

D. CHOOSING INTELLIGENT SERVE POSITIONING

You can serve from a position that creates the best angle to pick on the returner's weaker groundstroke. For example, if the returner has a weaker backhand, you can serve from closer to the middle on the deuce side or closer to the alley on the ad side. This will help the serve angle towards the returner's backhand. If you feel your opponent is in a groove on the return, try standing several feet left or right of your usual serving spot to present them with a different angle.

E. COMMUNICATING WELL

Talk with your partner about where you are going to serve so they can be ready to shift to the best position for the return. For example, if you tell your partner ahead of time that you are serving wide, they can be ready to cover

Jurgen Melzer's (*right*) prior knowledge of his partner serving down the "T" helps him to get a head start on his movement to the middle of the court.

the alley on the return. Or if you plan to serve up the "T," then your partner at net can be on high alert to attack any weak returns hit to the middle of the court.

After the serve you have two choices: serve and volley or serve and stay at the baseline.

1. SERVE AND VOLLEY: If you are serving and immediately moving forward to volley, it often makes sense to use more spin on the serve. Additional spin will cause the ball to travel more slowly through the air and enable you to get closer to the net for your first volley. Remember to follow the path of the ball as you move forward after the serve and perform your split step when your opponent hits the return (*right*).

The general rule for the server is to hit the first volley deep down the middle to limit the possible angles available to the returning team. If your opponents are playing in the common one-up, one-back formation to return serve (*see R and RP right*) and the return is hit below the net, the first volley should be hit low and deep to the receiver (R); the priority being to keep the ball away from the receiver's partner (RP). If the return is high, it often makes sense to hit the ball with power down at RP's feet.

2. SERVE AND STAY: Most recreational players elect to serve and stay back on the baseline; increasingly, professional players are doing the same due to the improvements they have made on the return of serve. This style of play leads to many cross-court rallies with one player up at the net and one player back at the baseline. The goal of the server during a cross-court rally is to hit (a) wide enough to keep the ball away from RP, (b) deep enough to keep R behind the baseline, and (c) fast enough to sometimes rush the opponents and set up their partner at net (SP) for an offensive volley.

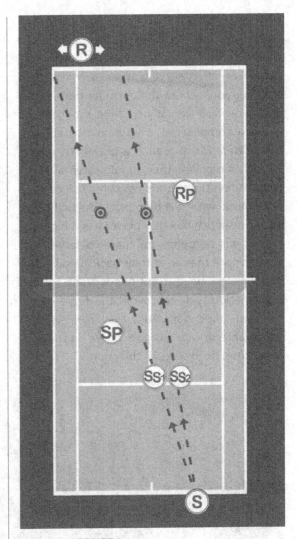

KEY: S - SERVER
SP - SERVER'S PARTNER
R - RECEIVER
RP - RECEIVER'S PARTNER

Your serve's location will influence where to split step when you serve and volley. Serving to the left side of the service box results in the split step also moving left (SS1). Serving to the right side of the service box, on the other hand, moves the split step to the right (SS2). The server's partner (SP) and receiver's partner (RP) should also move left and right following the direction of the serve to best cover the court.

Who should serve first on your team? If all other skills are fairly equal, the best server should serve first; this will result in the better server often serving more games. There are occasions where the stronger player may be the weaker server and then the decision is more complicated. The wind and sun are a consideration as well. If a player has a better kick serve, then they should serve with the wind. When the wind is assisting, the topspin of the kick serve will help bring the ball down into the service box. If a player has a high ball toss, it will be better for them to serve from the end with the sun at their back. If your team happens to be a right-handed/left-handed combination, you can avoid the issue of the sun and, additionally, use the cross wind to its advantage with a bigger curve on the slice serve from both sides of the court.

2. THE SERVER'S PARTNER

The server's partner can put a lot of pressure on the returner by being active and putting away weak returns. They can also induce errors and anxiety from the returning opponents due to distracting movements and memories of successful poaching (*see page 251*) on previous points.

A. POSITIONING

Where the server's partner stands at net during the serve is important. Usually, the best position is around the middle of the service box (*below, facing right*). Standing too far from the net makes the poach less effective because the opposing team has more time to react to the shot, while positioning too close to the net makes the server's partner vulnerable to the lob and reduces the chances of poaching on

Most players stand in the middle of the service box when their partner is serving (*facing right*).

Bob Bryan (*foreground left*) moves forward and split steps as his brother serves the ball.

returns hit in the middle of the court.

Exactly how far from the net you stand to begin the point will depend largely on how fast you can move backwards to defend the lob and the quality of your partner's serve. If you cover overheads well and your partner's serve is strong, you can play closer to the net. If the opposite is true, play deeper in the court. Your opponent's return of serve tendencies will play a role too. For example, if your opponent rarely lobs, you can play closer to the net. If they lob frequently, then play further away from the net.

You may want to start a little farther back in the service box and take one step forward as your partner hits the serve (*above*). This movement forward will get your body momentum started, making it easier to cut across the court and potentially pick off a weak return. Keep in mind that your opponents can't pick up on forward movement nearly as easily as sideways movement, so sneaking forward following your partner's serve or during the rally can be an excellent tactic.

How close you position yourself to the doubles alley is also an important consideration. If you stand too close to the alley, you might prevent yourself from getting beaten with a down-the-line passing shot, but you limit your chances of poaching and make the cross-court return easier for your opponents. Additionally, hugging the alley forces your partner to cover most of the court, leaving bigger gaps in the court for your opponents to exploit.

Once the rally begins, move quickly into the best position based on where the ball is located and how the point is progressing. That is, shift right and left following the direction of the ball, and move forward when the rally is in your favor and backward when the rally is turning negative.

Typically, the server's partner will follow the above positioning guidelines, but there are two other serving formations that can make strategic sense under the right circumstances: the "I" and Australian formation.

B. "I" FORMATION

The "I" formation starts with the server serving a foot from the center hash mark, and the net player straddling near the center line and crouching low to avoid getting hit by the ball (*below*). Before the serve, the net player and the server communicate as to the direction the net player will move. If the net player moves right, the server will move left, and vice versa. This formation can cause problems for opponents on their return because they don't know which way the net player will move after the serve. The "I" formation is not only an effective way to disrupt an opponent's rhythm, but also can get a strong net player more involved to positively influence the point.

In the "I" formation (*above*), the net player crouches near the center line on the opposite side of the server. In the Australian formation, the net player also stands near the center line but on the same side as the server.

C. AUSTRALIAN FORMATION

In the Australian formation, both the server and the net player line up on the same side as the court. The server serves a foot from the center hash mark, while the net player is approximately two feet from the center line.

Many players feel more comfortable returning cross court in the same direction from which they received the serve. Playing the Australian formation forces your opponents to change the direction of their return and hit down the line (and over the highest part of the net). If your opponents are consistently hitting strong cross-court returns, using the Australian formation is a terrific way to upset their groove.

The Australian formation, like the "I" formation, is also particularly effective when one partner is considerably stronger. A team can use this formation when the weaker player is serving; this allows the stronger player, positioned at the net, to take up more of the court, and be more involved in the point. It also allows a team to take best advantage of its strongest shots. For example, if your forehand volley is particularly strong, then using the Australian formation when your partner is serving to the ad side allows you to move to the right and poach using your forehand volley.

For all their advantages, the "I" and Australian formation should be used selectively by most players because the server is forced to move sideways after the serve, which can be troublesome. Performing the serve and volley tactic while using these formations can be risky for this reason. Still, when used under the right circumstances, or as a surprise move, these formations can be very effective.

3. THE RECEIVER

Generally speaking, the doubles return has to be more precise and faster than the singles return. The presence of the opposing net player places importance on hitting the cross-court return low and fast over the net.

If your opponents are serving and volleying, a good place to aim the cross-court return is to the outside "T" where the singles line meets the service line. This will place the ball at the server's feet if they serve and volley and wide enough to make the net player's poach very difficult. If the server is staying at the baseline, then the cross-court return should be aimed deep towards the baseline.

While the vast majority of returns will go cross court, if playing a team that poaches often, hitting down-the-line returns will keep the net person more stationary and less aggressive. It is a good idea to do this early in the match to send your opponents the message that their poaching is fraught with danger. Hitting the return down the line can also be an effective ploy if the net player is uncomfortable at net or a much weaker player than the server.

The lob return is also a good option against a strong poaching opponent. Like the down-the-line return, the lob return can foil an aggressive net player. A successful lob will also demand movement from your opponents and force them to defend against a high bouncing ball.

A. THE SLICE RETURN

While most doubles returns will be driven with topspin or lobbed, a terrific third option is to use the slice return. There are two main reasons why slice returns are an essential part of a good doubles player's return of serve repertoire. **First**, it is easier to control the height and depth of the ball. These are helpful qualities for

COACH'S BOX:

The mistake some receivers make on a down-the-line return is to try to put the ball in the alley. This leaves little margin for error. It is wiser to aim directly at the net person or at the singles line. This gives your shot a healthy margin for error and often results in an awkward volley from the net player. Also, don't let the fact that there is someone at the net make you anxious and cause you to rush the swing. Many players return more consistently cross court than down the line for this reason. To relax the mind, imagine the net person is invisible and visualize a down-the-line target deep in the court to aim your shot.

The compact nature of the slice backhand swing makes it a good shot to use on the return before attacking the net.

keeping the ball away from the opposing net player. **Second**, slice returns can be executed quickly and therefore provide different court positioning and tactical options. For example, if your opponents are holding serve comfortably when receiving your topspin returns from behind the baseline, take advantage of the slice swing's expediency, and try a slice return from inside the baseline. This movement forward may upset your opponents' rhythm as well as make a poach more difficult by shortening the time available for the opposing net player to cross to the middle of the court. Another option is to hit the slice groundstroke return from inside the baseline and immediately move forward quickly to the net: the "chip-and-charge" play. This places pressure on the server to hit a passing shot immediately following the service motion. You can also mix up your slice returns with drop shots if your serving opponent is staying on the baseline. The drop shot and the slice returns have similar backswings and therefore increase your ability to disguise the drop shot and surprise your opponent.

B. THE SECOND SERVE RETURN

A weak second serve effectively becomes a short ball that you can prepare for because the ball must land in the service box. It often represents the best chance to attack or use your favorite shot during the point. After the serve, your opponent has use of your entire side of the court and your ability to plan ahead is limited.

Before the second serve, you and your partner should move forward two or three feet and position yourselves in an aggressive formation, letting your opponents know that you intend to take control of the point following the return. Keep in mind, you can also favor your strongest groundstroke by positioning yourself more to the left or the right to increase

Serena Williams (*left*) stands well inside the baseline to attack a second serve return.

the chances of the second serve going to your preferred groundstroke. Because you have a smaller area to cover in doubles, positioning yourself to favor your strongest groundstroke doesn't put you hugely out of position like it would in singles. Therefore, be quick on your feet and try to dominate on the second serve return by using your best groundstroke as often as possible.

4. THE RECEIVER'S PARTNER

Receiver's partner is often the position that requires the quickest reflexes and fastest movements. Here, you must make quick adjustments forward and back and left and right, depending on the quality and direction of your partner's return.

A. POSITIONING

Against most teams, if your partner is receiving serve, you should stand around the service line slightly closer to the center line than the singles line (*opposite foreground*). Your stance should be angled so you are facing the opposing net player. Your focus should be on this player because they represent the closest opponent and, therefore, the person whose shot you will have the least amount of time to react to. Once the return is made cross court to the server, move forward towards the middle of the service box and face the server. During the rally, your feet should always pivot so you are facing the opponent who is hitting the ball to facilitate faster movement and a quicker reaction.

If your partner hits a powerful, low return, move forward to the net and put pressure on the server's first volley or groundstroke (*above*). If the server pops up the volley or groundstroke off your partner's strong return, move forward diagonally and intercept the ball with an aggressive volley. On the other

Nenad Zimonjic (*foreground*) recognizes his partner's good return and quickly moves forward.

hand, if your partner floats a high return, take a step back to buy some time and give yourself a better chance of returning the fast volley or groundstroke that will likely be fired to your side of the court. If your partner hits the return down the line at the net player, shift towards the "T" area to cover the gap in the middle of the court (*next page*). If your partner hits a sharply angled cross-court return, follow the flight of the ball and protect your alley.

B. TWO-BACK FORMATION

When your opponent has a powerful serve and your partner is struggling to return serve, you have the option to move back and start the point positioned near the baseline. This is

Above, we see the synchronization of movement executed by the pros. As Bob Bryan (*facing left*) begins his movement to the right to return a wide serve, Mike Bryan (*facing right*) pivots his right leg at the same angle as his brother and also begins shifting to the right. Below, after Bob Bryan attempts a down-the-line passing shot, Mike Bryan moves further to the right to cover the middle and defend his opponent's highest percentage shot option, the volley through the middle of the court.

With the receiver's partner positioned at the baseline (*right background*), the serving team doesn't have an easy target to volley through.

called the two-back formation and it is often a wise choice when you are facing a strong server, particularly when returning the first serve.

There are three main advantages to the two-back formation (*above*). **First**, moving back to the baseline removes an easy target for an aggressive net team's volley. Without a target to aim for, many volleyers become less confident in their shot decisions and make more mistakes. **Second**, by setting up in the two-back formation, there is less pressure to hit fast and low over the net to protect the receiver's partner, therefore, your team can hit returns with less speed and higher over the net for more consistency. **Third**, you can extend more points by using lobs and passing shots, testing your opponents' skill and patience. This formation is particularly effective if you and your partner's groundstrokes are superior to your volleys or if the opposing team hits groundstrokes poorly, making an extended rally work in your favor.

The pros follow the ball right and left to best cover the angles available to their opponent.

II. Court Positioning

WATCHING TOP PROFESSIONALS play doubles, you can see clearly how well they move without the ball and how hard they work to establish the best location on the court to cover the angles and likely shots from their opponents (*above*). They flow with the game moving quickly to the right, left, forward, or back following the ball around the court as if it was some kind of powerful magnet. Sometimes their movement to establish good positioning is large, but most times during a rally it is slight due to the brief time it takes for the ball to travel across the court. But even if the movement is small, they know it can make the difference between being able to reach shots or not or having a split second longer to play a balanced shot instead of being rushed.

Court positioning is a crucial aspect of doubles play and is something every tennis player can do well.

In this section, I first discuss why playing the net together in the two-up court position is a formation you should be striving to establish in your doubles play. Next, I talk about court position considerations for the two-up and one-up, one-back formations. There are also court positioning concerns when lobs and overheads are played.

1. ADVANTAGES OF THE TWO-UP FORMATION

Controlling the net as a team is an important goal in doubles. **First**, because there is such little time to react to a volley, doubles teams who attack the net well together can make the opposing team constantly feel rushed and

Serena Williams seizes upon a short ball to join her sister at net and gain the positional advantage.

defensive. **Second**, once a team is positioned at the net together, the opposing team must come up with a quality shot to stay in the point. If the opposing team doesn't hit the ball low, fast, or high and deep, the net team will seize the advantage. This pressure can result in many "hidden" points won by errors stemming from your intimidating presence at net. On the other hand, if one player is on the baseline, the opposing team can direct a mediocre shot to the baseline player and pay less of a price. **Third**, when the ball is above the net, the net team has the advantage of hitting down into a visible court, while the baseline player or players on the opposing team must hit up into a court blurred by the net.

For these reasons, while hitting from the baseline, players should be ready to pounce on the short ball and transition forward to the net (*above*). The service line represents a good demarcation of the court; balls that land inside the service box are usually appropriate opportunities to move forward from the baseline and attack the net. If the ball lands here, you will usually hit your first volley close enough to the net to be an effective volleyer. Other methods to move forward from the baseline include lobbing down the line, playing a drop shot, or hitting a high arcing topspin crosscourt shot that provides time to run forward and establish good net position.

Don't be discouraged if you don't see immediate results from attacking the net. Some players lose confidence with their net play too quickly after being on the receiving end of a couple of successful passing shots or lobs. Sometimes it takes a few games to pick up on your opponents' tendencies and time your volleys. Remember that over the course of the match playing the the net well together will place pressure on your opponents and help you win.

The Murray brothers have their weight forward as they split step together at the net always looking to attack the ball.

2. TWO-UP COURT POSITIONING

Once in the two-up formation, it is important you move as a team. For example, if your partner is pulled left to hit a volley, you should move simultaneously left the same distance. If you don't move together in this way, you will leave an exploitable gap in the middle of the court. A good rule of thumb in covering the court is to move with your partner as if you have a rope tied between you. This image reinforces the need for the movement around the court to be done in chorus. When the ball is on the other side of the court, you should also move as a team to counter your opponents' use of angles. For example, if you hit a cross-court volley to the ad side alley, you and your partner should shift right. The wider your team hits the ball, the greater the movement in that direction to cover the angles available to your

When the pros sense a lob isn't happening, they like to get as close to the net as possible.

Following a defensive volley, the Bryan brothers (*background*) move back to buy time and defend the point.

opponent on their passing shots.

Remember to be flexible with your court positioning at the net and adjust quickly to the circumstances. If your opponents are in trouble after a strong shot, move forward (*opposite bottom*). The closer you can position yourself to the net, the more pressure you will place on your opponents. Your court positioning at the net should be aggressive, all while watching out for a possible lob. Whether you are at the net with your partner or by yourself, the maxim to remember is: "Get as close to the net as possible, anticipate the lob." It isn't difficult to anticipate the defensive lob. If your opponent sets up with a short backswing and the racquet face very open, there's a good chance a lob is about to be hit.

Of course, you won't always be on offense; there will be times you need to defend the point. If you or your partner hit a weak shot, move backwards to buy some time to react to your opponent's likely aggressive response (*above*). Moving back a step or two will provide an extra moment of time that may allow you to get your racquet on the ball and extend the point. Watch the Bryan brothers play for a model of this flexibility. You will notice they are always in motion during the point, mov-

ing right and left following the flight of the ball as well as forward and backward, responding quickly to the offensive and defensive phases of the rally.

A. STAGGERING

If your opponents are in the common one-up, one-back formation, then you should play the net in a staggered formation with one player slightly in front of the other (*below*). When your opponent at the baseline is about to hit

The staggered formation at the net shown here by the team in the foreground leads to more aggressive poaching, improved lob coverage, and better communication on balls hit down the middle.

the ball, the player facing them straight ahead or down the line should be slightly closer to the net than the net player facing the baseline player at a diagonal or cross court.

This staggered positioning at the net has the advantage of giving each player a clear role to play. The down-the-line net player, sometimes referred to as the "terminator," will poach more on balls hit towards the middle. The cross-court net player, sometimes referred to as the "workhorse," will cover more of the lobs. The cross-court net player's deeper positioning helps lob coverage for two main reasons. **First**, the cross-court player is already left or right of the ball to swing and return the down-the-line lob. To return the same lob, the down-the-line net player would need to run extra distance left or right of the ball to comfortably swing the racquet. **Second**, the opponent's cross-court lob is hit into the longest court and requires the greatest distance to move and retrieve.

By having one player more focused on poaching and the other on the lookout for the lob, your net play as a team will feature a good mixture of offensive pressure and defensive court coverage. In contrast, having two terminators playing the net leaves the team very susceptible to the lob, and two workhorses at net will have a difficult time putting the ball away.

Staggering also leads to better communication when the ball is hit up the middle. The deeper player facing the cross-court shot has a split second more time to see the opponent's shot, know how their partner is reacting, and play the shot accordingly.

3. ONE-UP, ONE-BACK

The most common formation for recreational doubles is for each team to have one player up at the net and one player on the baseline.

If you are at the net in this formation, and a cross-court baseline rally is in motion, you should follow the flight of the ball, moving forward and backward diagonally with each shot to best cover the court (*below, A to B*).

For example, if your partner hit cross-court towards the alley (R1), then you move forward diagonally to the left to cover the down-the-line passing shot in the alley (*below A*). How-

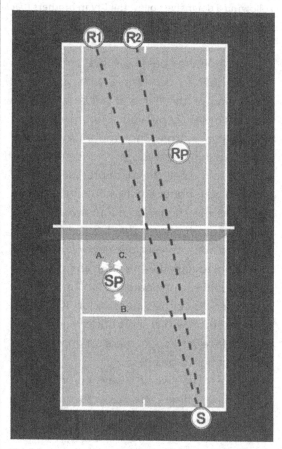

During a cross-court rally between the server (S) and the returner (R1), the server's partner (SP) will track the ball and move to "A" when R1 is hitting the ball, and then move backwards to "B" when S is hitting the ball. However, if S hits the ball deep and towards the middle of the court (R2), SP should not move to "A" but instead move to "C" and look to poach.

Occasionally, the pros look back (*foreground left*) to see the quality and placement of their partner's shot and get a head start on their next move.

ever, if your partner hits cross court towards the middle of the court (R2), then you move diagonally to the right and look to poach (*opposite C*). If your opponent returns the ball cross court to your partner on the baseline, then you move backward diagonally to the right (*opposite B*).

As you move backward diagonally to B, you should be facing the opposing net player (RP) because you want to be aware of their movement. However, if you feel your partner at the baseline is in trouble, it is okay to take a quick look back to see how your partner is faring (*above*). If you know that your partner is likely to hit a poor shot or short lob, you can start moving backwards more aggressively than usual to buy time for your opponent's likely powerful response. Too many recreational players blindly face forward *all* the time and, conse-

quently, react late and become easy targets for the opposing net player to hit through.

If you are the baseline player, you need to be ready to cover a lob over your partner's head or, if your partner at net is set up for an easy volley or overhead, move forward and establish more aggressive court positioning. The baseline player must also be ready to communicate with their partner at net. The baseline player is the "captain" of the team and responsible for issuing court position commands such as "switch," "stay," and "back up" to their partner at the net.

Sometimes while playing in the one-up, one-back formation your opponent at the baseline moves forward to join their partner at the net and, on your side of the court, you are alone at the net with your partner standing at the baseline. This means you are in the "hot seat"

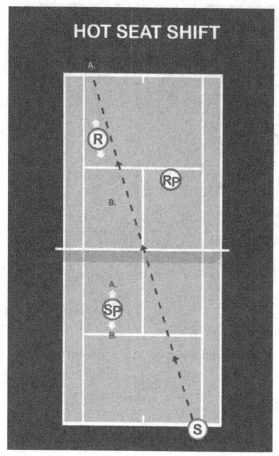

HOT SEAT SHIFT

When the returner (R) moves forward from "A" to "B," the server's partner (SP) should move backwards from "A" to "B."

ally defensive but can quickly turn offensive if your partner at the baseline hits a strong shot at the opposing net player's feet.

4. COURT POSITIONING IN RESPONSE TO LOBS AND OVERHEADS

Almost every lob will result in a significant change in court positioning. If a good lob gets over your opponents' heads, you and your partner should move forward and take over the net position. If you stay on the baseline after hitting a good lob, you are relinquishing pressure by letting your opponents reply to the bounce instead of hitting it in the air, allowing them time to set up and position themselves well to defend the point. Remember that the likely response to your lob is another lob coming back. Because of that, after a deep lob over your opponent's head, position yourself around the service line, not in the usual net position in the middle of the service box. On the other hand, if you are at the net and

position. If you find yourself in this scenario, you are in a vulnerable position and should shift backwards several feet from the middle of the service box to around the service line to buy time to defend against your opponents' volleys (*above*).

A mediocre shot from your partner at the baseline will spell trouble for you in the hot seat. However, your partner can neutralize the hot seat situation by hitting a deep lob or driving the ball with enough speed to rush the opposing net team. The hot seat position is usu-

Rohan Bopanna (*facing left*) sees his partner is going to end this overhead positioned in "no-man's land" and moves to the middle to protect him.

your partner hits a poor lob, you must retreat quickly towards the baseline. Don't forget to do your split step when your opponents hit the overhead; keep your hands in front of you and try to block the ball back in play with a short swing.

There are four main court positioning scenarios when playing the overhead. **First**, if you and your partner are both at the net and your partner is moving back for a deep lob, you should shift back with your partner. There is a good chance your partner will be hitting the overhead defensively in this situation, and therefore, you should move back in case the overhead is weak. **Second**, if your partner is balanced for the overhead but positioned several feet past the service line, you should move forward and towards the center line to cover more court and protect your partner who is caught in "no-man's land" (*opposite right*). **Third**, if your partner is hitting an overhead off a very short lob and positioned very close to the net, shift backwards to help cover for the possible lob over your partner's head. **Fourth**, if you are at the baseline and your partner is in good position to hit the overhead, move forward and join your partner at the net.

III. Poaching

POACHING REPRESENTS AN IMPORTANT part of doubles play. It occurs when the net player intercepts a shot that was directed at their partner (*below*). Poaching is a great way to hit winning volleys or to disarm opponents by forcing them to hit their shots faster, lower, and wider to avoid a poaching net player. It

Mike Bryan's outstanding poaching ability (*right*) leads to many winning volley situations.

An unplanned poach by Venus Williams means her sister Serena must move left quickly to cover the unprotected side of the court.

can also cause opponents to take their eyes off the ball or change their mind mid-stroke, causing them to make more errors and their game to deteriorate.

There are two types of poaches: the first one is planned off the serve, where your serving partner knows you are going to poach, and they immediately move to cover the other half of the court. The second type of poach is one of opportunity when you see your opponent rushed or off balance during the rally. Unplanned poaching calls for an extra aggressive volley because both teammates are momentarily on the same side of the court, leaving the other side unprotected (*above*).

You have to have thick skin when poaching and realize that you will sometimes get passed down the alley. But keep in mind that for every alley passing shot you give up by being aggres-

sive, you will usually win many more points by poaching and forcing your opponents into hitting riskier shots and making more errors. So while your opponents may win a point or two with an alley shot, the odds overall are in your favor. By poaching consistently and aggressively, you will help your team win the match.

In this section, I will discuss how to anticipate poaching opportunities, timing the poach, the movement required to poach effectively, and where to place the poached shot.

I. ANTICIPATION

Poaching involves anticipation of how well your opponent is likely to hit the ball given the shot circumstances. It takes extensive practice to learn the nuances of poaching and attain a good "feel" for the right time to take a chance and move to the middle of the court. Strongly

Bob Byran (*foreground right*) recognizes his opponent has an awkward volley and quickly moves forward and to the middle of the court looking to poach.

consider poaching when you see your opponent hitting any of these four types of shots.

A. LOW SHOTS

Low balls are good candidates for poaching because your opponents will be forced to hit at a slower speed to clear the net.

B. DEEP SHOTS

The deep ball gives your opponents less time to prepare off the bounce and control the direction of their shot to hit past you in the alley. An added benefit of the deep ball is that your opponent will have their head down to focus on the deep bounce of the ball and be unable to see you move to begin the poach.

C. RUSHED OR OFF BALANCED SHOTS

Any time your opponent is rushed or off balance (*above*) is another great opportunity to poach because their shot will lack power. It also likely that your opponent will not have the control necessary to aim their shot accurately in the alley's small area.

D. MIDDLE SHOTS

Shots hit from the middle of the court are favorable for a poach because of the limited angles available to your opponent to hit a passing shot by you in the alley.

COACH'S BOX:

Some opponents are easier to poach on because of their swing technique and the amount of spin they use. For instance, players with a large backswing or who use heavy spin are easier to poach on because their long swing forces them to commit to their shot direction earlier, and the heavy spin makes their shot travel more slowly through the air. In contrast, players with a compact swing or flatter shots can adjust the direction of the shot later if they notice the net player darting to the middle to poach, and their flatter ball travels more quickly through the air.

Jean-Julien Rojer moves towards the net's center strap to play this volley. His diagonal movement reduces the time available for his opponents to react to his shot, allows him to hit the ball at a greater height, and creates better angles.

2. TIMING

Learning to time your movement across the court is crucial. Don't begin to move across the court until your opponent has committed to their shot. If you move too early, your opponent will see the opening and hit behind you. The timing of the poach will vary depending on the speed of the game, but generally the poach can begin once the ball bounces on your opponents' side.

3. MOVEMENT

To poach, start in a crouched position and split step an instant before your opponent hits the ball. Your first move on the poach is forward and then diagonal to the ball. If you move diagonally with your first step, your shoulders will be turned, making quick adjustments more difficult. Instead, if you move forward first, you can better assess the type of movement required and how the steps needed can be performed best. Moving forward first also allows you to use your outside leg to push off and explode more quickly towards the ball.

After your first step forward, move diagonally towards the center strap of the net to rob time from your opponents (*above*). Also, by moving closer to the net you will hit the ball at a higher point and create better angles. After the poach, a quick decision has to be

By hitting left, Jurgen Melzer takes full advantage of the leftward momentum he gathered during his movement to this volley.

made about whether you continue over to the opposite side of the court or return back to your original spot. From behind you, your partner can help you by either saying "stay" or "switch." Good communication can avoid the dilemma of both of you being on the same side of the court for more than one shot.

4. SHOT PLACEMENT

Usually, you should hit the poach to the side of the court you are moving towards. By hitting to this side, you are using the energy generated by your movement to add power to your shot (*above*). Additionally, hitting the poach towards the opposing net player gives that player very little time to respond to your shot. After hitting this type of poach volley, a rapid fire exchange of shots typically ensues, so get the racquet ready quickly and be on high alert.

Hitting at the opposing net player's shoes or behind them through the middle should be

your two main shot choices when poaching. However, if you have more time to prepare and are positioned close to the net, the angled volley placed near or into one of the two alleys can win you many points. Or, if the ball is low and soft, a drop volley hit gently in the baseline player's service box can be a good choice.

COACH'S BOX:

Your doubles game should be filled with sabotage and surprise. One tactic to confuse your opponents is the "fake poach." The fake poach is when you make a large step towards the middle (*below*), appearing like you are going to poach, but instead quickly return to your original position. If you sell your opponents on the fake poach, you can tempt them to try a risky down-the-line passing shot and often receive an easy ball to volley. Keep in mind, the timing of the fake poach is a split second earlier than a regular poach. You want them to see you move and be distracted. The fake poach can done after any serve, but it works particularly well after your partner serves wide and your opponent thinks they have a favorable angle to pass you in the "open" alley.

IV. Shot Selection

IN DOUBLES, SHOT DECISIONS are often different than in singles because there is significantly more net play, and two players, often positioned in very different court locations, are covering the court instead of one.

To help you make the right shot choices in your doubles game, below I detail the various shot selection considerations including: hitting heights, hitting at the body and to the middle, hitting deep-to-deep and short-to-short, and hitting volleys and overheads. Keep in mind, when using this advice, you must take into account variations in the playing abilities of your opponents; that is, if one of the players on the opposing team is significantly less skilled than the other, the guidance in this section needs to be bent to accommodate for this difference in the opposing players' abilities.

1. HITTING HEIGHTS

In doubles, the height of the shot is sometimes more important than the power of the shot. For this reason, players who have finesse and can control the height of the ball well are often superior at doubles than more powerful players who may have less command on the height of their shot.

Doubles has two players covering the court, and because of that, there will be less outright winners, and you must accept that the ball will very often be struck by your opponent. Therefore, often the goal behind your shot is not to hit winners. Instead, the goal is to make it awkward for your opponents by hitting low, high, or at the body. Doing this can force a weak shot from the opposing team and allow you to take control of the point.

A. HITTING LOW

Because there is usually one and sometimes two doubles opponents at the net position, keeping the ball low is an important skill. Hitting low shots to the opposing net team forces them to hit the ball upward and defensively and can set you or your partner up at net for some winning volleys and good poaching opportunities.

Keeping the ball low can be the deciding factor in some situations. If all four players are inside the service box in a volley exchange, the team that gets their shot low at the feet of their opponent first generally ends up winning the point. In fact, unless your opponent is highly skilled, any ball during a rally that is below the height of your opponent's knees is usually going to tilt the point in your favor.

B. HITTING HIGH

Lobs are also an effective way to make things difficult for your opponents and force them into hitting an off balance shot. Furthermore, lobbing produces the benefit of forcing your opponent to play further away from the net for fear of being lobbed. This gives you more time to react to their volley and makes it easier to hit low at their feet.

On most occasions, the lob is the correct play whenever you and your partner are out of position. For example, when you and your partner switch sides of the court while in the one-up, one-back formation, the lob will allow your team time to move to protect the whole court and reset the point. The lob can also bail you out of a difficult cross-court rally when both teams are playing in the one-up, one-back formation. Here, if you feel there is any chance you will be late on your swing and forced to hit down the line to the opposing net player, then lob. Or, if your opponent's cross-

Bob Bryan is forced to play a defensive volley from a fast shot hit at his body.

court shot pulls you wide outside the doubles alley, a lob is often the right play not only to buy time, but also to thwart the opposing net player's chances of hitting a volley behind your partner (who has a large area to cover given your positioning outside the doubles alley).

Keep in mind it can be a smart shot sequence to drive the shot following a deep lob to the same player who plays the overhead. The player hitting the overhead off a deep lob will have poor court positioning and may still be recovering balance. The combination of a drop shot followed by a high lob is also a particularly effective shot sequence in doubles.

2. HITTING AT THE BODY

Hitting directly at your net opponent can make for an awkward shot (*above*). Hitting the ball at the right hip can tangle up your opponent and restrict the movement of their arms, limiting their ability to comfortably swing at the ball.

3. HITTING TO THE MIDDLE

In singles, where there is a larger area for your opponent to cover, placing your shot close to the sideline can be well rewarded, while hitting to the middle of the court can be an invitation for your opponent to take charge of the point. In contrast, in doubles, hitting to the middle is often a smart tactical choice. As in singles, hitting to the middle in doubles has the advantage of only needing to clear the lowest part of the net and eliminates the chance of missing your shot wide; however, in doubles, this shot can yield three additional benefits.

Hitting to the middle reduces the angles to defend against and can cause opponent indecision.

A. OPPONENT INDECISION

A shot down the middle can lead to confusion where either both to go to hit the ball (*above*) or both leave the ball alone thinking their partner will play the shot.

B. REDUCED ANGLES FOR YOU
TO DEFEND AGAINST

The doubles court is nine feet wider than the singles court; therefore, reducing the angles available to your opponent is a higher priority. This is amplified by the fact that there is more net play in doubles, meaning more volleys and less reaction time. If both opponents are at the net, a shot down the middle leaves them with fewer possible angles, making it more difficult for them to hit winning volleys or force you into a defensive situation. Or, if one or both opponents are at the baseline, a shot down the middle forces them to thread the needle on their passing shot attempts in the alleys.

The butterfly play first draws the opposing team towards the middle, leaving the alleys unprotected to place a winning volley.

C. SETS UP THE BUTTERFLY PLAY

When you hit in the middle of the court, it sometimes draws both players to the center, leaving the alleys wide open for your next shot (*opposite right*). This two shot sequence is called the butterfly play because of the way it resembles the closing and opening of butterfly wings. This play is especially effective when your opponents are in a one-up, one-back formation and you place your volley down the middle behind the opposing net player, drawing your opponents into an "I" formation.

4. DEEP-TO-DEEP, SHORT-TO-SHORT

As mentioned earlier, in most doubles rallies at the recreational level, each team has one player at the net and one player on the baseline. Usually the smartest tactic when in this formation is for the baseline player to hit towards the baseline opponent (deep-to-deep), and the net player to hit towards the net opponent (short-to-short).

The majority of doubles shots involve the deep-to-deep shot pattern with the two baseline players hitting cross court to each other.

> ### COACH'S BOX:
>
> Stroke biomechanics should play a role in your shot choices when your doubles opponents are both at net. If you choose to hit at your opponent's body, aiming at their right hip or forehand side produces the most awkward body positioning for them to defend the shot. However, if you choose to hit past your opponent with a power shot, aiming to the left or backhand side is often especially effective because the backhand requires an earlier contact point than the forehand.

There are three main reasons why hitting deep-to-deep makes strategic sense. **First**, it keeps the ball away from the greatest threat, your opponent at the net. **Second**, it allows your partner to use their net skills to poach and influence the point. **Third**, it is a diagonal shot hit to the longest court and over the lowest part of the net. Remember to be on the lookout for the short ball to attack during the

Mike Bryan (*facing left*) follows the short-to-short rule on this volley.

cross-court rally. Your goal here is to move forward off the baseline, join your partner at net, and thus, gain court positional advantage.

If you are at the net position, and the ball is above the net, it is usually wise to follow the short-to-short shot pattern and aim your shot to the opposing net player's half of the court (*previous page*). Due to the close proximity to you, the opposing net player will have little time to react and control their shot. This challenging shot will often result in an error or a pop up and you can take control of the point. To be more precise, hitting behind the opposing the net player, not right at them, is the very

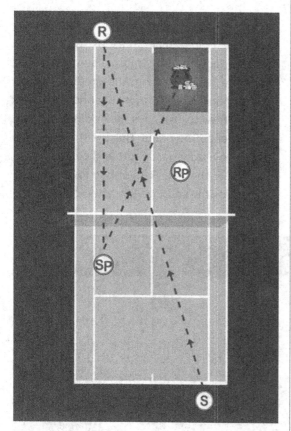

When playing the net, the area behind the opposing net player represents a prime location (or "gold mine") to hit winners.

best area to hit your volley in this scenario. I call this area behind the net player the "gold mine" because if you can hit the ball in this court location, you are usually "golden" (*left*).

The short-to-short tactic does not apply equally to low balls. If the ball is low, your volley should usually be directed back to the deep player due to the slower speed and higher degree of difficulty on the low volley (*opposite*). If you accidentally pop up your low volley, but direct the ball to the deep baseline player, you can salvage the point, whereas popping up your low volley to the opposing net player is likely to lead to trouble.

This tactic of hitting high volleys to the closest opponent and difficult volleys to the deepest opponent should become a consistent part of your doubles play. The quicker your shot placement decision is, the more decisive and well-executed your volley. When experienced players see a high ball or low ball, they automatically know the right shot to play, adding confidence to their shot.

The deep-to-deep and short-to-short guidelines can also be applied in less obvious and less structured situations. For example, if you are rushed or are making a difficult low shot from the baseline and both opponents are at net with one opponent eight feet from the net and the other 15 feet from the net, then, all things being equal, your shot should be directed to the opponent 15 feet away from the net. Regardless of how chaotic the rally or odd the court positioning becomes during a point, if you are in trouble, you must be aware of your opponent's court positioning and direct your shot to the deeper player to buy time and recover. Or, if you are hitting an easy overhead and both your opponents are retreating backwards with one opponent 15 feet from the net and the other 25 feet from the net, then, all

The low volley should be placed away from the opposing net player and to the deeper-positioned doubles opponent.

things being equal, your shot should be aimed at the opponent closest to you. To play shrewd doubles, you must cultivate good court awareness and know where your opponents are positioned. Use your peripheral vision to help you make the right shot choice and hit the ball in the correct half of the court.

5. VOLLEYS

One of the keys to being a good volleyer is knowing where to place the volley based on the height of the ball. As discussed earlier, if your opponent gives you an easy high volley, the object is usually to power the ball at the feet or behind the closest person on the other side. Remember to be disciplined and hit these volleys at the right speed. Don't try to hit a winner at 80 mph when 50 mph will do. You don't get extra points for that additional 30 mph; all you are doing is increasing the chances that you miss the shot. If the ball is low, the goal is to hit the ball to the deepest player. If you have time and are balanced, low balls can be good opportunities to use the short part of the court with drop volleys to the opposing baseline player.

In fact, any volley hit short and soft to the opposing baseline player can be a very effective shot, particularly at the recreational level. The drop volley is an effective shot on low balls, but for recreational players, the "bump" volley on chest-high balls can also be used to hit short or force the opposing baseline player to scramble forward and hit a low, awkward shot. On this volley, the racquet moves just a few inches and gently "bumps" the ball. You won't find this volley in the text books, but it has four advantages that I feel makes it an important shot to learn. **First**, because it is not a power shot, it is a shot available to everyone.

Even with an open court available to the right, Olga Savchuk hits her overhead left to the closer opponent's side of the court.

Second, recreational players usually move better laterally than forward. **Third**, even if your opponent reaches the bump volley they often will be off balance or positioned just beyond the service line in an unfavorable part of the court. **Fourth**, because most volleys are hit between waist and shoulder high, it is a shot that that can be used frequently. Watch the more experienced players compete at your club and note how often they use the bump volley; they know they know it is a winning play.

Timing also plays a large role in where you place your volley. If you are rushed, play your volley down the middle because it takes the chance of missing wide out of the equation at a time when your racquet control is compromised. If you have a good amount of time to prepare, shots aimed towards the alleys will often give you a bigger advantage than hitting to the middle.

6. OVERHEADS

In singles, with a larger area of the court to cover, the correct approach on the overhead is to be aggressive because a weak overhead can leave you in a vulnerable position. In doubles, this concern diminishes because you have a partner and you both have only half a doubles court to protect. The basic philosophy on the overhead in doubles is to be consistent and hit with some patience. Of course, if you can blast an immediate overhead winner from an easy lob you should do so, but sometimes in doubles you may have to hit three or four overheads to win the point.

If you have an opposing player positioned around the service line, aim your overhead behind or to the side of that player (*above*). If you have a short lob, it is often a good idea to angle the overhead off to the side. If you are hitting a deep, difficult lob, play more conservatively down the middle and towards the deeper positioned doubles opponent.

V. Game Plans

Most doubles teams you'll encounter will use a mixture of offensive and defensive play. Against such teams your strategic focus should be on the topics discussed earlier in the chapter — doing your job well in each of the four roles, executing the right court positioning moves, using the most effective formations, poaching aggressively, and making the right selection choices. However, you will play teams that are especially defensive or offensive, and while the above tactical principles of doubles still apply, there are several other strategic tips to consider to help tip the scales in your favor. I begin this section by discussing these tips, then I suggest ways to help you win when playing with a weaker player or against players of unequal abilities, and finish by considering how statistics can impact game plans.

1. DEFEATING A DEFENSIVE TEAM

In my 25 years of coaching, the doubles question I've probably been asked the most about is how to beat the team that moonball their way to victory. As I emphasized in Chapter 13, these players, like every opponent, are to be respected. With this mind set, you are less likely to get frustrated if you are losing, or let your guard down if you are winning. Don't dread playing defensive players either. You can feel relaxed and reassured in the knowledge that you won't be defending against power shots often and the stress of hitting the ball low and fast over the net will be infrequent. Besides entering the match with the correct mind set,

you should also tune-up your overhead. Remember the overhead is a confidence shot, and true confidence can only come from successful repetition. Before the match ask your partner to feed you some lobs and then switch roles. This will improve you and your partner's timing and belief in the shot. If your overhead is sharp, an opposing team that lobs a lot should be an eagerly awaited adversary.

Additionally, there are four tactics to consider to help you defeat a defensive team. Let's discuss these tactics.

A. USE THE DROP SHOT

Defensive players love to camp out at the baseline. They don't like to run forward off the baseline to reach a drop shot and find themselves drawn into the net position. Once they are positioned at net, their lobs are ineffective and they are forced to hit volleys. At the recreational level, I recommend using the drop shot frequently, especially when receiving serve. Once the serve is played, your opponents have the option to hit high and deep in the court, making the drop shot harder to execute.

B. ATTACK THE SERVE

Defensive players usually develop a defensively style game in part because they lack a dominating serve. Take advantage of this and be aggressive on the return. Drive the ball at the opposing net player sometimes and look to chip-and-charge as often as possible.

C. ATTACK THE NET

Defensive players like a predictable rhythm. They enjoy rallies that proceed in a baseline-to-baseline metronome beat. Attacking the net makes the rally unpredictable. It turns the rhythm of a baseline-to-baseline point from a waltz to a Metallica song full of lulls and cre-

Attacking the net produces pressure and a rhythm of play that defensive teams dislike.

scendos. That's what you want.

These players lob a lot, so when you attack the net play a little deeper in the court than usual, and make use of the swinging volley's power often to rush your opponents. Keep in mind, playing a little deeper will shrink the area of court available for your opponent's to lob successfully and often lead to more lob mistakes.

D. MIRROR THEM FOR THE FIRST TWO GAMES
For many players, the ten minutes allotted to warm-up is insufficient to get all the shots ready and the body loose enough to move quickly. During the first two games, mirror their defensive style of play and use this time to get fully warmed up and ready for the more aggressive game you will employ in the third game. Besides grooving your strokes, this

tactic can lead to two other positive developments. One, it shows your opponents that you don't mind the slower pace of play, and two, if you do well in these two games, your opponents will feel deflated knowing you beat them at their own game (and defensive players typically lack a dangerous plan B).

2. DEFEATING AN OFFENSIVE TEAM
Some teams like to play "first strike" tennis; that is, they intend to go for a winner early in the rally. They enjoy quick points, so therefore, the underlying theme of your strategy here is to make them "hit one more shot" and extend the rally as much as possible. Mentally, when playing a power team, you need to appreciate that they may have some hot streaks, but they rarely last a whole match. Hang tough

when they enter one of these streaks. Remember their sunny play will soon dip under some clouds and it won't be long before the momentum swings back your way.

To beat a power team you need the ability to hit strokes like lobs deep in the court and soft dink shots at the net player's feet. I don't see these type of finesse shots practiced enough on the recreational courts. I see a lot of baseline-to-baseline hitting out there, but not too many cat-and-mouse, lob and dink drills that successful professional doubles teams use frequently in their training. These shots are relatively easy, but they need to be practiced.

The next time you play against a hard-hitting doubles team, consider these four tactics.

A. USE THE TWO-BACK FORMATION

There's nothing a power team enjoys more than drilling volleys through the receiving team's partner positioned around the service line. When a power team is serving well, that player might as well have a bullseye painted on their shirt. A smart tactical move in this situation is to move your partner back to near the baseline and start in the two-back formation. With you and your partner at the baseline, your opponents don't have an obvious target. Instead, they have several shot possibilities which can make them less decisive volleyers. Also, the two-back formation takes the pressure off the returner to hit low, fast returns; they can instead hit returns with a higher margin of error and become a more consistent returner.

In the two-back formation, don't forget to use the lob return and the lob more often than usual during the rally. With your partner positioned back at the baseline, your lob doesn't have to be perfect. The goal here is to lengthen the point and let your opponent's lower

percentage shot-making do them in. Although not as common, you can also use the two-back formation when serving. If your opponents are successfully drilling balls at your partner at net on your serve, don't be shy about moving them back to the baseline to start the point; this has the positive effects of removing the target and lengthening the point.

B. HIT DOWN THE MIDDLE

Hitting down the middle limits the angle available for your opponents to move you around the court. Hitting to the alleys can be a risky shot against aggressive players because their power combined with the greater angles available can cause trouble. Also, power players can cause you to rush your shot and compromise your control. By hitting down the middle you eliminate the chances of missing wide and increase the chance of extending the rally.

C. INCREASE YOUR FIRST SERVE PERCENTAGES

Power players depend on dominating their opponent's second serve. Unlike defensive players, these competitors have the power to hurt opponents who possess a less than stellar second serve. I recommend slowing your first serve down slightly and expand your target to help you increase your first serve percentages.

D. USE THE "I" FORMATION

Power players typically take the return of serve early and fail to wait to see which way the opposing net player in the "I" formation is moving. This can lead to their returns being hit directly into the darting net player's hitting zone. Also, power players don't typically lob often, so the net player has license to not only dart left or right after their partner serves, but also forward to become a more effective volleyer.

3. PLAYING WITH A WEAKER PLAYER

At any level of tennis, you will sometimes play with a weaker player. To succeed in this situation, the first step is communication. It is important to be realistic and not only tell your partner to expect that more balls will be hit to them, but also to remind them that by working together you will be unified as a team and prevail.

Together, you should discuss match strategy, focusing on how to best minimize your partner's exposure and maximize your influence on the match. Playing the "I" or Australian formation is a good way for you to dominate the point because you are positioned around the middle of the court. You should also poach more often after your partner serves or returns serve to exert more influence on the match. Standing on the baseline with your partner can help you hit more shots. This formation is particularly useful if your partner is uncomfortable at the net. On the other hand, if your partner is more comfortable at the net than the baseline, it can make sense to place them close to the net to volley from that favorable position on the court.

You should play more aggressively than you would if teamed up with a partner of similar ability. Knowing that most balls are going to be directed at your partner, you should play offensively and attempt to dictate the point when the ball is in their half of the court. There is a tricky balance to strike here. The trick is not to overplay and try low percentage shots that lead to too many errors. You should be aggressive but not play outside your comfort zone. Don't forget to keep these tactics and advice in mind if you happen to be the weaker player on the team.

If you are playing with a weaker partner, look to dominate the middle of the court more.

4. PLAYING AGAINST A TEAM THAT HAS A WEAKER PLAYER

It is rare when playing doubles that both opposing players are of equal ability, so developing and utilizing a strategy to exploit the weaker player is as common as it is important. In this scenario, it is smart to use shot patterns that move the other team around, opening up the court to hit to the weaker player. Using softer, shorter angle shots more frequently can create greater movement from the opposing team and expose gaps in the court to hit to the weaker opponent.

Remember that it is easier for the stronger opponent to protect the weaker opponent from the baseline than at the net, so drop shot the weaker player and draw them towards the net. This leaves them with no place to hide. When your opponents are both at the net, hit to the weaker player. Don't shy away from hitting several shots in a row at the weaker player in this situation. When watching the professionals, it becomes obvious who they think is the weaker volleyer when their opponents are both at the net; they will fire ball after ball at the weaker net player. This can intimidate the weaker player and place greater pressure on them to perform and hold up their half of the court.

When playing a team with unequal abilities, the stronger player will sometimes cross to the weaker player's side of the court, leaving them both on the same side of the court. Don't hesitate to aim the ball to the open court when a strong player gives you the opportunity from "hogging" the weaker player's side. Even if the stronger player is able to play this shot, they will be moving sharply sideways and leave a large area of the court for the weaker player to defend. Lastly, if the stronger player is dominating with strong volleys, don't forget to lob to negate their effectiveness and move their starting position further away from the net.

5. STATISTICS

As you remember from Chapter 13, statistically speaking, if you can win 55% of the points, you will win the match the vast majority of the time. Extrapolating from that, if you have a doubles shot pattern that wins you the point 55% or more of the time, you should play the strokes and use the formation that encourages that shot pattern as much as possible. For example, if your baseline play is superior and you win 55% or more of the time from the baseline, stay with the cross-court rally. Play your shots deep and try to keep your opponent pinned at the baseline. Don't be eager to drop shot or lob the opposing net player to change that pattern. You will often find the opposing team knows its baseline play is inferior and will make a low percentage shot to bail out of it. This reaction will further raise the probability of your team winning the point.

If you are playing the net position during a cross-court baseline rally, your eagerness to poach and willingness to take risks should vary based on your partner's chances of success from the baseline. If your partner has the advantage there, your urgency to poach should be less. If your partner has the disadvantage, you might position yourself closer to the middle and take more chances, poaching more often on your opponent's wider or faster cross-court shots.

If playing the net as a team is the positioning that wins you 55% or more of the points, then the serve and volley and charging the net after the return of serve should be frequently used tactics. No strategy is 100% effective, so don't deviate from a winning tactic just because you lost a few points in a row. Yes, you will be lobbed over and miss some volleys, but remember that over the course of the match the irrefutable power of statistics will trump in the end. Having a big edge is not needed; exploiting a small edge can get you the same result.

You also have to be observant and realize that staying in a cross-court rally or rushing the net may make sense with your opponent who is playing the deuce side, while the opposite may be true with your opponent who is playing the ad side. The more you can tailor your strategy to the strengths and weaknesses of your opponents on each side of the court, the more successful you will be.

Obviously, within any winning strategy, you should mix things up occasionally to add the element of surprise and make the winning strategy even more successful. This is a balancing act that you have to figure out through intuition, observation, and experience. The higher the winning percentage of a tactic, the less the urgency should be to surprise your opponent.

If you are in the 45% or less side of the equation, do your best to get out of it in a timely, high percentage manner. For example, if you are winning 45% or less of the baseline rallies, look to drop shot, lob over the opposing net player, or move forward to play volleys by using the serve and volley and chip-and-charge tactics more often.

VI. Communication

TENNIS IS A SOLITARY GAME for a singles player, but in doubles you communicate and work together with your partner. If you watch doubles teams on the professional tour compete, they are always communicating, setting up plays, and lifting each other up to play the match in the best emotional state. They talk together to plan their objective for the next point, as well as discuss their opponents'

Discussing strategy before the point leads to quicker court position shifts and more assertive shot decisions.

strengths, weaknesses, and tendencies.

You and your partner should make the same kind of assessments, be tactically savvy, and communicate well to use the formations and strategies that best lead you to victory. To help you make the correct tactical choices, please refer to Chapter 13's strategy questions. You and your partner should answer these questions and highlight the more important ones regarding your opponents' strengths and weaknesses, positioning, and movement. By having open lines of communication, your strategy is more likely to be complete, as you might notice something in the opposing team's game that your partner didn't see and vice versa.

Good communication is also necessary to ensure that you stay positive as a team and in a good frame of mind. You can energize your partner by saying "great shot," or if your partner misses a shot, you can say "no problem, next time that shot is yours." What you say to your partner — and how you say it — can affect how they play and how you perform as a team. The longer you play with your partner, the more you will understand what words and expressions work to lift their spirits.

Stay upbeat at all times, especially if things are not going your way. That's because while it is important to be positive, it's even more important not to be negative. We naturally put enough pressure on ourselves, so the last thing we need is more pressure from our partner. Showing disappointment over your partner's miscues can make them more tense and tentative and ultimately hurt their performance. After a missed shot by your partner, you can explain it was your weak serve that put your partner on the defensive. Likewise, if you hit a winning volley, you can thank your partner for setting you up. Good partners share the blame

Always remember to congratulate your partner after a well-played point.

and deflect the praise.

There will be times when you might want to lighten the mood in a tense situation with some humor. At other times, if you are ahead in a match and sense your partner relaxing, you may need to remind your partner to stay focused and finish the job. Also, as their partner, you should monitor your partner's level of aggression. If you think they are over-swinging or playing too safely, you can suggest adjustments in their level of aggression to bring them back to their ideal swing speed.

HAND SIGNALS

Recreational players sometimes think that only advanced players use hand signals. But in fact, hand signals can be used by players of all levels and are a great way to harmonize with your partner and confuse your opponents.

The typical hand signal is from the server's partner to the server. The communication is done by placing the non-hitting hand behind the back and signaling to the server whether they plan to poach or stay still after the serve is hit. For example, an open palm means no movement, and a clenched fist means a poach is planned. A second hand signal could be given by pointing a finger in the direction of where to serve the ball. This gives the net player a head start on how to move at the net. For example, if you know that your partner is going to serve wide, then you can shift more quickly to cover the alley. While less common, the returner's partner can also give hand signals and point their fingers in different directions suggesting where their partner should hit their return. Knowing ahead of time where the ball is being hit allows the net player to gain a better position earlier in the point.

VII. Choosing a Partner

TO PICK THE RIGHT PARTNER, first you must understand fully your own strengths and weaknesses as a doubles player. Once you make an honest assessment of your game, you want to find a partner who complements your playing style, making the whole greater than the sum of its parts. For example, if you have a strong serve, try to find a partner who is skilled at the net and who can take advantage of the opportunities that stem from your power serve. Or, if you are player that uses a lot of spin on groundstrokes, then teaming up with a flat baseline power hitter will force your opponents to continually defend against shots coming at them at different speeds and trajectories. In general, a power player should team up with a consistent player and vice versa. A team of two power players may be susceptible to racking up unforced errors on a bad day, while two steady players together may lack the explosiveness to hit winners or place pressure on the opposing team to hit lower, faster and deeper in the court. Experiment and play with a variety of partners to discover what type of partner works well with your game.

In picking a partner, a major consideration is your partner's preferred side of the court to receive serve and whether that choice complements your favored side. If you or your partner have a weak backhand, then the ad side might be best because most balls come down the middle of the court, and the cross-court backhand is an easier swing than the inside-out backhand from the deuce side. Since most players prefer their forehand over their backhand, the direction in which you prefer to hit your forehand is usually more important.

Which side of the court you decide to receive serve on depends partly on which direction you prefer to hit your strongest groundstroke.

Just as baseball has pull hitters, tennis players usually have a preference as to what direction they like to hit their forehand. If you like the inside-out forehand playing singles or a later contact point, then you may prefer playing the ad side. If you prefer the cross-court forehand playing singles or earlier contact point, then you may feel most comfortable playing the deuce side. If your backhand is the stronger groundstroke, then the direction you prefer to hit that shot should be highlighted. Keep in mind, because you only have half a doubles court to cover, you can position yourself to use your strongest groundstroke most of the time.

There are other factors to contemplate

when picking a side: usually the stronger partner plays the ad side because that is the side with the vast majority of the break points, as well as the very important 15-30 stage of the game. Another argument for the better player to return on the ad side is that they can hit more overheads. This is because most lobs are in the middle third of the court, which will be on the right side of the body for the ad side player, putting them in a good position for the overhead swing. Furthermore, the poaching forehand volley is done from the ad side, and because the forehand volley permits more time and reach than the backhand volley, more opportunities will arise to intercept balls for the ad side player. If the ability level is fairly equal between partners, then the player with the better lob may play the deuce side because if the lob goes over the net player's head, it will be a difficult a high backhand for a right-handed server to defend.

While not as important as playing skills, personality is also a big consideration. Remember there is a lot of down time between points; it

If you get along well with your doubles partner, you will practice together more and understand each other's game better.

is important that you spend it with a partner with whom you produce a good match tempo and positive mental state. If you tend to rush through matches, choose someone whose internal clock runs a little more slowly than yours and who can get you to pause and gather your composure. A doubles team of two "fast-forward" players often play well when leading, but after losing two or three consecutive games, they are unlikely to slow down to stop the momentum. Conversely, if your mind works in a more deliberate fashion, pick someone who can turn up the emotional tempo of the match. I also think placing a quiet player with a chatty one can work well too. A doubles team of two introverts may not communicate enough, while two extroverts may talk too much, causing the flow of the match to become disjointed and the focus of their primary strategy diluted due to an overflow of information.

Remember that it is helpful to get along well with your partner. This helps keep your communication and coordination strong and makes it more likely that you will practice together more often and understand each other's game better. Spending a lot of time prac-

ticing together will help you determine who should defend the lob and balls hit towards the middle of the court. It will also help you to get to know your teammate's strengths and weaknesses as well as their cross-court and down-the-line tendencies. This knowledge will help you gauge the likelihood of whether a strong or weak shot is coming from your partner, allowing you to more quickly position yourself forwards offensively or backwards defensively. It will also help you get a jump start moving right and left on the court.

IX. Doubles Practice

PRACTICING FOR DOUBLES has the same guidelines as practicing for singles: you must keep up your intensity, be professional, and be prepared with a plan for practice. However, doubles differs from singles in many ways, and practice sessions should be geared with this in mind.

In doubles, the height of the shot is important and the ability to keep the ball low with finesse or high and deep with lobs takes on extra significance. Doubles places greater emphasis on movement forward and backward instead of the more common lateral movement used in singles. As compared to singles, there are many more opportunities to volley or react off the opposing net player's volley to either volley yourself or hit groundstrokes from the baseline.

The purpose of the serve and the direction and speed of the return is also different. In doubles, the placement and consistency of the serve is a higher priority. Also, the doubles return of serve is mostly hit cross court, and it must have the accuracy and power to avoid the serving team's net player. All practice sessions should focus on honing these doubles-specific skills. Lastly, communication between you and your partner in practice is vital for working out designed plays, poaching, defending lobs, etc. that obviously are not needed during a singles practice session.

1. DINGLES

Goal: To assess the situation quickly and move to the position on the court that will best help your team win the point.

With all four players on the baseline, both players on one team feed the ball cross court at the same time to their practice partners on the other side of the court. The four players rally cross court with one another, and once an error is made, the player who made the error calls out "Dingles" and the remaining ball is played out by the four players. First team to 11 points wins. Add a variation by hitting down the line to begin or with the four players hitting volleys from the service line.

2. AIR BALL

Goal: Move your opponent around the court to open up space for passing shots or low shots at the feet of the opposing net players.

Start with one team on the baseline and one team at the net. One of the net players feeds the ball to the baseline team who try to pass or lob the net team to win the point. Regular scoring is used unless the baseline team gets the ball to bounce on the net team's side of the court. If that happens, the baseline team wins two points instead of one. First team to 15 wins and then switch roles. Add a variation and play four games of doubles with serves where the only ball that can bounce is the serve.

3. LOB RETURN

Goal: Practice hitting the lob on the return of serve and then the overhead.

The net player on the serving team must be touching the net with their racquet when the server hits the ball. The returner hits the lob and plays out the point. First team to nine points wins, and then players rotate one position to the left and begin the next game with a new player serving. Add a variation by awarding two points to the lobbing team if their lob bounces and/or two points to the overhead team if they hit a winner on the overhead.

4. SEVENS

Goal: Learn to use different formations and to serve and poach as a strategic unit.

One player serves until either team reaches seven points. The net player of the serving team must use one of four choices for each point — poach, fake poach, Australian formation, or "I" formation. If the returning team wins the game, players rotate one position to the left and begin the next game with a new player serving. If the serving team wins, the receiving team begins the next game with a two point lead. If the serving team wins the second game, then the receiving team starts with a four point lead.

5. SMALL COURT, BIG COURT

Goal: Encourage poaching and aggressive net play.

Play out the point in the one up, one back formation with the server and receiver rallying cross court using the singles court only. The reduced court gives the net players more opportunities to poach. The two players at the net are looking to poach, and once a volley is struck, then the whole doubles court is available to use to play out the point. First team to 11 points wins, and then players rotate one spot to the left and begin the next game with a new player serving.

Federer's compo-
sure allows him to
think clearly during
matches.

CHAPTER 15

Psychology

I T IS TRUE THAT DEVELOPING THE STROKES and learning the strategies discussed in the previous chapters will give you an edge over your opponents. However, tennis is also a gritty mental sport, and if you are not focused and resilient, you will lose matches that you should win based on your strokes and knowledge. You need to be both mentally strong to stay determined and mentally positive so you compete in an emotionally elevated and energetic manner. Rafael Nadal, considering the importance of psychology in tennis, wrote, "Tennis is, more than most sports, a sport of the mind; it is the player who has those good sensations on the most days, who manages to isolate himself best from his fears and from the ups and downs in morale a match inevitably brings, who ends up being world number one."[1] While you might not aspire to be "world number one," your tennis goals are much more likely to be accomplished if during your matches you can remain focused, stay positive, and think clearly in the heat of the battle.

Improving mentally doesn't happen overnight but rather, like everything else in tennis, takes training and experience. Roger Federer and Bjorn Borg are two examples of professional players who have a good temperament on the court. But this wasn't always the case. As kids, their parents revoked their playing privileges after angry outbursts on the court. Over time, both players learned to control their emotions and made the mental side of their game a strength. For most of us, like Federer and Borg, becoming mentally strong is a skill that must be nurtured and developed.

In this chapter, I'll give you a mental training regime that will help you both gain a cerebral edge over your opponents and enjoy the game more. The chapter is divided into eight sections: the inner voice, concentration, confidence, overconfidence, overcoming adversity, nervousness, body language, and visualization.

I. The Inner Voice

THE FIRST THING YOU MUST LEARN is to navigate the challenges of play with a positive and constructive inner voice. The inner voice is crucial in every sport, but it is especially so in tennis since a proportionally small amount of the time is spent actually playing the point. The rest of the time goes to picking up balls, changing ends, and getting ready for the next point. You want to spend that time thinking coherently and staying emotionally upbeat.

The messages spoken by your inner voice are energy impulses that affect how your brain processes the match. You can be winning but feel flat, or you can be losing but still feel energized, all by the messages sent through the mind. Mentally tough competitors know that thoughts control emotions and emotions affect performance. It is important to remember that if you have positive thoughts, you will be in a good emotional state and play at a higher level.

How can you work on improving your inner voice? Through mindfulness. That is, during the match, ask yourself if your thoughts are making you play better or worse. Train yourself so that when a negative thought enters your mind, you recognize it, dismiss it, and replace it with a positive thought. A dysfunctional inner voice that says "I hate my serve" will compromise your serve and make it worse — thoughts can become self-fulfilling prophecies. Instead, after a double fault, adopt self-talk such as, "I've hit great serves countless times before

and I'm going to do another one right now." Or, if you start a match poorly, don't tell yourself, "Today just isn't my day." Instead, tell yourself, "It's early in the match and I know my timing and rhythm will improve as the match progresses." All these inner thoughts have emotional consequences, but the latter ones are much more productive to your performance. Playing well comes from confidence and trust in your game, and your thoughts should reflect that confidence and trust.

Of course, every mind is different and your mind will respond to words in its own unique way, so experiment with different words and phrases until you discover the ones that motivate you and overpower your negative sub-

"Be good to yourself," Murray once wrote in a notebook that he read on court; he knows that his negative inner voice has sometimes adversely affected his performance. [2]

Karolina Pliskova responds positively after winning a point.

INNER VOICE TRAINING

After the point is over, you have approximately 15 seconds to get ready for the next point. During that time there are four stages the inner voice must navigate through to stay constructive.[4] By doing this and establishing your own pace and rhythm between points, you will feel in control and gain confidence from that feeling and its familiarity.

STAGE 1: RESPOND TO THE LAST POINT

If you win the point, you should use the positive feelings to spur your energy; if you lost it, quickly reflect on what can be learned and get back into a positive frame of mind.

STAGE 2: RELAX AND RECOVER

During this stage, your breathing should be deep, your body language positive, and your inner voice quiet, ensuring that the mind is relaxed and feeling reassured.

STAGE 3: PREPARE

Begin lifting your emotional state and become excited about playing the next point. Now you are thinking strategically about how you are going to serve or return and what level of aggression will give you the best probability of winning the point.

conscious. After the match, analyze how well your inner voice spoke to you and assess the negative-to-positive message ratio. The positives should vastly outweigh the negatives.

Also, don't weigh down your mind with too much self-talk on technique during the match. Save working on technique for the practice court. During matches, self-talk should focus on staying positive, tactics, and overall competitiveness. Thinking about technique during the match can lead to "paralysis by analysis," when attempts to improve synchronized brain activity and muscle movement instead makes it worse. As Serena Williams once said, "When I think too much, I don't serve well. When I just say, 'Serena, just hit the ball and serve,' that's when I serve really well."[3]

STAGE 4: PERFORM RITUALS

Rituals may include how many times you bounce the ball on the serve or how you move around on your feet before the return of serve. These rituals before you start the point place your body on autopilot and allow your mind to become unencumbered, deepening your focus for the task ahead.

All professionals develop their own methods to figure out how to use their inner voice as a positive force through each of the four stages. Practice and develop your own way of staying upbeat between points and use that process to be in an optimal emotional state as you begin each point.

Sometimes the professionals use rituals such as straightening their strings to gather their thoughts.

II. Concentration

TENNIS REQUIRES STEADY concentration. If you can sustain concentration, you will make good shot choices, stay true to your prepared game plan, and take a big step forward toward maintaining the energy level and determination needed to win the match.

It can be difficult to concentrate because our minds naturally tend to shift focus when presented with novel stimuli. This bias towards new sights and sounds once alerted our ancestors to dangers in the wild, but it is a destructive force in the game of tennis. In a typical match, you will bombarded with internal and external stimuli, thoughts, and emotions. If you are fully focused, you should be able to block out everything extraneous to your game plan, whether it is an unruly supporter of your opponent, another match happening on an adjacent court, or an opponent who takes an inordinate amount of time between points. Players with good concentration can control the direction of their thoughts and block out these types of distractions.

It is important to know not only what to concentrate on, but also how to maintain concentration over a long period of time. Many players are able to focus fully for a set, but few are able to do it continuously for two or three sets. Fortunately, concentration is a mental skill that can be developed through repetition and practice. It is also helpful to develop inner voice catch phrases like "only the ball matters" or "right here, right now," and add rituals such as straightening your strings or bouncing the ball on the ground to bring a distracted mind back to where it should be.

Jelena Jankovic let frustration from losing a lead in the second set cloud her focus during the third set at the 2015 Indian Wells final.

1. STAYING PRESENT

Concentration requires staying present. After any setback, whether losing a big lead or missing an easy shot, it can be difficult to stay focused. Many players, even the touring pros, dwell on setbacks and end up frustrating themselves even more. Jelena Jankovic, in the third set of the 2015 Indian Wells women's singles final, was still thinking about blown chances earlier in the match. During a change-over in a close third set, I heard her on television say to her coach, "I haven't been able to hold my serve...That's why I lost that second set." She went on to lose the match, and her lack of present thought didn't help.

Your mind should be clear at the beginning of each point. Dwelling on your previously missed shot only reinforces that mistake in your mind and increases the likelihood of making the same mistake again. If you are distracted in any way by the previous point, bring your mind back to the present and keep your focus on the next serve or return of serve.

This is not to say that you shouldn't learn from what just happened, but rather that you should not dwell on past mistakes. For instance, if you missed the previous point because you attempted a risky shot, you can remind yourself to be more patient next time. Or, if your opponent hits a winning volley from close to the net, you can make a mental note to lob more frequently.

Remember that the negative mental characteristics of overconfidence and lack of confidence are both future-oriented qualities that share the absence of present thought. For example, relaxing when you are ahead 40-0 because you assume the game is yours can be costly. If you lose the 40-0 point through a careless shot and then lose the subsequent point, the score is suddenly 40-30 and not only has your opponent regained the momentum, but the possibility of losing the game that you were well ahead in may raise your anxiety and cause you to play the 40-30 point poorly.

The bottom line: don't procrastinate. Fight to stay present in every game one point at a time, because the momentum of a game can quickly shift quickly away from you. If you are down 0-40, don't give up on winning the game; your opponent may suffer from lack of present thought, play a loose point, and allow you back in the game. This can be huge in a match. Winning a game from 0-40 down can demoralize your opponent and sometimes change the complexion of the set.

2. FOCUS ON THE PROCESS

Players who are able to stay present have trained their mind to focus on the process and not the outcome. Don't obsess on winning or losing. Think of the match more as a probability gambit and focus on performing the actions that will tilt the odds in your favor.

The negative effects of focusing on the outcome were apparent in Serena Williams' loss to Roberta Vinci at the 2015 U.S. Open. The pressure to win that tournament and complete the historic Grand Slam contributed to Serena's nervous play and loss to a player she had defeated in four previous match-ups without losing a set. Even in the relaxed environment of my group lessons, the negative impact of focusing on the outcome is sometimes easily recognizable. If a game of first to eleven points ends up being nine points all, the swings that were confident at the beginning of the game sometimes become less assured. Instead of raising their level of play when it counts the most, often the closer players get to the outcome, the lower their performance.

To keep your level of performance consis-

Andre Agassi once wrote, "Freed from the thoughts of winning, I instantly play better. I stop thinking, start feeling. My shots become a half-second quicker, my decisions become the product of instinct rather than logic."[5]

tently high, focus on the process. You can think of the process of the match like a GPS guiding you to a desired destination. Similar to GPS giving you a sequence of street directions, the point-to-point tennis process that guides you to victory involves staying mentally positive, moving your feet well, using the right tactics, and hitting with the appropriate level of aggression. If you concentrate in this manner, you will more than likely arrive at your desired destination at the end of the match: victory.

View focus on the process with a sense of fascination and enthusiasm. Tennis has many strokes and variables all filtered through the imperfection of humankind, and therefore, the process can never be predictable or mundane. That's a wonderful quality of tennis; take advantage of it. After winning match point, you should feel great about winning, but also slightly let down that the enjoyment from being immersed in the process is over. If you are able to feel this way, you will play enthused and relaxed, and reach a sublime state that not enough players experience.

III. Nervousness

NERVOUSNESS CAN PRODUCE SPECIFIC physical and mental stresses. It can lead to an elevated heart rate, tension in the legs and arms, and a racing mind. In turn, this can slow down your movement, tighten your grip, and cloud your concentration. Your swing speed may change from one of controlled aggression to either hitting tentatively and hoping the ball will go in or swinging aggressively to end the point as quickly as possible. Of course, the great irony of nervousness is that players get tight because they are driven to win, but unfortunately it can lead to a style of play that takes them further away from achieving that goal.

To be sure, a level of nervousness is built into the sport itself. Due to the way tennis is scored, comebacks are encouraged, so players can feel a lack of security when ahead. The sudden nature of the scoring system can raise anxiety as well. For example, at 5-5 in a third set tiebreak, both players are two points away from winning a very long match. There is a lot of time, effort, and emotion invested in the match up to that point so it is understandable that players can get nervous. Furthermore, there are no time constraints in tennis, and therefore, there is no way to safely hold on

to a lead by running out the clock. You must finish the job.

You can work to overcome the nervousness inherent in tennis. Here are five mental tips that can reduce your nervousness.

1. PERCEIVE THE SITUATION CORRECTLY

Anxiety's effect on your level of play is largely based on your perception. Embrace the mindset that you are lucky to be healthy and playing a worthy competitor in a sport that you enjoy. Feelings of gratitude will stimulate a key part of the brain that lowers stress.

Also, it is helpful to develop a wider perspective of the game and view your tennis career as an evolving process of learning, adventure, and self-discovery. The more you can fuel your performance with feelings of introspective enthusiasm and positive self-development, the more relaxed and better you will play.

"Success is a journey, not a destination. The doing is often more important than the outcome." [6]

- Arthur Ashe

2. FOCUS ON THE PROCESS, NOT THE OUTCOME

As mentioned earlier, concentrate on executing the steps that help you move the match in a winning direction and avoid thinking about the end of the match.

3. KEEP MOVING AND BREATHE DEEPLY

If you are struggling with nerves, keep your feet moving and do some shadow swings to help you stay loose. Feel free to turn your back on your opponent for a few seconds between points and take some deep breaths before setting up for the serve or return.

Even the greats can let their nerves get the best of them. Nadal's self-described nervous play led to some uncharacteristic losses in 2015. After his early loss at the 2015 Miami Open, he said, "It's not a question of tennis, the thing is the question of being relaxed enough to play well...I am still playing with too much nerves for a lot of moments." [7]

4. RELAX AND TRUST

Ironically, it is by letting go slightly that your nerves recede and you play better. You will play your best when you trust your swing and have the confidence that your body will do the right thing. Think about how many times you have hit a great return on a serve that is a foot or two is out. Once you realize the serve is out, you surrendered control of the conscious mind and allowed your swing to flourish unencumbered by anxiety.

5. REMEMBER THAT YOUR OPPONENT IS LIKELY TO BE NERVOUS TOO

If you are nervous, you can take some solace that your opponent is likely to be nervous too. If you can effectively use the advice discussed above, you can seize the psychological advantage and increase your chances of winning the match.

Using this advice to reduce nervousness during the fury of the match isn't easy. It must be practiced and honed with diligence. Additionally, you must be able to distinguish harmful nervousness from a small tingle of nerves — the positive pressure — that pushes you to play your best. A small level of nervousness at a pivotal stage of the match is normal and can be a catalyst for peak performance. It will produce adrenaline which, when channeled in the right way, can help you play better, with heightened awareness and increased muscle readiness. Learn to appreciate it and train yourself to equate a mild dose of nerves with excitement and an opportunity to play your best tennis. Developing the ability to enjoy pressure and play well in a close match will be a great source of pride and a memory that you can reflect upon fondly.

IV. Confidence

PLAYING WITH CONFIDENCE resides at the opposite end of the performance spectrum from nervousness and will often play a significant role in the outcome of the match. When you are confident, your body flows and you play in a relaxed and assertive manner. Many times in my coaching career I've seen the positive effect a boost of confidence can have on students. For example, if an inexperienced player wins a serving game during a group lesson aiming for targets, the confidence gained from that win will often have that student looking forward to serving more, practicing the serve more, and improving their serve more quickly from that win and increase in belief.

Confidence can affect a player's game in a variety of ways. For example, if you believe in your forehand, you are going to be more decisive on that stroke. If you are very fit, you will have confidence late into a long match because of your superior endurance. Confidence also leads to good decision-making. If you have confidence in your baseline game, you will remain patient during the rally, playing high percentage tennis. However, if you lack confidence in your groundstrokes, you may attempt to end the point quickly with a low percentage serve or overly aggressive baseline shot.

Confidence builds on itself, largely from winning matches. When you win, you become more self-assured, and from this feeling you play better and enjoy the benefits of this fortuitous cycle. The way Marin Cilic swept through Thomas Berdych, Roger Federer, and Kei Nishikori in straight sets to unexpectedly win the 2014 U.S. Open is an example of how confidence can power a player's game to new heights. In describing Cilic's run, Federer put it succinctly, "No fear and just full-out confidence." [8]

Confidence can be a positive cycle; however, the cycle can suffer a setback or reversal after losses. Remember that your confidence will go up and down over your tennis career, and therefore, it is wise to appreciate it when

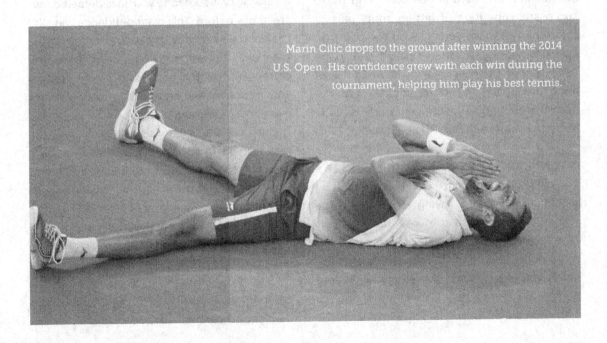

Marin Cilic drops to the ground after winning the 2014 U.S. Open. His confidence grew with each win during the tournament, helping him play his best tennis.

it's present and not be discouraged if it fades, because it will return.

If you lose trust in your game, you should look for ways to reestablish that trust — even the greats do this. After losing in the second round at Wimbledon in 2013, Federer quickly decided to enter a small tournament in Hamburg with the hope of accumulating wins and restoring faith in his game. He said, "Right now I just want to win a lot of matches, hopefully win a couple of tournaments, and then sort of build confidence."[9] If you experience a bad patch of form, you can do what Federer did and enter a tournament a level down from your usual level. Winning a series of matches against players that give you a little more time to set up for your strokes can bring back the positive virtues of confidence.

Here are three additional tips suggested from noted tennis coach and psychologist Allen Fox that you can use to restore faith in your game.

1. PREPARE BEFORE THE MATCH

Spend time on the practice court and make successful repetition of hitting shots part of the remedy. Before you walk on the court do an extended visualization session (*see page 296*) to get yourself in a positive frame of mind and loosen up your muscles through dynamic stretching to ensure your body is ready for action before the first ball is struck.

2. PLAY HIGH PERCENTAGE TENNIS

You can build confidence during the match by extending rallies and playing your shots a little higher over the net and more inside the lines than usual. The cumulative effect of hitting more shots will improve your timing and belief in your game. Once self-assurance in your game returns, you can play with more aggression and risk.

3. PRACTICE HARD TO CORRECT FLAWS IN STROKE TECHNIQUE

If you have a technical flaw in your game, practice hard to correct it so your swings stay smooth at all stages of a match. If you have good technique, you are much more likely to be confident. For example, if you have a glitch in your second serve, your faulty technique and subsequent lack of confidence will likely show up in double faults under stress. When faced with a weakness in your game, take the mental approach that every player has strengths and weakness and understand that your strokes are as good as they are going to be at this point in time. Unify psychologically behind the "cards you were dealt" mentality and always stay positive in a good emotional state.

V. Overconfidence

CONFIDENCE IS GOOD, but overconfidence can be costly. Never assume that the match is yours simply because your opponent has a lower ranking or is someone you have defeated several times before. This overconfidence can lead to poor mental and physical preparation before the match that will hurt your performance. The correct mental approach is to always respect your opponent and prepare conscientiously for every match, without exception.

Overconfidence can also strike during the match. Even if you have played a small amount of competitive tennis, there is a good chance that you have let down your guard and experienced the awful feeling of blowing a 5-1 or 5-2 lead in a set. When you have full command of a match like this, there is a danger of falling into the "comfort trap" where you feel satisfied with the situation and play without the competitive intensity to finish the job. This can lead to careless shots and usher your opponent back in the match. Another thing to keep in mind when playing with a lead is that many opponents play their best when they are losing and throw caution to the wind. This attitude can relax them, leading them to play better and possibly wrestle the match back in their favor.

Here are four tips for preventing overconfidence from affecting your level of play.

1. KEEP YOUR MENTAL INTENSITY CONSISTENTLY HIGH

If you notice some overconfidence creeping in, take a quick timeout, walk to the back fence, and remind yourself that playing tennis with a lack of mindfulness is perilous. Then jog in place for a few seconds to help raise your energy level. This regrouping can assist you in getting back to the right mental zone and awake your killer instinct to finish off the match.

2. STAY WITH YOUR WINNING PLAN

Continuing to play well and focusing on your winning game plan will give your opponent the sense that a comeback is almost impossible. If they see you play a few loose points due to overconfidence, you are giving them hope and opening the door for a comeback.

3. ACKNOWLEDGE THE SCORING SYSTEM AND THE DANGER THAT LURKS BEHIND A FREE-SWINGING OPPONENT

The combination of the scoring system and a carefree opponent can combine to make a lead in tennis fragile, which can turn overconfidence swiftly into consternation. For example, if you are ahead 40-30 you might be one point away from winning but, at the same time, your opponent may be one point away from tying the game and three points away from a new game and a fresh start.

4. RECOLLECTION

A quick recollection of a match you lost after having a big lead can act as the reminiscing smelling salt needed to wake you up and put a jolt back into your intensity.

VI. Overcoming Adversity

TENNIS INVOLVES some unpredictability, so you are guaranteed to play some matches that will test your resolve. For example, there will be days when your timing is off and fluent winners are unusually hard to come by. Sometimes it will be very windy or the temperature very hot. You will experience bad luck, such as an unfortunate net cord on a big point or an opponent's mis-hit off the frame that ends up being a winner. To overcome adversity, you must hone your ability to keep your emotions in control and persevere.

Perseverance is an essential trait in overcoming adversity, and perseverance is a derivative of the will to win. It may be cliché, but it is true — the player who wins the match is often the one who wants to win the most. Legendary NFL coach Vince Lombardi said it well: "Winning isn't everything, but wanting to win is." The will to win helps you soldier on during the trying situations that occur during a match. Use professional players such as Dominika Cibulkova as your competitive role model. The diminutive Cibulkova has won many matches through her fight and tenacity. Or maybe you know someone at your local club who often wins because of their steely resolve and determination. Having players such as these to look up to can give you direction and inspiration.

When things aren't going your way or match conditions are challenging, try the following four tips.

1. TAKE YOUR TIME

Take a five second pause and walk away from the action. A step back can help you see a problem from a new perspective and increase your ability to control your emotions. During this short break, keep your inner voice optimistic and focus on the strategy for your next serve or return of serve.

2. BE HONEST

Acknowledging that your emotional state has been compromised can make you calmer. Looking inward from an outside perspective can help you to be more rational and assess the situation more objectively.

3. USE PHYSIOLOGICAL TOOLS

Taking deep breaths and bouncing around on your feet are terrific physiological tools to keep the muscles loose and get you back to the correct emotional state.

4. COMBINE ACCEPTANCE WITH A POSITIVE RATIONALE

Accept bad luck as a comically incongruous part of the game and remind yourself that you will get your share of fortunate net cords and mishits too. Usually the number of lucky breaks each player receives evens out over the course of a match. Accept that days where your timing is off is part of being human and be motivated by the fact that victories on such ill-fated days are even sweeter and more admirable. Lastly, accept that inclement weather is part of the game and remind yourself that your opponent is dealing with the same conditions.

On some days, tennis will test your temperament; just ask Djokovic.

VII. Body Language

YOUR BODY LANGUAGE WILL AFFECT your mental state — and your opponent's. Most players exhibit positive body language when they are winning. Their head is high, shoulders up, and they pump their fist more frequently. This body language can invigorate a player's game by adding adrenaline and increasing focus while deflating an opponent. The challenge in tennis is to have positive body language when losing. Bad body language includes dropping the shoulders, shaking your head, or muttering to yourself. This poor physical presence will lower your energy level and send encouraging

COACH'S BOX:

Never be intimidated by an opponent's higher ranking or go into a match with a defeatist attitude. On the professional tour, a player defeats an opponent with a significantly higher ranking in almost every tournament. This occurs at all levels of the game. Human variability along with the weather, court surface, injuries, and other factors make every match unique. Your competitive mantra should be to fight for every ball and play every match on its merits. If you maintain this philosophy, you will maximize your abilities and have many "surprising" victories.

signals to your opponent.

Professionals are mentally trained to be aware of the power of body language. When watching great players like Federer and Nadal, you can't tell if they are winning or losing the match by their appearance. They always look focused and eager to compete. Such players are wonderful role models for the poise needed for good body language; however, both players do it in slightly different ways. Nadal walks quickly with a dogged determination, while Federer walks slower in a more relaxed manner. You too need to find the type of body language and walking pace between points that puts you in the best mood and match rhythm to produce your best tennis.

To improve your body language, try these techniques.

1. DISASSOCIATE

When a point is lost, train yourself to emotionally move on and walk to set up for the next point with good posture and confidence.

This may require both disassociating yourself from your emotions and a little bit of acting skill. Good body language doesn't always require loyalty to feelings in the name of authenticity, but rather rebelling against negative impulses and acting "right" even when you don't feel like it. You can maintain a positive appearance after losing a point by using routines like contentedly straightening your strings or bouncing around from foot to foot before returning serve.

2. GOOD SPORTSMANSHIP

As I tell my students, it's okay to acknowledge your opponent's good shot. I've seen Djokovic do this many times by tapping his hand on his strings or giving his opponent the thumbs up sign. Besides exhibiting good sportsmanship, this will put the shot behind you and give you

By giving the thumbs up to an opponent's good shot, Djokovic puts the point behind him and keeps his mind in a positive state.

"One who smiles rather than rages is always stronger."
- Japanese Proverb

closure. Plus, it shows your opponent that you are not concerned and enjoying the competitive experience.

3. SMILE

A smile stimulates brain activity associated with positive emotions. In a pressured situation, a smile can help you to defuse negative feelings and allow you to think clearly and remain in the present.

VIII. Visualization

AS MENTIONED EARLIER, improving the mental side of your game doesn't happen by chance; you must work at it and practicing visualization techniques should be part of the process. Using visualization techniques before

and during the match can help you play with more confidence and stay in the right emotional state. Such techniques can set up a blueprint for your body's subconscious to follow in order to play your best tennis. In contrast, if you don't visualize, you can quickly lose confidence and good emotions when things aren't going your way, leading the match to spiral downward out of your grasp.

I. BEFORE THE MATCH

Begin the visualization process the night before or morning of the match by finding a quiet place and spending at least ten minutes rehearsing in your mind. Visualize hitting great shots, staying calm and focused, walking confidently, and even shaking hands as the victor at the end of the match. Picture yourself in long and short rallies and executing shot patterns that you predict will work well. For example, if you know you will be playing an opponent who stands a long way behind the baseline or is a poor mover, you might visualize yourself hitting successful drop shots during a rally. Setting clear on-court goals like this will help bring order during an unpredictable match. Visualization can also improve any mental weaknesses you may have. For example, if you struggle with your temperament, then visualize yourself remaining composed even under difficult circumstances.

Imagine not just points, but also games and sets to prepare you best for the upcoming reality. The closer the visualization represents reality, the more relevant and helpful the imagery will be. See in your mind hitting great shots to specific areas of the court, feel the impact of the ball on the strings, and hear the sound of the ball. It is important to feel the emotions of joy and enthusiasm associated with hitting great shots in your mind. This positive reinforcement will encourage your mind and body to reproduce it later on the court. While visualizing hitting great shots, clench your left hand at the same time. Then at crucial times during the match, you can clench your left hand and positive feelings will immediately enter your mind.

To be realistic and prepared, it is also important to picture losing some points. If you plan only for success, you will be too relaxed and less likely to achieve your goal. Blind optimism can trick your mind into thinking that the job is done. Being mindful during the visualization process of not only your positive hopes, but also of the impediments, will energize you best before the match.

2. DURING THE MATCH
Visualization can help you play better during the match too. All tennis players visualize during the match to a greater or lesser degree. Unfortunately, it is often done in a way that hurts, not helps, their performance. Too often players visualize failure and frequently are not even aware they are doing so — it can be very ingrained in some of us. For example, as a player prepares to hit an overhead off a high lob, a picture of their overhead being dumped into the net may flash before their mind. Or, as they are getting ready to return serve, the memory of a missed return may enter their brain. Just as you must be aware of the words you say to yourself, you also must be conscious of the images that play out in your mind. Be alert and train yourself to notice and delete negative images and replace them with positive ones.

If you have encountered a slump during a match, the first step is to calm your mind so the visualization process can work best. Take a five second break between points or while changing ends and imagine yourself hitting

COACH'S BOX:

Part of the visualization process should be to develop and write out a positive pre-match script. After completing the pre-match visualization process, read your pre-match script and vow to hold yourself accountable to it. An example could be, "I am fortunate to play this great sport and appreciate the opportunity to play today. I understand that my emotions play an important role in my performance, and knowing that, I will remain resolute, energetic, and positive 100% of the time. I will stay focused on and committed to the process on each and every point. Win or lose, this match will end with me taking another step forward in improving my game and feeling satisfied knowing that I came prepared and gave my very best effort. Now play hard and have fun!" Reading a motivational paragraph like this can get you excited to play before the match and help you stay in the right emotional state during the match.

aggressive, fluent strokes. It is helpful to have specific shots in mind that have happened in the past. For example, if you hit an ace at a critical time in a memorable match, use that memory to assist getting your confidence back on the serve.

Conducting shadow swings while visualizing can further lift your confidence. If you miss an easy forehand, shake it off by doing a forehand shadow swing. As you do it, imagine the ball going exactly where you intend. This has a positive double effect — it stops you from dwelling on the missed shot and will have you mentally prepared when that shot arrives again.

Djokovic celebrating his
2012 Australian Open
marathon victory — all his
hard work improving his
fitness paid off.

CHAPTER 16

Fitness

YOU CAN KNOW HOW TO USE YOUR BODY for balance, powerful swings, and efficient movement. You can know how to swing the racquet, the strategy, and how to stay mentally positive and focused, but if you become physically tired, those skills dissipate and renders that knowledge moot.

Fitness underpins every aspect of tennis, and while it has always been a crucial part of the game, in the modern era it has become even more important. This is especially true on the professional tour. The pros are using their incredible fitness to cover the court and extend points like never before. ATP player Janko Tipsarevic spoke of how difficult it can be to win a rally, "It takes five winners to finish a point. One point now seems like a full workout."[1] The grueling rallies have made a long professional singles match one of the most physically and mentally exhausting experiences in all sports. Take the six-hour 2012 Australian Open Final between Nadal and Djokovic, in which chairs were carried onto the court for the trophy presentation because both players were so fatigued they could barely stand. The pros fully understand the increased physicality of the game and now spend almost as much time working out off the court as they do on the court hitting balls. Some top players even hire teams of fitness experts that include a conditioning coach, nutritionist, and physiotherapist in a effort to gain an advantage over their competitors.

There are many examples of professional players whose rankings have soared after taking their fitness to new heights. After experiencing a mid-career slump, Andre Agassi took to the gym daily and ran up hills in Las Vegas' searing heat in between tournaments. He went on to win five of his eight Grand Slam titles after he turned 28, an age typically associated with a decline in a player's skills and speed.

Agassi attributed his late career success to his improved fitness. He knew his faster movement permitted him to reach more shots balanced and his improved endurance allowed him to remain energetic even at the end of a very long match. This meant he could win points by encouraging extended rallies and exhausting his opponents, leading them to resort to low percentage shots. He said, "If your body is weak, it tells you what to do. If your body is strong, it will actually listen to you when you tell it to do something."[2] Obviously, recreational players don't need to dedicate their lives to fitness the way Agassi did, but there is a good lesson to be learned for players of all abilities: improving your fitness will significantly improve your performance.

Tennis is a uniquely athletic sport that requires a special type of fitness. Tennis players need agility to maintain balance on a difficult volley or wide ball, quick bursts of speed to run down shots hit all over the court, and the endurance to last a long match. In addition, they need to be flexible and strong from head to toe. On most shots, the energy is transferred up the body, building such that each body

Andre Agassi won most of his Grand Slam titles after devoting himself to improving his fitness late in his career.

segment benefits from the movements and power of the previous body segment, utilizing the kinetic chain. Being inflexible or weak in one body part will reduce the power gathering and moving to the next body part and result in a less forceful shot.

It is not surprising then, knowing the full body nature of tennis and the variety in type and intensity of movements it requires, that tennis is considered one of the best sports to play to improve one's overall health and fitness. A study released by the British Journal of Sports Medicine found that people who played racquet sports had the lowest risk of death of all sports participants surveyed in the study.[3] As former U.S. Open Champion Samantha Stosur once said, "Tennis takes care of everything. It requires agility and quickness to get to the ball, core strength to get power into your shots, and stamina to last for an entire match. In addition to toning your arms and shoulders, it's a total body workout for your legs and abs, and works your heart and core unlike any other sport."[4]

In this chapter, I will explain six components of fitness that are crucial to tennis players: flexibility, agility, quickness, core stability, strength, and endurance. I share exercises that will help you improve these components, including 15 flexibility exercises and four exercises each for the other five components. There are hundreds of exercises that can help you improve your fitness in these areas: I have provided some samples that have worked well for my students. Your job is to mix up your workout routine with an assortment of exercises and to tailor your fitness regime to your age and fitness level. As with any fitness program, please consult your physician before using the exercises listed in this book. After explaining the six components of fitness, the chapter concludes with a section on nutrition and hydration that will help you choose the right fuel for your body to feel energetic all match long.

I. Flexibility

NOVAK DJOKOVIC'S FLEXIBILITY sets him apart from other top ATP players. He stretches throughout the day and sometimes spends more than two hours stretching, knowing it helps him recover more quickly after matches and increases the chances of him having a long career. On the court, the benefits are im-

Djokovic prides himself on being extremely flexible and works on it constantly. He has been known to continue casual conversations with friends while resting his leg on their shoulder to stretch.

mediate and obvious. His flexibility allows him to contort his body into different shapes under duress while still maintaining balance, enhancing his ability to control the racquet and hit an effective shot. His flexibility also allows him to hug the baseline during the point and "shrink" the court; he achieves this by doing near splits to cover his opponents' best shots and extend rallies, pushing his opponents to hit harder and harder and aim closer to the lines, ultimately forcing errors. The role of Djokovic's flexibility in his success has highlighted the value of being limber and motivated many of his peers to become as physically elastic as possible.

Flexibility is not only crucial for the top professionals; it is necessary for players of all levels. I'll discuss the advantages of flexibility in greater detail before moving on to different types of stretching.

I. ADVANTAGES OF FLEXIBILITY

A. MORE POWER
Any restrictions in elasticity will limit your range of motion and the amount of power your muscles can generate during the swing. The serve is a good case in point. The longer the shoulder muscles can stretch on the serve, the stronger the force produced when the muscle contracts. Also, greater shoulder joint flexibility will produce a longer swing path to build up racquet speed from the bottom of the racquet drop to contact.

B. IMPROVED BALANCE
Greater flexibility allows you to stay balanced in challenging situations. For example, when reaching for a low, wide shot, being flexible through your core will allow you to widen your stance, keep your balance, and thus control the racquet well. After playing that low, wide

Serena Williams' dedication to stretching is plain to see at the end of this point at the 2015 U.S. Open.

shot, it will also allow you to drop your body down and load up good power in the legs to change directions and recover quickly back to the middle of the court.

C. LESS INJURIES

Flexibility is also important in reducing injuries, lessening the likelihood of tears and pulls by lengthening the muscles and providing a good framework for strengthening the muscles and joints that experience extreme motions. Tennis involves a wide range of movements, such as hip rotations on groundstrokes, abdominal and back twisting on the serve, start and stop movements that put pressure on the knees and groin, explosive running using the various leg muscles, and elbow extensions and wrist flexions during the swinging of the racquet. Therefore, players need to be flexible throughout their whole body to reduce the chance of injuries.

Flexibility also reduces the strain of opposing muscle groups. Tight muscles cause limited range of motion, and when a primary muscle can't move properly, other muscles must work harder to support it. In the short term this means muscle tension and fatigue. More seriously, over the long run this often turns into muscle imbalances, inflammation, and injuries. Another consideration specific to tennis players is that the constant use of the racquet arm can cause imbalances in the muscle structure. Consequently, tennis players must maintain elasticity equally throughout their bodies to keep the potential problems associated with muscle imbalances to a minimum.

D. SPEEDS RECOVERY PROCESS

Stretching after your match or practice session will reduce inflammation, lengthen and relax your muscles, and leave you feeling less sore and stiff the following day.

2. DYNAMIC AND STATIC STRETCHING

There are two basic types of stretching that contribute to increased flexibility. Both have an important place in a tennis player's warm up and cool down. The first type of stretching is "dynamic stretching," or exercises that increase blood flow and range of motion before you play. Dynamic stretching should be done only after some general activity that raises the body temperature. A good example of this sequence would be to jog lightly for three to five minutes, then do eight to 10 minutes of dynamic stretching.

The second type is "static stretching." Static stretching is done as part of your cool down and involves stretching a muscle or group of muscles to a point of tension and holding the stretch. After a practice session or a match, you should dedicate some time to static stretching to prevent injury, increase flexibility, and prevent muscle soreness.

For your static stretching to be safe and effective, there are several points to remember. **First**, emphasize slow, smooth movements and coordinated deep breathing. Inhale deeply through your nose and exhale through your mouth as you stretch, then ease back gradually. Hold the static stretch position for 20-25 seconds as you breathe normally. **Second**, you should feel no pain. If it hurts or if you feel intense burning, you are stretching too far. **Third**, do not lock your joints and do not bounce. Instead, keep a nice steady stretch. **Lastly**, try to make stretching a daily routine and stay consistent to achieve the best results and maximum flexibility of your body.

A. DYNAMIC STRETCHES

1. CARIOCA STEPS: Your left foot crosses in front of your right, then your right foot steps right, then your left foot crosses behind your right, then your right foot steps right. Move across the court several times from doubles alley to doubles alley. Next, face the opposite direction and repeat.

Carioca step

COACH'S BOX:

Too many recreational players jump onto the court for a practice session and spend little time getting their body prepared for the rigors of playing tennis. Make sure that before you hit your first ball, your heart rate is slightly elevated and you are sweating lightly. Also, I recommend doing shadow swings for all the shots for a minute or two to warm up the arm and shoulder muscles.

eral times lifting the opposite arm and leg on each step, i.e. raise your right knee towards your chest and left arm in the air and right arm in the air when you lift your left knee.

3. LUNGE AND TWIST: Take a large step with the leading leg and drop the trailing leg towards the ground until both knees are at around 90 degrees. Raise your arms up to shoulder and rotate upper body in a circular fashion. Stand up, progress to the next lunge and move back and forth across the court two or three times.

Lunge and twist

4. ARM CIRCLES: Stand up and lift your right arm straight out to your sides at shoulder height. Move your right arm forward in small circular motion for 15 seconds. Gradually allow the circle to get bigger until you are making as big of a circle as you can for another 15 seconds. Repeat with the left arm. Next, moving both arms simultaneously, do the same build up of circles from small to large over 30 seconds.

B. STATIC STRETCHES

1. WRIST FLEXION: Straighten your elbow and hold your arm out parallel to the ground. With your right palm facing up, use the left hand to push the fingers of the right hand backwards towards your body. Switch arms and repeat.

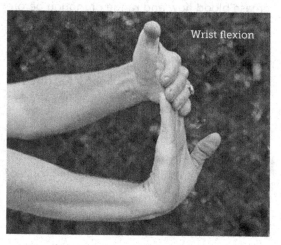
Wrist flexion

2. FOREARM EXTENSION: Straighten your elbow and hold your arm out parallel to the ground. With your right palm facing down towards the floor, use your left hand to pull the back of the right hand gently down. Switch arms and repeat.

3. TRICEPS STRETCH: Extend one hand down the center of your back and use the other hand to grasp the elbow. Exhale slowly and gently pull your elbow downward. Switch arms and repeat.

4. SHOULDER STRETCH: Straighten your left arm across your right shoulder. Hold the left arm with your right arm above the elbow and gently pull it backwards. Switch arms and repeat.

5. QUADRICEPS STRETCH: Stand near a wall or table for support. Grasp your ankle and gently pull your heel up and back towards your buttock until you feel a stretch in the front of your thigh. Keep your back straight and knees close together. Switch legs and repeat.

Quadriceps stretch

6. HAMSTRING STRETCH: Lie on the floor near the outer corner of a wall or a door frame. Raise one leg and the heel against the wall and keep your knee slightly bent. Gently straighten that leg until you feel a stretch in the back of the leg. Switch legs and repeat.

7. CALF STRETCH: Stand at arm's length from a wall. With your feet facing the wall, place your right foot behind your left foot wider than shoulder width apart. Lean forward slowly and bend your left foot, keeping your right knee straight and your right heel on the floor. Hold your back straight and your hips forward. Switch legs and repeat.

8. SEATED GROIN STRETCH: Sit on the floor with the soles of your feet together close to your body. Grasp your feet with both hands and position your elbows on the inside of your lower legs. Press your knees towards the floor with your elbows and hold the stretch.

9. KNEE TO CHEST STRETCH: Lie on your back on a firm surface and gently pull one knee up to your chest until you feel a stretch in your lower back. Keep the opposite leg relaxed in a comfortable position. Switch legs and repeat.

10. HIP FLEXOR STRETCH: Kneel on your right knee and place your left foot in front of you, bending your left knee and placing your left hand on your left thigh for support. Place your right hand on your right hip and keep your back straight. Lean forward and feel the stretch in your right thigh. Switch legs and repeat.

11. COBRA STRETCH: Lay on your stomach, put your hands and arms next to your chest and stretch your arms so they are perpendicular to the floor. Relax your body and let your arms support your weight. You should feel the stretch in your lower back and abdomen.

Maria Sharapova's improved agility helped her win the French Open.

II. Agility

PLAYING TENNIS WELL REQUIRES good agility. Tennis is a sport of continual adjustments because every shot hit by your opponent arrives with varying velocities, heights, and spins and lands in different parts of the court. Therefore, you must be agile enough to stop and start quickly after moving in a variety of directions, all while maintaining balance to hit the ball effectively.

Even the pros must work to improve their agility, as Maria Sharapova discovered when stymied by clay courts early in her career. She famously described her lack of agility on clay courts as mimicking a "cow on ice." To remedy that, she worked hard on her agility, develop-

ing her ability to slide and move with increased assurance and hit more of her shots with good balance on the clay courts. Her dedication to improving her agility was a big reason why she finally won the French Open in 2012 and again in 2014.

AGILITY EXERCISES

1. LATERAL ALLEY DRILL
Start outside the doubles alley facing the net. Shuffle with side steps into the court getting both feet over the singles line. Quickly reverse direction and side step until both feet are over the doubles sideline. Do this for 20 seconds, rest, and repeat several times depending on your fitness level.

Cone slaloms

Agility ladder

2. CONE SLALOMS

Line up 10 cones along the baseline about three feet apart. Start at one end of the cones facing the net and weave in and out of the cones using small steps until you reach the end of the cones. Jog back to the starting position and repeat several times depending on your fitness level. Add a variation and face the side fence and weave in and out of the cones running forward with small steps until you reach the end of the cones.

3. BALL DROPS

Stand 15 feet away from your training partner and have them throw the ball in different directions. You run and try to catch the ball before it bounces a second time. After 15 catches, switch roles. Add a variation and throw two balls in the air at different heights for you or your partner to catch. Alternatively, have the player catching stand with their back facing the player tossing. The thrower tosses

and then says "go" when the ball they toss hits the ground.

4. AGILITY LADDER

Place the agility ladder on the ground and go through a series of movements as fast as you can to decrease your contact time on the court while still maintaining your balance. Move forward up the ladder with one foot stepping in each ladder step and then do it with both feet stepping individually in each ladder step. Then do the same two movements skipping across sideways. Add a variation by doing one forward or backward step outside the ladder before moving sideways up the ladder.

Murray uses his anticipation and foot speed to extend points and frustrate his opponents.

III. Quickness

QUICKNESS IS BEING ABLE to anticipate, re-act, and then move with speed to maximize the time you have to set up for the stroke. Any extra time you have to hit your shot allows you to swing in a more balanced state and hit with more power and accuracy. Quickness will also help you reach more balls and extend more rallies. Using your speed to force your opponent to hit one, two, three, or more shots often results in you winning the point either by their mistake or by changing a defensive situation into an offensive one.

Quickness is not all about foot speed. It starts with anticipation and reaction time. The first key to developing anticipation starts with focusing on your opponent's body position-ing during their backswing. For example, if your opponent sets up with a large shoulder turn, there is a good chance they are hitting down the line. The second key is knowing the possible shots your opponent can hit based on their racquet face and the amount of time

they have to prepare for their shot. For ex-ample, if your opponent has an open racquet face on the backswing and is rushed, you can move forward to anticipate a slow or short re-ply. In contrast, if they have a closed racquet face and are not rushed, you can expect a fast and deep shot. Third, it's important to pick up on your opponent's tendencies. Some players like to drop shot frequently while others like to hit cross court or down the line. You can an-ticipate and adjust your position accordingly. After you have positioned yourself in the best location on the court based on these observa-tions, perform a strong split step and react as quickly as possible when the ball leaves your opponent's racquet.

QUICKNESS EXERCISES

1. FIGURE EIGHT

Place two cones about five feet apart along the baseline. Start behind one of the cones facing the net. Move around the cones later-ally and diagonally, always facing the net and tracing a figure eight around the two cones.

COACH'S BOX:

The key to quickness is not just accelera-tion, but also deceleration. Therefore, avoid quickness drills which only involve running in one direction. Running straight or in one direction can develop speed and cardiovas-cular strength but won't improve all the skills needed to be a good mover on the court. Instead, train your body for explosive move-ment with short multi-directional sprints and by activating the fast twitch muscles.

Racquet touches

Spider run

Complete as many figure eights as you can in 30 seconds. Rest for a minute and repeat several times. Add a variation and place the two cones five feet apart along the center line and trace the figure eights while facing the net.

2. RACQUET TOUCHES
Standing on the center line, sprint and touch the singles line with the racquet, and then sprint back and touch the center line with the racquet. Use the cross over step to reach out and touch the lines with your racquet. See how many lines you can touch in 30 seconds and then rest for a minute. Repeat several times. Add a variation by touching the line using open stances instead of cross over steps.

3. BOX JUMPS
To perform the box jump, you will need a sturdy box that is 12 to 30 inches high depending on your ability. Stand approximately one to two feet in front of it, with your feet slightly wider than shoulder width apart. Swing your elbows towards your hips and jump up onto the box. Maintain your balance and absorb the jump by bending your knees at impact. Do two to three sets of 15 jumps with a 30 second break between sets.

4. SPIDER RUN
Place three balls evenly spaced out along the service line, three by the net and two at the baseline corners. Set a racquet on the ground by the center mark of the baseline. Starting at the center mark on the baseline, sprint around the court and collect the eight balls. Place the balls one at a time on the strings of the racquet. Use a stopwatch to time your spider run and try to decrease your time with practice.

IV. Core Stability

ONE OF THE MOST IMPORTANT PARTS of the body for tennis players is the core, that is, the central third of the body including the lower back, hips, and abdomen. The core is the central pillar of strength in the body; if your core is strong, it sets the foundation for your legs and arms to be strong too.

Rotational core strength is key to transferring power into your shots. For example, the forehand groundstroke uses rotational core strength to store energy during the backswing as the shoulders coil and subsequently releases that energy during the forward swing as they uncoil. Similarly, on the serve, your abdominal muscles lengthen to stabilize the spine as it extends back during the trophy position, and then following the trophy position, your oblique muscles assist with the upward rotation of the torso as you reach up to hit the ball.

Core training not only helps your strokes, but also improves your movement. Players who are strong in their core can change directions more quickly. When you change direction your upper body tilts against the momentum. Being strong through the torso provides the body with strength to lean against the momentum, stop quickly, and begin to change direction as the legs then match the upper body tilt and push off in that direction (*below*).

A strong core can also speed up your first movement following the split step in a more stationary situation. After the split step, the upper body leans in the direction of the ball and the legs and arms begin to pump. If you are strong in your core, you provide your legs and arms with a sturdy foundation from which they can pump, thus improving your first step and, as a result, your subsequent steps as well.

CORE STABILITY EXERCISES

1. OBLIQUE CRUNCHES

Begin the oblique crunch exercise by lying on your back with your knees bent and feet flat on the floor. Slowly drop your legs to the left and let your knees rest near the floor. Place your fingertips to the side of your head, just behind your ears. Push your lower back into the floor and curl up slowly so both your shoulders lift off the floor a few inches. Hold for two seconds and return to the start position. Use your obliques to lift you up rather than using your hands to pull you up from behind your head. Repeat for 10 to 12 repetitions for three to four sets using both sides of the body.

Djokovic's core muscles help him to stop quickly after running down a wide forehand.

Medicine ball throws

The plank

2. MEDICINE BALL THROWS

Place your legs in a forehand neutral stance. Then throw the medicine ball 15 times against a wall or with a partner using a two-handed forehand swing. Next, switch into a backhand neutral stance and do the same thing using a two-handed backhand swing, then rest for a minute. Repeat three times.

3. SUPERMAN

Lay flat on your stomach with your arms straight out in front of you and your legs straight out behind you. Keep your arms and legs about shoulder width apart. Lift your legs and arms simultaneously several inches off the ground, hold for a few seconds, and lower your arms and legs back to the ground. Or do the exercise by raising your left arm and right leg simultaneously and switch. Complete three sets of 10.

4. THE PLANK

Begin by getting into the pushup position on the floor. Then bend your elbows 90 degrees and rest your weight on your forearms. Your elbows should be directly beneath your shoulders, and your body should form a straight line from your head to your heels. Hold the position for as long as you can and perform three to five times. If regular plank is too difficult, begin the plank resting on your knees.

V. Strength

IN THE PAST, there were a significant number of teenagers ranked in the top 100 on the ATP tour; today there are less than a handful. Most tennis experts agree that this change is attributable to the increased physicality of the game and players needing more time to develop the strength now required to be successful.

Strength for tennis must not only be explosive, but also long-lasting; you must have the endurance to perform explosively for the hundreds of movements needed to win a match. Leg strength is vital to be able to accelerate and decelerate well in various directions as well as to store energy that is released upward throughout the upper body during the swing. Similarly, you need strength in the core, shoulders, and arms to generate power on the various strokes.

There are two main types of strength exercises. Single-joint exercises, where one primary muscle is worked, are especially beneficial when strengthening a particular muscle group to alleviate a muscle imbalance. For instance, hitting thousands of balls can lead to an over-development in the muscles in the front of the body; strengthening the upper back muscles balances out this over-development and reduces the chance of injuries.

The other type of exercise is the multi-joint

form, which works several muscles and joints at once. These are more relevant to tennis players. The squat is an example of a multi-joint exercise that works primarily the gluteal muscles, quadriceps, hamstrings, and calf muscles with movement occurring at the hip, knee, and ankle. These exercises can help strengthen the muscles in a "kinetic chain" approach that helps the serve and groundstrokes.

Strength training should also involve some isotonic resistance. Isotonic resistance is a constant weight or tension where shortening and lengthening of the muscle occurs along with joint movement. These types of muscle movements are required on the various swings and while running around the court. Isotonic exercises can be performed with free weights, body weight, medicine balls, and many types of weight machines. Any isotonic exercise that involves standing up or forcing you to keep bal-

anced are particularly good for tennis because that is the way the game is played. Also, because many shots rely on the dominance of one leg, step-ups and lunge variations should be a significant part of your leg strength training.

Body weight, free weights, and machines are all useful in building strength, but your workout regime should utilize resistance bands as well. Resistance bands rightly have become a very popular form of isotonic exercise for tennis players; they are light and portable and can be easily used to mimic tennis strokes. Also, they are a low impact exercise that reduces the incidence of injury in addition to providing constant tension to strengthen and stretch the muscles.

With any strength exercise, gradual increase in weight is the best way to achieve results and avoid injury. It's always better to start with less weight and focus on proper form

Nadal uses a resistance band to warm up his shoulder before a practice session.

before increasing the weight. Additionally, by doing exercises at a faster speed using lighter weights, you can work on increasing your rate of force production, that is, your ability to create maximum force in the least amount of time. Enhanced force production will help you gain explosiveness. Of course, your strength training should not be confined to using light weights. A well-balanced workout schedule also should employ exercises that involve lifting heavy loads to add power to your swings and movement.

STRENGTH EXERCISES

1. PUSH-UPS

Assume the high plank position and place your hands slightly wider than your shoulders. Keep your body in a flat plank and lower your torso until your chest hovers just above the ground with your elbows forming a 90 degree angle. Raise yourself up, continuing to push until your arms are almost straight (but not locked). Repeat lowering and raising yourself at a steady pace in a controlled manner. Complete the number of repetitions and sets appropriate to your level of strength.

2. HIGH CABLE WOOD CHOP

Using a cable machine, hold the cable handle with both hands and arms outstretched slightly above your head. With your arms in this position, keep your shoulder blades flat against your back. From here, pull the cable down across the front of the body, then return to the start. The goal is to maintain your back angle while completing the exercise, using your torso and not your arms for momentum. Complete three sets of 12 to 15 repetitions doing the right side followed by the left side.

Walking lunges

3. WALKING LUNGES

Stand tall with good posture while holding the dumbbell pair in your hands. Step forward with one leg keeping back straight. Then bend your knees and drop your hips downwards straight towards the ground. Push up with your front leg and bring your back foot forward. Take another step forward with the opposite leg and repeat the lunge. Complete 20 steps, rest, and repeat three times.

4. ONE ARM/ONE LEG CABLE ROW

Using a cable machine, set up in the single squat position with your left leg on the ground and reach down for the lower cable with your right hand. Raise your right leg in the air behind you to balance out the body. Drive your body up from a single squat position to a standing position and pull the cable backwards to your side in a rowing motion with your shoulders back and down. Finish the motion by flexing the extended knee and hip forward into the ending position. Complete two or three sets of ten repetitions on both sides of the body.

VI. Endurance

MANY MATCHES, especially longer matches, boil down to the player who has the better endurance being victorious. At the end of a long match, fit players can still move quickly and stabilize their feet before swinging and uncorking the kinetic chain. In contrast, tired players will more frequently hit the ball off balance as they are unable to commit to the movement necessary to get into the correct position to hit the ball well. They often will play a low percentage shot to end the point quickly. It is very reassuring to feel fit late in a match and look over the net to see your opponent hunched over and breathing heavily. That type of body language is usually a signal that the match is about to be your victory.

Tennis is a sport that requires both aerobic and anaerobic endurance. The body's aerobic energy system supplies fuel to muscles for endurance and the anaerobic energy system provides power for bursts of activity. Therefore, endurance training should be a mix of running drills that build lung capacity and short, high intensity footwork and agility drills.

Endurance training should also be geared to tennis' unique pacing. Each match is different, but an approximate timeline for an average point is around five seconds and the average rest time taken between points is approximately fifteen seconds. This means there is a work-to-rest ratio of 1:3, and consequently, tennis training should be geared to this ratio.

Tennis drills and activities used to improve aerobic fitness and anaerobic power should follow a 1:3 work-to-rest cycle and include relatively short, multi-directional movement patterns, decelerations, and strength exercises. While going out and running five miles may improve your cardiovascular endurance, there

Murray breathes heavily after an intense point. His superior cardiovascular endurance allows his body to recover quickly and be ready for the next point.

are better and more specific ways to improve your tennis fitness without subjecting your hips, knees, and ankles to added prolonged stress. Running two or three miles of interval sprints at high intensity and jogging slowly in between the sprints following an approximate 1:3 work-to-rest ratio is a much better tennis conditioning exercise than running five miles at a steady pace.

ENDURANCE EXERCISES

1. 50, 40, 30 DRILL

Start at a given point and put markers down 30, 40, and 50 yards away from you. Sprint from the start point to the 30 yard line and back. Rest for 15 seconds. Next, sprint from the start point to the 40 yard line and back. Rest for 30 seconds. Lastly, sprint from the start point to the 50 yard line and back, and then rest for 45 seconds. Repeat three to five times.

Two, four, six, eights

4. SERGEANT DRILL

On the court, have your training partner shout the directions, "Right, left, forward, and back" at varying time intervals. Follow his or her directions skipping sideways right and left and running forward and backwards. Do sets of 60, 45, and 30 seconds with 15 second breaks in between and then switch roles with your partner. Repeat several times.

2. TWO, FOUR, SIX, EIGHTS

Begin standing on the baseline. Sprint to the net and back (this counts as "two") and rest for 15 seconds. Next, run from the baseline to net and back twice (this counts as "four") and rest for 30 seconds. Continue going from baseline to the net and back three times, then four times, and resting 45 seconds in between each set. Repeat two or three times.

3. 20 MINUTE INTERVAL TRAINING

On a bike, treadmill, or track perform a 20 minute cardio interval workout following these guidelines. Start with a five minute warm up. For a total of 20 minutes start with a fast pace for 30 seconds followed by a medium-to-slow pace for 60 seconds. Finish with a three minute cool down.

Sergeant drill

VII. Nutrition

THE FITNESS COMPONENT of your game isn't complete without a good nutritional base. Nutrition has become an integral part of tennis, and at the elite levels, it has become a science. Touring pros are now getting groundbreaking blood tests that analyze how their body digests certain types of food. Many drink personalized powdered sports beverages in order to direct their diet to improve performance. Novak Djokovic, for example, discovered through blood tests that he was highly intolerant to wheat and dairy products. He changed to a gluten-free diet and his endurance reversed from being an obvious weakness to a well-recognized strength.

You may not go so far as to take blood tests or brew your own personalized shake, but you should recognize that a well-nourished and hydrated body can give you a competitive edge. It can mean the difference between feeling strong and energetic for the entire match or feeling sluggish throughout and faltering at the end. Also, poorly nourished players take longer to recover and muscle aches and stiffness are common post-match conditions for such competitors.

A good tennis diet includes a balance of carbohydrates for energy, proteins for muscle recovery and strength, a small amount of healthy fats for slow-release energy, vitamins, minerals, and water. Many unhealthy foods, especially processed foods like high fructose

Eating a meal consisting of some lean protein and vegetables or salad is a wise choice three or four hours before your match.

corn syrup, hydrogenated fats, and chemical additives should be restricted from your diet.

1. EATING SCHEDULE

The timing of when and how you eat before the match is important. Breakfast is key for building strength as muscles are depleted of glycogen after the body fasts through the night. It is important to choose a breakfast that is substantial enough to get your body ready for the day. Some great breakfast foods are whole grain cereals, Greek yogurt, egg whites, and fruit. On match days, breakfasts should be a bit larger than normal and have more carbohydrates.

Three or four hours before the match eat a meal that's high in complex carbohydrates, moderate in protein, and low in fat. Fruits, vegetables, and grains should make up approximately seventy percent of your plate, with the rest devoted to proteins like dairy products or lean meats. Your pre-match meal should be something that you are familiar with so choose a nutritious meal that has worked for you in the past. Carbohydrates are stored in our muscles and liver, and they are the first fuel used in a match. Therefore, the closer you get to match time, the smaller the amount you should eat and the purer the carbohydrates consumed.

One hour before the match eat a snack like a banana or an energy bar and drink some water. Once the match starts, there is only a short time during changeovers to refuel. Here, energy bars or gels are very convenient products to consume to keep your energy up. Be careful of the ingredients and avoid energy bars or gels that are high in sugar. Sugary foods can give you a small burst of energy followed by a sudden crash when your blood sugar spikes and then quickly falls. An energy bar or gel with a good level of carbohydrates can effectively

The pros monitor their fluid consumption to ensure they stay sufficiently hydrated during their matches.

provide the 30 to 60 grams of carbohydrates needed for every hour of tennis exercise. To help speed up the muscle recovery, replenish the nutrients within two hours of the completion of the match and eat a high carbohydrate meal with a lean source of protein, like chicken with steamed brown rice and vegetables.

2. HYDRATION

Hydration should begin the night before a match. Make sure to drink plenty of water the night before and 10 to 15 ounces in the hour leading up to the match. Plain water is the best choice just prior to the match. Once the match starts, however, and especially if it is hot or humid, sports drinks are a good choice because they not only have carbohydrates, but also a good ratio of sodium to potassium to replenish the electrolytes you have lost. Remember to be consistent with your fluid intake during the match and set a schedule of consuming two to four ounces of water or sports drink at every change over. You should continue to consume water or sports drink after the match to replenish any fluids and salts that may have been lost during the match, especially if another match is a short time away.

Conclusion

TENNIS IS MY LIFE'S PASSION and work. The sport has been so generous to me, and I am grateful that I had the opportunity to share my knowledge and experience with you in *Absolute Tennis*. Whatever your motivation for reading the book, my hope is that you learned a lot, are enjoying your tennis more, and are playing better than ever.

Of course to raise your game, the knowledge you gained from this book has to be combined with hours of practice. Nothing worthwhile comes easy, and this is particularly true in a skillful game like tennis where small deviations — like being a degree or two off with the racquet face — can result in an error. Improving your game takes mindfulness, commitment, and resolve. I urge you to be patient with the process; you will be very glad in the long run.

Remember too that it is important not to be overly critical of yourself. Judging yourself too harshly will hurt rather than help you. Instead, practicing and playing matches with a sense of gratitude and a smile will lead to more time on the court and faster improvement. The right internal approach is to salute your dedication and savor your progress along the way; raising your level of play is an accomplishment of which you should be very proud.

If you hit a speed bump during your training, which everyone invariably does, take a step back and remind yourself of the many positive qualities of tennis: how its incredible variety makes every shot different and every opponent unique; how its innate malleability leaves you free to put your own stamp on each ball struck; and how it can be very individual, but at the same time permits you to play doubles or in a league and feel part of a team. It is also a sport that vindicates self-belief and ac-

tivates the mind to think deeply and problem solve. As Andre Agassi once said, "There can be thousands of people watching or you could be in your back yard, and either way, you are dealing with simple elements that cause you to ask yourself to believe when you might not. To ask yourself to find a way, when you don't think there is. It's a great sport and very symbolic of life and prepares you for life."[2] Tennis offers a lot, and I think it is helpful to appreciate this as you train and work on your game.

Playing better is well within your grasp, and if you do, the rewards are notable. There's the joy of winning more often and the satisfaction derived from hitting skillful shots that were not previously part of your game. Also, playing better usually results in playing more often and you reaping the health benefits that stem from increased time on the court. I know you can improve and experience these rewards: I've seen it happen countless times in my life. With constructive stroke repetition, tactical knowledge, and a mind and body in good shape, it will happen.

For those of you learning a new stroke or beginning the game, don't forget to use progressions to structure your practice sessions. There's no question that swing technique is learned faster and cemented stronger when tennis training is broken down into gradually more challenging steps. Try not to be in a hurry to jump through the progressions. Wait until you are competent and confident executing each progression before moving on to the next one. Also, remember to keep the proper order of learning — that is, consistency, placement, and then power. Consistency is the first principle; it slows down the swing to assist the grooving of proper stroke mechanics, encourages repetition, and reinforces the winning match philosophy of keeping errors

"Wait until you see
what I'm going to be
doing with this."

to a minimum. After consistency comes placement, which improves as you learn the correct
timing of the swing and which part of the ball
needs to be struck to direct the ball. Power is
the third variable. It is the most fun part of the
learning process, but at the recreational level, it is also the least important. My advice is
don't be enticed by power's glamor until you
have good consistency and placement in your
game first.

And what about a key question raised in
the book — the future? Compare the speed
of the game 40 years ago to today. What will
it look like 40 years from now? Tennis players will continue to get taller and faster, and

the equipment and training methods will keep
improving. With these advancements, will
the extra power, reach, and time of Ambitennis lead to it becoming an accepted style of
play? Will future players curve the ball rightward with reverse serves or "spike" their volleyball serve? Will the "best of both worlds"
hybrid backhand become a recognized shot?
No one knows but the advancements certainly
will lead to some changes. Whatever happens,
I am excited, curious, and ready for the future,
and my advice to you is to be on the lookout
and embrace the changes too. It is always better to lead and be in front of the curve than to
follow and play catch-up.

SOURCES

CHAPTER ONE BALANCE

1. Welby Van Horn, "Welby Van Horn: Secrets of a true master," *Tennisplayer.net,* October 2016, https:// www.tenisplayer.net/. [page 1]

CHAPTER THREE MOVEMENT

1. Pat Dougherty, "Advanced Reaction Steps," *Tennisplayer.net*, 2005, https://www.tennisplayer.net/. [page 17]
2. Tom Perrotta, "How Rafael Nadal Wrestles with the Anxieties of Age," *Wall Street Journal*, May 19, 2016. [page 23]

CHAPTER FOUR GRIPS

1. Tony D'Avino, "The Forehand Grip and Finger Anatomy," *Deciding Point*, October 1, 2016, http://www.decidingpoint.com/?s=the+forehand+grip+and+finger+anatomy. [page 27]

CHAPTER FIVE SERVE

1. Lou Marino, "Like a Baseball Pitcher, Try 'Changing Up' Your Serve," *The Bluffton Sun*, May 16, 2016, http://www.blufftonsun.com/like-a-baseball-pitcher-try-changing-up-your-serve-cms-1378. [page 37]
2. Tom Perrotta, "Why Serena Williams Rules Tennis: It's All in the Serve," *Wall Street Journal*, September 9, 2015. [page 44]
3. Craig O' Shannessy, "Keeping Score: Giving Foes the Runaround," *The New York Times*, August 28, 2011. [page 64]
4. Christopher Clarey, "Focused Ferocity by Williams on a Stage She Owns," *The New York Times,* September 6, 2014. [page 66]

CHAPTER SIX RETURN OF SERVE

1. ATP World Tour, "Infosys ATP beyond the numbers: Andy's Answers." Accessed December 27, 2015, www.atpworld tour.com. [page 68]
2. *2014 Women's Wimbledon Final Eugenie Bouchard versus Petra Kvitova*, ESPN, July 5, 2014. [page 69]
3. Kenny Hemphill, "10 Ways that Tennis Has Quietly Changed in the Last 10 Years," *Mental Floss*, March 18, 2015, http://mentalfloss.com/uk/sport/27746/10-ways-that-tennis-has-quietly-changed-in-the-last-10-years. [page 69]
4. *2016 Apia International Sydney Men's Final Viktor Troicki versus Grigor Dimitrov*, Tennis Channel, January 16, 2016. [page 77]
5. Craig O' Shannessy, "Brain Game: Federer's Tactical Change." Accessed March 22, 2016, www.atptour.com. [page 78]
6. Craig O' Shannessy, "How to Watch Tennis: Trust Numbers, Not Eyes," *The New York Times*, August 28, 2016. [page 81]

CHAPTER SEVEN FOREHAND

1. Craig O' Shannessy, "Brain Game: Nadal Wins Forehand Festival." Accessed March 19, 2013, www.atptour.com. [page 83]
2. Rafael Nadal and John Carlin, *Rafa* (Hyperion Books, 2011), p. 6 [page 85]
3. Tom Perrotta, "How Rafael Nadal Wrestles with the Anxieties of Age," *Wall Street Journal*, May 19, 2016. [page 95]
4. Stuart Miller, "Out of a Perceived Weakness Is Born an Act of Aggression," *The New York Times*, September 6, 2015. [page 112]

CHAPTER EIGHT BACKHAND

1. "ATP Stats Leader Boards." Accessed December 30, 2016, http://www.atpworldtour.com/en/stats. [page 120]
2. John Yandell, "Modern Pro Slice: Spin Levels," *Tennisplayer.net*, October 2011, https://www.tennisplayer.net/. [page 144]

CHAPTER NINE DROP SHOT AND LOB

1. "Federer's secret weapon," *tennishead*, August 20, 2012, http://www.tennishead.net/news/on-tour/2012/08/20/federers-secret-weapon. [page 150]

CHAPTER 10 APPROACH SHOT

1. Craig O' Shannessy, "Brain Game: Federer's Tactical Change." Accessed March 22, 2016, www.atpworldtour.com. [page 157]
2. "Daily Data Viz: The steady decline of the serve and volley," *Sports Illustrated*, June 28, 2016, http://www.si.com/tennis/2016/06/28/wimbledon-grass-serve-and-volley-approach-stats. [page 162]
3. Craig O' Shannessy, "A Misguided Departure from the Serve-and-Volley," *The New York Times*, June 21, 2014, https://www.nytimes.com/2014/06/22/sports/tennis/a-misguided-departure-from-the-serve-and-volley.html. [page 162]

CHAPTER 11 VOLLEYS

1. "Tennis Instruction: Is the One-Handed Backhand a Thing of the Past?" *Tennis-XBlog*, March 16, 2009, http://www.tennis-x.com/xblog/2009-03-16/956.php. [page 188]

CHAPTER 12 FUTURE STROKES

1. Christopher Clarey, "Nadal Captures 4th French Open Title," *The New York Times*, June 8, 2008. [page 195]
2. Gretchen Reynolds, "Learning a New Sport May Be Good for the Brain," *The New York Times*, March 2, 2016, http://well.blogs.nytimes.com/2016/03/02/learning-a-new-sport-may-be-good-for-the-brain/?_r=0. [Page 198]
3. Florian Loffing, Norbert Hagemann, and Bernd Strauss, "Left-Handedness in Professional and Amateur Tennis," *PLoS One* (2012); 7(11),

accessed December 30, 2016, https://www.ncbi.nlm.nih.gov/pmc/articles/PMC3492260/. [page 204]
4. Ben Shpigel, "Seahawks Punt Team Is Flashy With Play, Not Name," *The New York Times*, January 10, 2014, https://www.nytimes.com/2014/01/11/sports/football/moniker-for-seattle-punt-team-call-it-no-1.html. [Page 211]
5. Robert Philip, "Fosbury's life never the same after famous flop," *The Telegraph*, August 12, 2001, http://www.telegraph.co.uk/sport/othersports/athletics/3010663/Fosburys-life-never-the-same-after-famous-flop.html. [page 211]

CHAPTER 13 SINGLES

1. Damien Saunder, "Shot Charts in Tennis," *GameSetMap*, February 9, 2016, http://gamesetmap.com/?p=1261. [page 223]
2. Craig O' Shannessy, "How Nadal Dominates the French Open," *The New York Times*, May 24, 2014. [page 228]
3. Craig Lambert, "Numbers are the language of success," November 12, 2016, http://www.universaltennis.com [page 228]
4. U.S. Open, 2016 Men's Finals IBM SlamTracker Statistics. Accessed on December 31, 2016, http://www.usopen.org/en_US/slamtracker/index.html. [page 229]
5. Andrew John, "Cheers, ovation greet Serena's triumphant BNP return," *The Desert Sun*, March 17, 2015, http://www.desertsun.com/story/sports/tennis/bnp/2015/03/14/serena-williams-indian-wells-bnp-paribas-open/70320218/. [page 231]
6. Craig O' Shannessy, "Brain Game: Federer's Tactical Change." Accessed March 22, 2016, http://www.atpworldtour.com/en/news/brain-game-federer-beats-wawrinka-london-2015. [page 233]

SOURCES

7. Craig O' Shannessy, "Breaking it Down: Nadal vs. Federer," *The New York Times*, January 24, 2014, https://www.nytimes.com/2014/01/25/sports/tennis/breaking-it-down-nadal-vs-federer.html. [page 235]

8. Christopher Clarey, "Federer overcomes age, and a longtime adversary." *The New York Times*, January 30, 2017. [page 234]

9. Jon Wertheim, "Nadal talks history, Wimbledon, spirituality," *Sports Illustrated*, July 16, 2010, http://www.si.com/more-sports/2010/07/16/nadal-interview. [page 236]

CHAPTER 15 PSYCHOLOGY

1. Rafael Nadal and John Carlin, *Rafa* (Hyperion Books, 2011), p. 7. [page 283]

2. "'Be good to yourself:' Andy Murray's motivational on-court notes revealed," *The Guardian*, February 17, 2015, https://www.theguardian.com/sport/2015/feb/17/andy-murray-motivational-court-notes. [page 284]

3. Tom Perrotta, "Why Serena Williams Rules Tennis: It's All in the Serve," *Wall Street Journal*, September 9, 2015. [page 285]

4. James Loehr, "Mental toughness training: The 16 second cure," *Tennisplayer.net*, March 2008, www.tennisplayer.net. [page 285]

5. Andre Agassi, *Open* (Vintage, 2010), p. 365. [page 288]

6. Len Berman, *The Greatest Moments in Sports* (Sourcebooks Jabberwocky, 2009), p. 46. [page 289]

7. Simon Briggs, "Nervous Rafael Nadal worried he is losing mental edge," *The Telegraph*, March 30, 2015, http://www.telegraph.co.uk/sport/tennis/11505396/Nervous-Rafael-Nadal-worried-he-is-losing-mental-edge.html. [page 290]

8. "Marin Cilic defeats Roger Federer in three sets for spot in final," *Sports Illustrated*, September 6, 2014, http://www.si.com/tennis/2014/09/06/us-open-live-blog-marin-cilic-vs-roger-federer-live-scores-updates. [page 291]

9. "Federer looks for confidence boost in Hamburg." Accessed July 15, 2013, www.atpworldtour.com. [page 292]

10. Allen Fox, "Confidence game: Five steps to battling your way out of slump," *Tennis*, April 2014, p. 17. [page 292]

CHAPTER 16 FITNESS

1. Eli Saslow, "Freak of Nurture," *ESPN Magazine*, July 13, 2012, http://www.espn.com/tennis/story/_/id/8132800/has-novak-djokovic-b(10)ecome-fittest-athlete-ever-espn-magazine. [page 299]

2. Jack Groppel, "Age respects hard work and will to win," *ADDVantage Magazine*, October-November 2006, http://www.addvantageuspta.com/(S(yw2ma5ex3zffow552kp3i445)X(1))/default.aspx/act/newsletter.aspx/category/ADD-askprof/menuitemid/502/MenuGroup/Ads/NewsLetterID/698/startrow/30.htm. [page 300]

3. "Playing Tennis Linked to Longer Life," Tennis Industry Magazine, (please write Tennis Industry Magazine in italics) February 2017 [page 302]

4. Jennifer D'Angelo Friedman, "Defending U.S. Open Champ Sam Stosur Reveals her Favorite Tennis-Inspired Workout Moves," *Self Magazine*, August 31, 2012. by [page 302]

CONCLUSION

1. Iris Watts Hirideyo, "Andre Agassi on the Beauty of Tennis," *Iris' Journal*, September 12, 2011, http://www.hirideyo.com/journal/iris/andre_agassi_beauty_of_tennis. [page 318]